Borderlands and Liminal Subjects

Jessica Elbert Decker • Dylan Winchock
Editors

Borderlands and Liminal Subjects

Transgressing the Limits in Philosophy and Literature

palgrave
macmillan

Editors
Jessica Elbert Decker
California State University
San Marcos, California
USA

Dylan Winchock
California State University
San Marcos, California
USA

ISBN 978-3-319-67812-2 ISBN 978-3-319-67813-9 (eBook)
https://doi.org/10.1007/978-3-319-67813-9

Library of Congress Control Number: 2017955273

Cover design by Fatima Jamadar

Printed on acid-free paper

This Palgrave Macmillan imprint is published by Springer Nature
The registered company is Springer International Publishing AG
The registered company address is: Gewerbestrasse 11, 6330 Cham, Switzerland

Acknowledgments

We would both like to thank Amy Invernizzi and Phil Getz at Palgrave for their guidance, support, and infinite patience throughout the creation of this book. Dylan Winchock would like to thank Susan Strehle for her encouragement to investigate the ambiguities of speculative fiction. He would also like to thank the Southwest Popular/American Culture Association for feedback on much of what would become a chapter in this book. Jessica Elbert Decker would like to thank her colleagues in the Ancient Philosophy Society for all of their helpful feedback, especially Danny Layne, Emanuela Bianchi, Jill Gordon, Michael Shaw, and Sara Brill for their expertise in approaching Plato's *Timaeus*, a most intimidating dialogue. She would also like to thank the presenters and participants of the 2012 *Collegium Phaenomenologicum* in Città di Castello, Italy, for riveting discussions of ancient philosophy; special thanks to Claudia Baracchi for her inspiring week-long seminar on Plato's *Timaeus*. Finally, a heartfelt thanks from both of us to Monika Elbert for proposing this fruitful collaboration.

Contents

Notes on Contributors

Jessica Elbert Decker is an associate professor of philosophy at California State University, San Marcos, where she teaches in the philosophy, environmental studies, and women's studies departments. Her research focuses on Ancient Greek texts in both philosophy and mythology, using the tools of feminist theory and psychoanalysis. Her work has been published in *Epoché: A Journal for the History of Philosophy*, *philoSOPHIA: A Journal of Continental Feminism*, and *Women's Studies: An Interdisciplinary Journal.* Her current research project is a monograph on the fragments of the Presocratic philosopher Heraclitus.

Salvador Fernández is a professor of Spanish and French literary studies at Occidental College, in Los Angeles, California. He has published a book entitled *Gustavo Sainz: Postmodernism in the Mexican Novel* and co-edited a collection of essays titled *El norte y su frontera en la narrativa policíaca mexicana*. He was a Fulbright scholar in Barcelona, Spain.

William Koch is an adjunct assistant professor at the New York City College of Technology. His recent publications include "Phenomenology and the Impasse of Politics" in *Phenomenology and the Political* and "Phenomenology as Social Critique" in *The Horizons of Authenticity: Essays in Honor of Charles Guignon's Work on Phenomenology, Existentialism, and Moral Psychology.*

Tereza Jiroutová Kynčlová is a professor of gender studies at Charles University, in Prague, Czech Republic. Her publications include "Gender Aspects of Education in the Czech Republic," "Prospects of Anzaldúan Thought for a Czech Future," and "Constructing Mestiza Consciousness: Gloria Anzaldúa's Literary Techniques in Borderlands/La Frontera – The New Mestiza."

Adia Mendelson-Maoz is an associate professor in Israeli literature and culture at the Open University of Israel. She investigates the relationships between literature, ethics, politics, and culture. Her latest book, *Multiculturalism in Israel – Literary Perspectives*, was published in 2014 by Purdue University Press. She has just completed a manuscript titled *Borders, Territories, and Ethics – Contemporary Hebrew Literature in the Shadow of the Intifada.*

Filippo Menozzi is a professor of postcolonial and world literature at Liverpool John Moores University. His research interests are world and postcolonial literature, South Asian women's writing, critical theory, migration narrative, and Marxism. He is the author of *Postcolonial Custodianship: Cultural and Literary Inheritance.*

Paromita Mukherjee is an assistant professor of English literature at Amity University in Kolkata, India. Her doctoral work focused on twentieth-century British women writers, and her recent publications include international journal articles and book chapters.

Irina Negrea is an assistant professor of humanities at Shaw University in Raleigh, North Carolina. Her publications include book chapters entitled "On the Margins of a Movement: Passing in Three Contemporary Memoirs," in *Passing Interest: Racial Passing in US Novels, Memoirs, Television, and Film, 1990–2010*, and "'Mama, I Think I Broke Something': Thinking about the Environment in Behn Zeitlin's *Beast of the Southern Wild*," in *Movies in the Age of Obama: The Era of Post Racial and Neo-Racist Cinema.*

Andrea Oppo is an associate professor of aesthetics and philosophy of religion at the Pontifical University of Sardinia, in Italy. He is the author of the books *Philosophical Aesthetics and Samuel Beckett* (2008) and (ed.) *Shapes of Apocalypse. Arts and Philosophy in Slavic Thought* (2013).

Numerous articles written by him on the relationship between philosophy and literature have been published.

Danielle Russell is an associate professor of English studies at Glendon, York University, in Toronto, Ontario, specializing in American and Victorian literature. She is the author of *Between the Angle and the Curve: Mapping Gender, Race, Space and Identity in Cather and Morrison*, and her publications include chapters on *The Color Purple*, *The Madwoman in the Attic*, and Neil Gaiman.

Dylan Winchock is an adjunct professor of literature and writing at California State University, San Marcos, where his research focuses on border studies, as well as city and utopian fiction. His most recent presentations include "Margaret Atwood's *MaddAddam Trilogy* and the Failure of Memory at the Edge of Apocalypse" and "Tearing Down Silence: The Subversion of Rented Rooms in Gloria Naylor's *The Women of Brewster Place.*"

Heather Hei-Tai Yeung is an assistant professor of English language and literature at Bilkent University, in Ankara, Turkey, where she focuses on poetics, literary theory, and contemporary literature and the arts. She is the author of *Spatial Engagement with Poetry.*

Introduction: Borderlands and Liminality Across Philosophy and Literature

Jessica Elbert Decker and Dylan Winchock

A border is but a line extending infinitely, widthlessly, and abstractly; yet the moment this line is delimited and inscribed upon a map or etched within the earth, it takes on new social meaning. Borders are found nowhere in nature but where human beings impose them, and they are imposed with a purpose. A border, then, may be better understood as being more than a line: it is a physical limit. Useful, it locates the division between things, their beginnings, and their endings. We draw borders between nation states, transforming rivers, mountains, and other arbitrary features into the difference between the sovereignty of "us" and "them." We build fences around property to distinguish between that which we possess and that which we do not. We delimit with borders those things which we identify as part of our self from those things that we have rejected as "outside."

A border, however, is more than just a physical limit: it is also the limit of ideas. It is the line we draw with words through definition, sketching out the edges of a concept, as well as the edges of the categories we use to contain the world around us. It is the radical break we impose on time through eras, epochs, and movements—between the past, present, and future. It is the oppositional line drawn between good and evil, true and false, white and black, male and female, dominant and subordinate: the hierarchical binary pairs constructed and upheld by Western society.

J. Elbert Decker (✉) • D. Winchock
California State University San Marcos, San Marcos, CA, USA

J. Elbert Decker, D. Winchock (eds.), *Borderlands and Liminal Subjects*, https://doi.org/10.1007/978-3-319-67813-9_1

The study of borders is a critique of these purposeful lines drawn on the world around us, and so, too, is it a critique of the hierarchical power structures that produce such lines and are in turn reinforced by them. Both physical and conceptual, the production of a border is never a neutral act. Borders are invisible lines crisscrossing social spaces, worldviews, and perception. They are drawn to distinguish between races, between genders, and between socioeconomic classes. As such, with every border drawn, a structure of power materializes alongside it. Hierarchies are justified through the naturalization of unnatural lines; for to naturalize a border is to naturalize privilege as well as oppression. Borders, in whatever form they may take, are always political.

There are some who would argue that proper analysis comes only in the form of the physical, geopolitical border between nations. Josiah Heyman, a major proponent of this position, contends that conceptual borders obscure the very real political and economic issues that emerge and manifest at the concrete border. The metaphorical use of border, he claims, abstracts and de-localizes the issues at hand through "momentarily satisfying but paper-thin imagery."[1] Academic criticism that focuses on images of the US-Mexico border, he suggests, results in a reproduction and reinforcement of the binary oppositions of "Mexico/U.S., illegal/legal, poor/rich."[2] Instead of producing a genuine critique, it reifies the hierarchical contrasts between the two sides of the border.[3]

While the geopolitical is certainly of great importance and should be studied at length, Heyman's dismissal of the conceptual is itself far too reductive. Akhil Gupta and James Ferguson argue that space is "a neutral grid on which cultural difference, historical memory, and societal organization are inscribed."[4] Each organizational map produced—including that of economics or politics at the national border—is thus only one of the many ways in which meaning is inscribed upon geography. Furthermore, Gupta and Ferguson suggest that "the fiction of cultures as discrete, object-like phenomena occupying discrete spaces becomes implausible for those who

[1] Josiah McC. Heyman, "The Mexico-United States Border in Anthropology: A Critique and Reformulation." *Journal of Political Ecology* 1 (1994): 43–44.

[2] Ibid., 47–48.

[3] Ibid., 60.

[4] Akhil Gupta and James Ferguson. "Beyond 'Culture': Space, Identity, and the Politics of Difference." *Cultural Anthropology* 1 (1992): 7.

inhabit borderlands."[5] As culture shifts, flows, and transforms across space well beyond the border, it seems negligent to focus on a singular narrative-organizational map rooted along but one thin line. Instead, if the metaphorical is genuinely acknowledged, then its "paper-thin imagery" is revealed as a layered and complex thing. The act of crossing is carried around the world on the back of every border crosser, be it a migrant worker or a transnational businessperson.[6] Everyday acts far from the border are thus influenced by the act of crossing, and this influence politicizes otherwise mundane behavior, transforming the "neutral grid" of place into a contesting Borderland space. Indeed, as border crossing increasingly becomes the norm, "space and place can never be a 'given', and [...] the process of their sociopolitical construction must always be considered."[7] Based on this argument, Borderlands are not fixed in place, but rather exist as the unstable space *between* places,[8] or the shifting stream of marginalized narratives beneath the surface of the dominant organizational maps, striving to be heard over the din of an overarching ideological system.

The ubiquity of Borderlands in an age of late capitalist globalization makes simple definitions of nation and region untenable, problematizing the containment of any space through the use of a singular, unbroken border line. The blurred "interstitial zone" thus displaces static maps with palimpsestic intersections produced by the "hybridized subject."[9] Rather than reinforcing the binary, as Heyman suggests, the metaphorical images of the border and conceptual Borderlands call into question the validity of the binary and its inscribed structures of power. This is not a refutation of the importance of the geopolitical border, but a call for an inclusive analysis that looks across disciplines and perspectives, understanding that with each narrative trajectory explored, a more complete picture of a phenomenon may be revealed.

One only needs to look to the production of physical borders to find a simultaneous production of metaphorical Borderlands. Victor Turner, in *The Ritual Process*, defines liminality as a state of existence evoked within the particular context of rites of passage. This ritualized marginalization—

[5] Ibid.

[6] Ibid.

[7] Ibid., 17.

[8] Ibid., 18.

[9] Ibid.

ceremonially marked out in bordered physical space—produces a metaphorical connection between the unknown and the known, or the mysterious and the intelligible.[10] Liminality is thus the in-between or marginal state, in which an individual resides before becoming integrated into his or her new position in society.[11] It is a temporary, interstitial residence used to mark the transformation of an individual into a part of the whole. It thus legitimizes not only individual inclusion, but the ability of society to have mastery over that which is outside of its limits—or at least the ability to reinforce the exclusion of the other as an opposing binary to the cultural dominant. As a result, the ritual process places the liminal subject in neither its previous identity nor its newly integrated one. It is instead a blank slate: "They have to be shown that in themselves, they are clay or dust, mere matter, whose form is impressed upon them by society."[12] Within Turner's framework, we see how liminality can exist for the benefit of the dominant, where the marginal subject is passively transformed, and society actively enacts this transformation upon them.

Gloria Anzaldúa attempts to subvert the passivity of the marginal into an active position of ambiguity that questions the binary structure of hierarchical worldviews. The Chicana perspective, according to Anzaldúa, is a permanently liminal location of silence and obscurity for the racially "prohibited and forbidden" within both the United States and Mexico.[13] In this way, Chicano/as are excluded from Mexican, Indian, and Anglo culture, while paradoxically being part of all three. Victor Turner argues that the liminal subject "elude[s] or slip[s] through the network of classifications" and that "liminal entities are neither here nor there; they are betwixt and between."[14] Anzaldúa agrees, but complicates his exclusionary "neither/nor" position by suggesting that her identity is both between *and* among: "what I want is an accounting with all three cultures – white, Mexican, Indian."[15] She locates within liminality a space/state/process of agency for the marginal through its inherent inclusivity rather than the automatic exclusion of the other. A Borderland identity is a potentially powerful position in that such a subjectivity has access to a multiplicity of

[10] Victor Turner, *The Ritual Process* (New Brunswick: Aldine Transaction, 1997): 15.

[11] Ibid., 125.

[12] Ibid., 103.

[13] Gloria Anzaldúa, *Borderlands/La Frontera* (San Francisco: Aunt Lute Press, 1999): 25.

[14] Turner, *Ritual*, 95.

[15] Anzaldúa, *Borderlands*, 44.

perspectives and bridges the unnatural divide formed between them. As a permanently liminal outsider, one gains a sensitivity and insight—*la facultad*[16]—that allows the individual to tactically navigate monocultural biases and exclusionary practices that tend to form within isolated in-groups. Anzaldúa thus empowers the permeability of the Borderland and delegitimizes the authority of the impenetrable border.

In her later works, Anzaldúa grew dissatisfied with the limitations of a theory rooted specifically within one ethnic experience. While her Chicana identity would most certainly remain of great importance to her, so too would her experiences as a woman and a lesbian. She therefore expanded her ideas beyond the geopolitical border that she so earnestly criticized. The term "Borderland" too quickly evoked the US-Mexico border in her readers, which prompted her to change the language so that her theories could more easily shift between the geopolitical and conceptual. Drawing from a personal mythology (loosely based on Nahúatl stories), she suggests *nepantla*, or a kind of liminality that allows for individuals to "question old ideas and beliefs, acquire new perspectives, change worldviews, and shift from one world to another."[17] Nepantla is more than just the physical, but also the psychical territory between the conscious and unconscious, "where image and story-making takes place."[18] Anzaldúa asserts that it is within this metaphorical and performative space that transformation occurs.[19] To transgress borders, then, we must do more than simply cross a line: we must be willing to break apart our old worldviews and reassemble them into something that allows us to navigate, survive, and bridge the liminal territory between binaries. It is also not something that begins and ends with the crossing of a line: it is an open-ended and fluid process toward the Coyolxauhqui Imperative, a desire to repair that which is broken or wounded.[20] It is not an act of breaking from the old by crossing into the new, but rather an assemblage of both old and new, a re-mixture from both

[16] Ibid., 60–61.

[17] Gloria Anzaldúa, "(Un)natural bridges, (Un)safe spaces," *The Gloria Anzaldúa Reader* (Durham: Duke University Press, 2009): 248.

[18] Gloria Anzaldúa, "Speaking Across the Divide," *The Gloria Anzaldúa Reader* (Durham: Duke University Press, 2009): 291.

[19] Gloria Anzaldúa, "Bearing Witness," *The Gloria Anzaldúa Reader* (Durham: Duke University Press, 2009): 278.

[20] Anzaldúa, "(Un)natural bridges, (Un)safe spaces," 247.

sides of the binary, and an ephemeral perspective that cuts across many layers of palimpsests.

Just as Anzaldúa did in her later works, Chela Sandoval moves border theory beyond the limitations of a Chicana perspective by suggesting the importance of what she calls US third world feminism. She argues that feminists marked with marginal labels such as "mestiza," "queer," and "women of color" have developed forms of feminism that tactically combine differing worldviews into a shuffling set of palimpsests, thus highlighting the Borderland as a "shifting place of mobile codes and significations."[21] Rather than locking the marginalized and silenced into a single strategy of resistance, Sandoval's "differential consciousness" allows individuals and communities to move "'between and among' ideological positionings."[22] While one could argue that this de-localizes border politics (as Heyman cautions about the conceptual border), its ability to shift perspectives produces a "tactical subjectivity" that disavows the supremacy of a dominant narrative by continually re-centering one's identity, narratives, and tactics of survival in relation to the greater context at hand.[23] From this perspective, it becomes increasingly clear that race, ethnicity, gender, sexuality, class, nationality, politics, and economy—to name a few—cannot be properly understood in isolation. Through differential consciousness, or a subversion of the liminal state, one may shift from one storyline to another, with the awareness that each is informed by the others.

The subversive readings of the liminal found in Anzaldúa and Sandoval should certainly not be thought of as emerging outside of an oppositional worldview; rather, they are built into the very structure of binary oppositions—an idea more directly explored by Homi Bhabha. Bhabha, in *The Location of Culture*, argues that meaning is produced across two subjects through a process of liminality in which the two are "mobilized in the passage through a Third Space."[24] Therefore, at a border, one side can only be understood in relation to the other, and it is at this Borderland intersection of the two that meaning emerges for both. Identity can no longer be understood singularly, and reified concepts of "unity," "the

[21] Chela Sandoval, *Methodologies of the Oppressed* (Minneapolis: University of Minnesota Press, 2000): 32–33.

[22] Ibid., 57.

[23] Ibid., 58.

[24] Homi Bhabha. *The Location of Culture.* (London: Routledge, 1994): 53.

authentic," and "the original" are called into question.[25] Similarly, teleologically fixing a culture in time and space obscures the idea that culture is an interactional process rather than permanent state. Bhabha instead calls for an acknowledgement that when an encounter occurs that "exceeds the frame of the image," our binary erasure of the other nevertheless "leaves a resistant trace, a stain of the subject, a sign of resistance."[26] When the Third Space opens up to us, like Anzaldúa's nepantla or Sandoval's differential consciousness, we can see identities for what they are: relational interactions and processes of mutual change and transformation. This is not to say that oppressive power structures do not exist, and Bhabha is not arguing for "the exoticism of multiculturalism or the *diversity* of cultures"—rather, he urges for us to consider an international culture through "the inscription and articulation of culture's *hybridity*."[27] It is through the inexorable ties among differences that meaning is made.

Western metaphysics has historically been dominated by dualistic categories—Plato's separation of the sensible from the intelligible seems a foundational move in this tradition, and yet, this notion of a Third Space outside of binary oppositions appears in Plato's thought. In the cosmology of the *Timaeus*, Plato suggests that the division between sensible and intelligible depends upon a third kind, which he names *khora* (space); this ambiguous Borderland space is the medium that allows for transmission between the sensible and the intelligible realms. Jacques Derrida emphasizes the disruptive effect of *khora*, which is somehow neither of the categories it mediates and somehow both at once. He points out that "at times the khora appears to be neither this nor that, at times both this and that, but this alternation between the logic of exclusion and that of participation. . .stems perhaps only from a provisional appearance and from the constraints of rhetoric, even from some incapacity for naming."[28] This problem of naming surfaces in the multiple names that Plato gives to *khora* (mother, nurse, third kind, receptacle, and space) meanwhile saying: "it must always be called by the same name."[29] Binary categories inevitably

[25] Ibid., 54.

[26] Ibid., 71.

[27] Ibid., 56.

[28] Jacques Derrida, *On the Name*, trans. David Wood, John P. Leavey, Jr., and Ian McLeod (Palo Alto: Stanford University Press, 1995): 92.

[29] Plato, *Timaeus*, trans. R.G. Bury (Boston: Harvard University Press, 1929), 50c.

create a Borderland between them, which has been conceptualized in various guises, and certainly not always by the same name.

In Plato, the problem is how to bridge the divide between the mortal, sensible world and the divine, intelligible world; in Aristotle, it is the problem of matter and form; in later Cartesian models, it presents as the mind-body problem; and in phenomenology, it appears as the chiasm. For thinkers before Plato, such as Pythagoras or Parmenides, the problem of the one and the many was paramount: if there is an underlying unity to the cosmos, how to account for the appearance of multiplicity? This problem of binaries can be traced through the history of Western philosophy, in various guises, but always with a similar structure: what is the relation between these opposing terms? How can they be opposite, and yet, seem utterly dependent upon one other for their existence or meaning?

In the poem of Parmenides, widely regarded as the origin of logic, an unnamed goddess diagnoses the pitfalls and deception of mortal thinking; in a section of the poem referred to as "the third way," she explains precisely what is flawed about mortal perception. She has offered a teaching to the young man (Parmenides, presumably): everything *is*, and nothing is not. But she warns him that human beings do not recognize this simple truth; instead, they conjure up a third path of their own making, a path that somehow combines *is* and *is not*, not realizing that they cannot possibly think or say what is not. The goddess tells the young man:

> I hold you back as well from the one [route or way, *hodos*] that mortals fabricate, twin-heads, knowing nothing for helplessness [*amechania*] in their chests is what steers their wandering minds as they are carried along in a daze, deaf and blind at the same time: indistinguishable, undistinguishing crowds who reckon that being and non-being are the same but not the same. And, for all of them, the route they follow is a path that keeps turning backwards on itself.[30]

As Peter Kingsley has pointed out, this identification of human beings as twin-headed indicates not only the human tendency to think in opposites, but subtly invokes the crossroads, referred to as "twin-heads" since Ancient

[30] Parmenides DK 6, Kingsley's translation in *Reality* (Inverness: Golden Sufi Press, 2003), 83.

Greek crossroads were shaped like a "Y."[31] Crossroads are liminal places associated with the goddess Hekate, who presides over magic, prayers, and offerings, and often acts as a *psychopompous*, one who guides travelers between worlds. Parmenides' use of "twin-heads" suggests ambiguity, danger, and trickery, as crossroads were also places where one might meet thieves, sorcerers, and con artists of various kinds. The human beings that Parmenides' goddess describes are trapped in a loop, walking a road that, like a Mobius strip, never goes anywhere. The human inability to think logically, according to the goddess, is bound up in our use of language—the way in which we distinguish things, name them, and categorize them.

Throughout Parmenides' poem, the goddess is describing "it": a pronoun without a referent; she speaks in depth of what *is*, but her speech is all verbs with no subject. Commentators generally choose an appropriate noun as the subject and say that the goddess is describing Being, or Existence, or Reality; but, as Mitchell Miller suggests, the subject of the poem is strategically elided.[32] In fragment DK 8, the goddess says of this "it," so far unnamed: "its name shall be everything—every single name mortals have invented convinced they are all true: birth and death, existence, non-existence, change of place, alternation of bright color."[33] If all is one, then every name refers to "it." The hapless state of human beings described by the goddess in the "third way" passage of the poem is, at least in part, a problem of language and naming: our categories bind and limit our thinking. Binary categories are especially limiting, as the goddess' witty mocking of human beings as "twin-heads" conjures up comical images of a two-headed creature perpetually at war with itself.

At the very least, what this text implies is that human thought is somehow paradoxical, slippery, even dangerously deceptive—this theme, of course, is picked up by Plato in his famous Allegory of the Cave, though

[31] Kingsley, *Reality*, 99–101 and notes on 565. The Ancient Greek word *trihodos*, literally "three ways," refers to a crossroads shaped like a "Y" where a traveler must choose between two paths forward ("twin-heads").

[32] Mitchell Miller, "Ambiguity and Transport: Reflections on the Proem to Parmenides' Poem," *Oxford Studies in Ancient Philosophy* 30, (2006): 3. "The goddess picks out or highlights 'is' by pointedly suppressing its subject (and, possibly, predicate). The effect is to reverse the usual order of the conspicuous and the inconspicuous: by eliding the normally conspicuous subject (and, possibly, predicate), the goddess brings the normally inconspicuous 'is' to the front and centre and challenges us to reflect upon it."

[33] Parmenides poem DK 8, Kingsley's translation in *Reality*, 190–191.

in Plato's narrative, the escaped prisoner finds his way out in the light. In the picture painted by Parmenides' goddess, the human beings are being steered by "helplessness," *amechania* in Ancient Greek, a term associated with complete paralysis and inability to act; literally, without a *mechos*, a scheme or trick, like the prisoners bound in place in Plato's cave. This image of paralysis, trapped between two binary pairs, is remarkably similar to Anzaldúa's description of the coatlicue state. This state of paralysis can lead to transformation, but it must first be recognized, just as the prisoners in Plato's cave must first realize they are prisoners, to have any hope of escape. In Parmenides' poem, the goddess offers hints on how to slip from these trappings of human thinking, when she warns the young man: "and don't let much-experienced habit force you to guide your sightless eye and echoing ear and tongue along this way, but judge in favor of the highly contentious demonstration of the truth contained in these words as spoken by me."[34] Habit is named as *force*, dragging dazed human beings along paths of thinking that they do not consciously will or choose. The habit of thinking in binaries seems especially persistent, if the canon of Western philosophy is any indication.

The limitations that appear in any binary system are rigid, and the borders between categories always bleed into one another—a tendency that suggests the violence required to enforce these borders, in which identities and power are often deeply invested. The work of Irigaray emphasizes the crucial role of sexual difference, understood as the binary opposition between male and female, in grounding patriarchal metaphysical systems—systems that she dubs "phallogocentric." Like Derrida, Irigaray suggests that the metaphysical understanding of the subject, as constituted by the Western philosophical canon, privileges certain categories over others; Derrida emphasizes the privileging of presence over absence, Irigaray argues that male identity has been constructed against female *lack*. The psychoanalytic tradition is replete with examples of this, as Freud characterizes libido as purely male and Lacan erects the phallus as master signifier and exiles women to a place outside of the Symbolic. This operation involves a conceptualization of the subject, often unconscious, where that subject's identity is defined over against a category constructed as "other." The fact that this process is almost entirely unconscious does not mitigate any of its oppressive effects; instead, it makes these effects all the

[34] Parmenides poem DK 7, Kingsley's translation in *Reality*, 120.

more pernicious as they are taken to be natural and inevitable. Perhaps the best example of this binary thought procedure in action is the notion of the universal subject, which has its beginnings in Ancient Greek thought but is fully realized in Enlightenment models of rationality. Here, despite the fact that only certain identities have access to the creation of culture—wealthy, white, male individuals, and so on—the notion of the universal subject insists on the homogeneity and equality of all subjects, flattening out any difference as irrelevant, or worse, non-existent.

Critiques of this fantasy of the universal subject have come from multiple disciplines; critical race theorists, queer theorists, and feminist scholars have all challenged this paradigm in the contexts of their respective discourses. Patriarchal, white supremacist, and heteronormative systems share a foundation in binary thinking. Ecofeminist scholar Karen Warren calls this foundation an "oppressive conceptual framework," arguing that such systems are deeply hierarchical, constructing dualistic categories such that one is always superior while the other is inferior (e.g. men versus women).[35] These oppressive conceptual frameworks maintain themselves through a "logic of domination" that attempts to justify unjust subordination; "a logic of domination is offered as the moral stamp of approval for subordination, since, if accepted, it provides a justification for keeping the Downs down."[36] As Warren notes, a frequent justification in the history of Western thought is the attribute of mind or reason—women, people of color, animals, and other marginalized subjects that do not conform to the dominant paradigm of the universal subject have all historically been denied autonomy for their alleged lack of reason.

Binary thinking, as Parmenides warned thousands of years ago, is a deeply entrenched habit of Western culture, and habits are notoriously hard to break because they are unconscious. One strategy for addressing this problem is to make these destructive habits visible so that their assumptions and effects can be challenged, sabotaged, and eventually, dissolved. Close examination of the boundaries between binary categories reveals that they are not so rigidly separated, but, as Donna Haraway suggests, these distinctions prove "leaky."

[35] Karen Warren, "Quilting Ecofeminist Philosophy" in *Environmental Ethics: Convergence and Divergence*, eds. Richard G. Armstrong and Susan J. Boltzer (New York: McGraw Hill, 2004), 418.

[36] Ibid.

Haraway argues that the binary pairs of human/animal, animal-human/machine, and physical/non-physical have all been effectively breached in our contemporary culture.[37] The permeability of these Borderland spaces opens up possibilities for reimagining our categories and creating new paradigms that recognize difference and resist hierarchical structures of identity.

A careful study of borders and Borderlands often begins with the most concrete example: national borders. These geopolitical lines designate the limits of political sovereignty, as well as that of culture and identity declared as legitimate representations of a nation. These national spaces are rarely as simple as this, however. Sovereign action within a nation inevitably affects other nations beyond its borders; nor is culture and identity shed and replaced upon crossing such borders. At the border, we instead see an interactional process between and among nations, where discrete national distinction is called into question. The Borderlands between nations that "bleed" across supposedly impermeable borders and produce an intermingling of cultures suggest a relationship across the border—between self and other, us and them—that potentially breaks down myths of sovereignty and reified hierarchy. The essays in the first section of this volume address the complex political, social, and cultural effects of geographic Borderland spaces.

Filippo Menozzi, in "On Being a Border: Reading Across Literature and Philosophy," bases his research on the recent influx of immigrants entering Italy through the Mediterranean island of Lampedusa. These dispossessed immigrants living inside the island's detention center find themselves defined by a space that is neither European Union nor home; they are subjects produced by territoriality and the stratifying process of global capitalism. Menozzi focuses on a group of European poets who have borne witness to the immigrant experience through a collection of poems, *Sotto il Cielo di Lampedusa*. An ethical obligation to testify to the urgency of an otherwise silent struggle demands that they attempt to give voice to the interaction between the "inside" and "outside" of European citizenship and experience. While this transnational communication places the poets in the difficult position of possessing voice among the voiceless, it is done as a call for solidarity and a multiplicity of subject positions. Such discourse of the

[37] Donna J. Haraway, *Simians, Cyborgs, and Women: The Reinvention of Nature* (London: Free Association Books Ltd., 1991), 151–153.

European border moves the margins into the center and challenges the definition of European identity.

Israeli national identity, argues Adia Mendelson-Maoz, is also challenged through an investigation of borders and Borderlands. In "Land, Territory and Border: Liminality in Contemporary Israeli Literature," Mendelson-Maoz explores the ways in which Intifada-era novels critique the strict political borders set between Israel and Palestinian Occupied Territories while also reinforcing the importance of a sense of difference at the border. The characters of these novels experience a Borderland process of moral and psychological transition, where liminality results in a loss of ethical certitude. Civil identity is thus often replaced by patriarchal aggression, emotional dissonance, and madness. Using Deleuze and Guattari's concept of nomadism and infinite becoming, Mendelson-Maoz suggests that these authors offer poetic alternatives of presenting and dismantling borders, deterritorializing both the liminal space of the Occupied Territories and the national space and sovereignty of Israel.

Heather Hei-Tai Yeung, in "Zones of Maximal Translatability: Borderspace and Women's Time," explores Emily Apter's *The Translation Zone*, Julia Kristeva's *Murder in Byzantium*, and Marina Warner's *The Leto Bundle*, attending to acts of border crossing, both physical and imaginary. In her essay, Yeung focuses on both physical borders and temporal ones, analyzing problems of translation not only between texts, but also in cultural contexts. Adopting Apter's notion of the moment of maximal translatability, Yeung examines crossroads—border zones where translation breaks down and collides with the exercise of state sovereignty. Yeung's focus on temporal borders emphasizes the manner in which physical borders create temporal limits as well as geographic ones, creating both physical and temporal points of convergence and permeability.

National identity is only one of the many places in which border and Borderland politics are present. Drawing the focus into a single nation, we can see both material and conceptual borders formed between racial and ethnic positionings. We see in the wake of "New World" colonialism a discourse founded on the supremacy of white, European civilization over a perceived savagery of indigenous American and African culture. Therefore, the attempted erasure of indigenous and African identities in the Americas through genocide and enslavement led to a return of the repressed in the forms of the Chicano/a and African American identities. The intersection of cultures produces new positionings that navigate the margins of society, subvert the borders, and reveal Borderlands of ambiguity that challenge the racial binary. The second section of this volume explores racial and ethnic Borderlands, focusing on liminal and marginalized identities created through binary models of race.

Salvador Fernandez, in "A Search for Colonial histories: *The Conquest* by Yxta Maya Murray," examines the significance of Murray's juxtaposition of a colonial narrative of cross-cultural contact with a contemporary narrative of postcolonial deterritorialized and displaced communities. Focusing on magical indigenous characters, Murray produces a Borderland narrative that moves across time and between intersecting accounts of oppression. She reinforces the idea of "polyphonic meaning" rather than a singular colonizing narrative, and by utilizing pre-Hispanic mythology as a foundational narrative, she non-violently critiques and resists the overarching European colonial project.

Danielle Russell, in "Transforming Borders: Resistant Liminality in *Beloved*, *Song of Solomon*, and *Paradise*," investigates liminality as a space and state of resistance in Toni Morrison's novels. Racial marginalization in America is symptomatic of a hierarchical and supremacist power system that privileges a dominant culture of whiteness. Toni Morrison suggests that the liminal position of people of color is potentially empowering in that her characters' actions denaturalize the racial border, revealing its artifice. This racial border manifests itself throughout the oppressive geography of her novels; marginalized characters transform these places into spaces of resistance through acts of transformations, redefinition, and naming. Doing so reveals instead of a concrete line between races a Borderland in which both sides of the binary change in relation to one another.

While Russell investigates several forms of liminal spatial resistance, Irina Negrea focuses specifically on the spatio-performative act of passing in "Gone Over on the Other Side:" Passing in Charles Chesnutt's *The House Behind the Cedars*." Within a nation of binary and supremacist racial politics, "mulatto" characters in Chesnutt's turn-of-the-century novel found themselves living "in-between" legally deemed "black" regardless of cultural upbringing. While the protagonist John Walden succeeds in being accepted by white culture by internalizing a white identity and passing as a white man, his sister Rena continues to identify as black and finds herself unable to successfully pass as a white woman. Negrea argues that Chesnutt's novel is itself a Borderland narrative in that John's ability to completely disappear into white society shatters myths of the impossibility of successful passing and of an impermeable racial border. John tactically reshapes an oppressive geography into a space of resistance and subversion.

The third section of the volume explores borders of gender and sexuality, focusing in particular on the ways in which Borderland identities challenge binary models of sexual difference and the heteronormative structures of Western patriarchal society. Sexuality and gender are categories that, in contemporary discourse, are understood as much more fluid than traditional models of sex and gender. While gender has long been recognized as socially constructed or performative, to use Judith Butler's term, the binary understanding of sex (male versus female) might also be challenged as an effect of rigid dualistic thinking and models that privilege the masculine over the feminine. Each of the essays in this section approaches gender and sexuality through the lens of queer identity.

Tereza Jiroutová Kynčlová, in "Queering and Gendering Aztlán: Anzaldúa's Feminist Reshaping of the Chicana/o Nation in the U.S.-Mexico Borderlands," argues that the patriarchal and exclusionary nationalistic rhetoric of *El Movimiento* demanded a response from Chicana feminists. Through the creative writings of Gloria Anzaldúa, Kynčlová reveals a feminist Borderland reconceptualization of Azltán, where patriarchy is subverted through combinatory narrative structures that merge the personal with the grand historical. These queered narratives of territory and family undermine hierarchical authority by transforming nationalistic male sovereignty into an inclusive non-heteronormativity. Anzaldúa emphasizes that external forces of oppression are not the only kinds that marginalized Chicana/o subjects confront; the dominant hierarchical distinctions are also internalized, creating subjects that perceive themselves as abject. Kynčlová suggests, following Anzaldúa, that queer identity (which Anzaldúa identifies as parallel to her notion of mestiza consciousness) offers a path of resistance to heteronormative, hierarchical, and androcentric discourse and its corresponding power structures, where Borderland spaces can become sites of transformation.

In "Borderland Spaces of the Third Kind: Erotic Agency in Plato and Octavia Butler," Jessica Elbert Decker interrogates binary structures of sexual difference, especially in models of sexual reproduction. Plato's metaphysics is usually understood as a dualistic system, where the categories of the sensible and intelligible are opposed to one another, but in the *Timaeus*, Plato introduces a third kind that he names *khora*, or space; he tells us that this third kind is necessary for any transmission between the sensible and the intelligible to occur. This third kind introduces an ambiguous Borderland space that is neither of the categories that it separates and unites, but somehow partakes of both. In the cosmology of the *Timaeus*, Plato uses the model of the family: father, mother, and offspring, as the foundation for his description of the cosmos and its origin. Consistently, he identifies the male as active and the female as passive, grounding these binary categories in such a way that renders only male subjects as autonomous beings. Using the models of sexual reproduction in Octavia Butler's *Wild Seed* and her *Xenogenesis* series, Decker argues that the third kind disrupts the binary models of sexual difference that Plato's dualistic system attempts to ground.

William Koch, in "Achilles and the (Sexual) History of Being," examines the figure of Achilles as he appears in Homer's *Iliad*, arguing that Achilles is the first literary figure in the history of Western thought to exhibit the persistence of the Drive, in Lacan's sense. Koch analyzes the famous rage of Achilles as a *pathe*, or passion, that challenges the heroic paradigms of epic and the fantasy of immortality. Starting from Zizek's suggestion that Heidegger's conception of temporality can be grounded in the underlying Drive, as it is described by in the texts of Freud and Lacan, Koch argues that the Drive is not merely an unconscious process, but ontological in nature. Fantasy is a future-directed activity, but the *pathe* of Achilles rejects this future-oriented desire and instead focuses desire on the present; Koch argues that Achilles is emblematic of what Lee Edelman has called the *sinthomosexual*, and as such, he challenges the borders of the Symbolic system in which he finds himself. The rage of Achilles does not conform to the logic of the dominant paradigms of his era; instead, in challenging the boundaries of both desire and logic, he opens up new horizons for change.

The final section of the volume explores the limits of meaning, memory, sense, and temporality. Speculative literature—the fantastical, magical, and supernatural—creates experimental spaces in which non-material borders may be materialized and critiqued. Fanciful girls traveling down rabbit holes can experience the impossibility of separating sense from nonsense; ghostly figures can blur the distinctions between self and other; decomposing cities can collapse the opposition between utopia and apocalypse, as well as memory and forgetting. Such investigations reveal the potentially vast scope of border studies when approached across disciplines.

In his essay, "Alice's Parallel Series: Carroll, Deleuze, and the 'Stuttering Sense' of the World," Andrea Oppo examines the border between philosophy and literature, a boundary that was first delineated in Ancient Greek philosophy with Plato's dismissal of art and myth from his Republic. Oppo frames his reading of Lewis Carroll using Deleuze's analysis in *The Logic of Sense*, arguing that the border between philosophy and literature must be explored in the context of language, meaning, and reference.

The contrasting perspectives of objectivity (the world of "facts") and subjectivity, where meaning is relational, is one way of conceptualizing this Borderland; in Deleuze's *Logic of Sense*, he conceives of this border as the contrast between surface and depth. Oppo argues, following Deleuze, that sense has a dynamic structure where inside and outside are entangled, as in a Mobius strip, and that this structure reveals that all sense is rooted in *nonsense*. In approaching the question of meaning in this manner, Oppo suggests the fragility and instability of sense, as it constantly "stutters" and threatens to fall into the abyss of nonsense. This reading emphasizes the permeability of the border between philosophy and literature, as the logic (*logos*) of sense and meaning cannot be understood through a simple division between facts/objectivity and aesthetics/subjectivity.

In "Cultural Liminality: Gender, Identity, and Margin in the Uncanny Stories of Elizabeth Bowen," Paromita Mukherjee explores the liminal figures in Elizabeth Bowen's stories, focusing on female characters engaged in transition; Mukherjee argues that these liminal identities destabilize cultural assumptions about selfhood and challenge traditional notions of female subjectivity. In reading Bowen's stories, Mukherjee focuses on experiences of the *phantasm*: ghostly, hallucinatory, and irrational experiences that challenge the borders of what is accepted as normal or real. Characters in these texts gain access to the other only through these ambiguous, ephemeral, and phantasmatic experiences. The experience of the uncanny (*unheimlich*), defined by Freud as paradoxically both familiar (*heimlich*) and strange, can have the effect of destabilizing identity; the boundaries between self and other can temporally dissolve, and the self—especially because of its imminent mortality—can be figured outside of itself and become other. Through close analysis of these female characters in transition, the manner in which identity becomes fluid is revealed, and the binaries of real versus supernatural and self versus other become permeable.

Dylan Winchock, in "Crossing the Utopian/Apocalyptic Border: The Anxiety of Forgetting in Paul Auster's *In the Country of Last Things*," utilizes Paul Ricoeur's philosophy of memory and narrative to study the human need to locate identity at the intersection of spatio-temporal narratives. The modernist Utopian project attempts to flatten narrative interaction through an apocalyptic erasure of the past in order to maintain a singular, self-contained, and uncontested narrative of the present. This highly policed border between apocalypse and Utopia is a fantasy, however, where Borderland testimonies "rooted" in fragmentation and mobility become tactics of political resistance against disappearance and amnesia.

Postapocalyptic novels describe instead of an erasure, a place of ruin—a space of *incomplete* or failed apocalypse where the tatters and shreds of a multiplicity of former perspectives hang onto a fragile, monovocal Utopian narrative. Winchock argues that Paul Auster's postapocalyptic novel reveals the importance of testifying to the "last things" cleared away by apocalypse as though it were "the first time," thus allowing oneself to see the familiar from new and shifting perspectives. It is through these tactical testimonies that the forgotten, erased, and silenced can be recalled and reconfigured in order to produce an ephemeral sense of wholeness.

Bibliography

Anzaldúa, Gloria. 1999. *Borderlands/La Frontera*. San Francisco: Aunt Lute Press.
———. 2009a. Bearing Witness. In *The Gloria Anzaldúa Reader*, ed. AnaLouise Keating, 277–279. Durham: Duke University Press.
———. 2009b. Speaking Across the Divide. In *The Gloria Anzaldúa Reader*, ed. AnaLouise Keating, 243–248. Durham: Duke University Press.
———. 2009c. (Un)natural Bridges, (Un)safe Spaces. In *The Gloria Anzaldúa Reader*, ed. AnaLouise Keating, 282–294. Durham: Duke University Press.
Bhabha, Homi. 1994. *The Location of Culture*. London: Routledge.
Derrida, Jacques. 1995. *On the Name*. Trans. David Wood, John P. Leavey, Jr., and Ian McLeod. Palo Alto: Stanford University Press.
Gupta, Akhil, and James Ferguson. 1992. Beyond 'Culture': Space, Identity, and the Politics of Difference. *Cultural Anthropology* 1: 6–23.
Haraway, Donna. 1991. *Simians, Cyborgs, and Women: The Reinvention of Nature*. London: Free Association Books Ltd.
Heyman, Josiah McC. 1994. The Mexico-United States Border in Anthropology: A Critique and Reformulation. *Journal of Political Ecology* 1: 43–66.
Irigaray, Luce. 1985. *This Sex Which Is Not One*. Trans. Catherine Porter with Carolyn Burke. Ithaca: Cornell University Press.
Kingsley, Peter. 2003. *Reality*. Inverness: Golden Sufi Press.
Miller, Mitchell. 2006. Ambiguity and Transport: Reflections on the Proem to Parmenides' Poem. *Oxford Studies in Ancient Philosophy* 30: 1–47.
Plato. 1929. *Timaeus*. Trans. R.G. Bury. Boston: Harvard University Press.
Sandoval, Chela. 2000. *Methodologies of the Oppressed*. Minneapolis: University of Minnesota Press.
Turner, Victor. 1997. *The Ritual Process*. New Brunswick: Aldine Transaction.
Warren, Karen. 2004. Quilting ecofeminist philosophy. In *Environmental Ethics: Convergence and Divergence*, ed. Richard G. Armstrong and Susan J. Boltzer, 416–428. New York: McGraw Hill.

PART I

National Borderlands

Ethics at the Border: Transmitting Migrant Experiences

Filippo Menozzi

Europe is everywhere outside of itself.[1]

What happens when the border, from being a simple space of transition or embarkation, becomes a permanent ontological condition, an enclosed and enclosing place of habitation defining new subjectivities? How does the standpoint of the border reframe central ethical questions about representation, witnessing and identification? The borders of contemporary Europe offer a privileged ground for exploring these issues. After the civil and political unrest that affected various countries in North Africa and the Middle East since 2011 and the civil war in Syria, the number of migrants, refugees and asylum-seekers trying to reach Europe by sea has increased dramatically. According to the UN Refugee Agency, during the first seven months of 2014 more than 87,000 people arrived in Italy by sea, mainly from Eritrea and Syria. From 2013 to 2014, the "Mare Nostrum" operation, launched by the Italian government, rescued more than 100,000 people. The route across the Mediterranean is fraught with risks. The UN Refugee Agency reports that in 2014 alone, some 3500 people lost their

[1] Etienne Balibar, *Politics and the Other Scene*, translated by Christine Jones, James Swenson, and Chris Turner (London: Verso, 2002), 100.

F. Menozzi (✉)
Liverpool John Moores University, Liverpool, UK

J. Elbert Decker, D. Winchock (eds.), *Borderlands and Liminal Subjects*, https://doi.org/10.1007/978-3-319-67813-9_2

lives in their attempt to reach Southern Europe. In April 2015, more than 700 people drowned in a single accident, the shipwreck of a vessel south of the Italian island of Lampedusa, the point of arrival of many routes from the Southern Mediterranean. The situation urged intense talks on the migrant crisis in Europe.

The response of governments and institutions has been uncertain and highly controversial. In 2014, the "Mare Nostrum" operation was replaced by a much smaller project, "Triton," with substantially reduced resources and powers. During the first months of 2016, the migrant crisis in Europe remains unsolved: migrant riots in the French port of Calais and various locations in Eastern Europe testify to a social, political and economic conundrum that is testing the European Union (EU) as a whole. Places like the island of Lampedusa (Southern Italy) and Lesbos (Greece) have become the center of an intense migrant movement and a symbol of the borders of Europe. Rutvica Andrijasevic has provided a vivid analysis of the situation in Lampedusa in the past years. Her research has brought to the fore the island's detention center, which has been denounced repeatedly in the last decades for human rights violations and legal irregularities. Lampedusa reveals what Andrijasevic describes as "the continuity of European space as it expands beyond its geo-political borders and the movements of migration that incessantly traverse that space."[2] The southern coastline of the EU shows the transformations of the reality of borders and complicates the very limits of Europe, questioning the logic of inside/outside and the meaning of European citizenship. As Heidrun Friese notes, after the 2011 unrest in the Middle East and North Africa, thousands of people reclaimed the right to mobility and reached the island of Lampedusa, which is today at the center of a growing "migration industry"[3] benefiting formal and informal economies, as well as the systems of national security, reception and detention of migrants. The current migrant crisis compels a rethinking of the very idea of Europe and demonstrates that Europe's borders are not at the margins, but rather at the center of the European political space and identity.

[2] Rutvica Andrijasevic, "From Exception to Excess: Detention and Deportations across the Mediterranean Space," in Nicholas de Genova and Nathalie Peutz, *The Deportation Regime: Sovereignty, Space, and the Freedom of Movement* (Durham NC: Duke UP, 2010), 148.

[3] Friese Heidrun, "Border Economies. Lampedusa and the Nascent Migration Industry," *Shima: The International Journal of Research into Island Cultures* 6, no. 2 (2012): 68.

In 2015, an international collective of poets, "multiVERSI," which includes poets from Italy, Iraq, Somalia and the USA, published a poetry anthology in two volumes, entitled *Sotto il Cielo di Lampedusa* (*Under the Sky of Lampedusa*). The poetry anthology is important because it presents the response of poets and writers to the current migrant crisis. In the brief introduction, the book outlines the central question about the significance and role of poetry when politics and economics seem to be powerless to stop the suffering of migrants. The authors state that poetic response to the tragedy of migrants is not only important, but actually fundamental and necessary. Reading such claims in the face of the concrete everyday suffering of refugees, migrants and asylum-seekers can raise a difficult ethical question about the claims of poetry in violent historical situations. In the European tradition, these claims relate to Theodor Adorno's influential (and often misunderstood) observation that the "abundance of real suffering" makes the writing of lyric poetry "barbaric" and yet, at the same time, it "also demands the continued existence of art while it prohibits it; it is now virtually in art alone that suffering can still find its own voice."[4] Poetry is not only impossible or "barbaric" when faced with extreme human suffering. Paradoxically, suffering demands the continued existence of poetry as faithful form of witnessing, its only true human response beyond any mere factual report or representation.

According to the "multiVERSI" collective, poetry is able to reclaim the fullness of life and the full humanity of the migrants. These poems are hence introduced as forms of protest, denunciation and testimony of the suffering of migrants. The majority of these poems are not, however, written by those who are currently traversing or have recently traversed the Mediterranean to reach Europe. Especially in the second volume, significantly subtitled 'No Man is an Island'—a subtitle inspired by John Donne's 1624 'Devotions upon Emergent Occasions'—most of these poems are not authored by today's migrants. While focusing on Lampedusa, these poems epitomize what Carlo Ginzburg would call a "noninsular vision" of literature,[5] which imagines the island as a point of connection and transition. The text is written as a *response* to migrant lives. The problem raised by *Under the Sky of Lampedusa* has hence to do with the possibility of expressing solidarity

[4] Adorno, Theodor, "Commitment." In Ernst Bloch et al. *Aesthetics and Politics*. Translated by Ronald Taylor. (London: Verso, 1980), 188.

[5] Carlo Ginzburg, *No Island is an Island* (New York: Columbia University Press, 2000), xi.

and speaking to, for or on behalf of people who come from the other side of the border of Europe. *Under the Sky of Lampedusa* captures the ethical dilemma symbolized by that "tie between a possibility and an impossibility of speaking," that, according to philosopher Giorgio Agamben, constitutes the vital dimension of the testimony.[6] Indeed, the main authors of the compositions included in the anthology are not those who are perishing in the Mediterranean or arriving at Lampedusa after extremely violent and exhausting journeys. Only a few letters and messages from those arriving in Lampedusa are reproduced in the book. The majority of the poems are responses, caught between the possibility of speaking and its impossibility. On the one hand, the poetic responses bear witness to the tragedy and deaths in the Mediterranean. They create an opportunity to speak about the experience of migrants and testify to its dramatic reality and urgency. On the other hand, the voices that are heard through the anthology are not the voices of the migrants. For this reason, the authors of the anthology claim no "authority" to speak for the migrants. This positioning does not fully prevent these poems from running the risk of becoming a new sort of 'dominant' voice telling the experience of others. Rather, the poems inhabit a transient, precarious ethical borderland, which oscillates between the ability to transmit experiences that might be lost and the potential appropriation of these experiences for establishing the voice of the poet. This problem is not solved, but rather constantly inhabited and re-proposed by the poems, which makes them a site to discuss the ethics of representing and transmitting the experience of migrants. This unstable location resonates with the ethics of "postcolonial custodianship" I have explored elsewhere, as a mode of cultural transmission of experiences that does not end up in claims to ownership and establishment of a sense of identity, but rather keeps the process of passing on open-ended (see my *Postcolonial Custodianship*).

The possibility of writing a poem on the migrant seems to coexist with the impossibility of doing full justice to the lost lives and deafening silence of migrants and refugees in current public debates in Europe. What enables these poems to take place is not the idea of speaking for the migrants, but rather the fact of speaking from the space of Europe as a border. It is the experience of the border that becomes, through these poems, a central

[6] Giorgio Agamben, *Remnants of Auschwitz*, Translated by Daniel Heller-Roazen (New York: Zone, 2002), 157.

location for mapping the ethical value of writing about migrant experiences. Acknowledging borders involves assuming the impasse between speaking and not speaking as an unavoidable task for working toward social justice. It entails neither claiming the authenticity of the migrant nor denying it or silencing it. An ethics of the border goes beyond inclusion and exclusion, and recognizes the politics of exclusion and inclusion as material precondition for thinking subjectivity. The poems collected are a response to the suffering of migrants, whereby the poets place themselves in the unstable and difficult position of the witness. These poems are forms of testimony because they epitomize the testimony as attempt, as Agamben writes, "to place oneself in one's own language in the position of those who have lost it."[7] At the border, ethics means responding to experiences that cannot be coded within established paradigms of subjectivity: European vs non-European, self vs other, included vs excluded, citizen vs refugee. For this reason, the poems attempt to get closer to the life of migrants—those who survived and those who perished—by questioning the location of the writers themselves. The poetic collective "multiVERSI" assumes an impossible position by siding with the migrants and trying to speak from their standpoint or *as* their standpoint, from their point of view, constantly negotiating the impossibility of speaking for human beings that are denied basic human and civil rights, including the right to speak.

These poems are hence extremely urgent and valuable as acts of impossible witnessing, unfinished solidarity. These are borderline poems, testimony of a deferred identification with the migrants arriving from the other side of Europe's borderlands. Through the poems of the anthology, the image of the border assumes a central relevance as symbol of this ethical ambivalence and impasse. The poems testify to a life across and along a border, the border of Europe. *Under the Sky of Lampedusa* bears witness to the fact of living on a border—or, as I will explain in this essay—the fact of assuming the border as a crucial ethical location in the contemporary world. Before proposing a reading of some of the poems from the anthology, this chapter will introduce the question of the border, especially the key concept of "being a border" that the poems exemplify and explore. From the border location, my reflections move to the textual location of *Under the Sky of Lampedusa*, which redefines the experience of borderline through the written word. The conclusion of the chapter explores the question of

[7] Agamben, *Remnants of Auschwitz*, 161.

subjectivity and advances a new "ethics at the border" that falls neither into claiming to speak on behalf of the migrant nor simply dis-identifying with the migrant. A borderline ethics envisages a spacing for a new map of witnessing and solidarity that reframes the very meaning of poetry as testimony of suffering.

Being a Border

In an essay included in *Politics and the Other Scene,* philosopher Etienne Balibar makes an important phenomenological distinction between different ways of experiencing borders in the contemporary world. According to Balibar, borders are polysemic and overdetermined; they are difficult to define because each definition presupposes in itself a preliminary act of bordering, a demarcation, and a limitation. The theorist trying to define the border "is in the danger of going round in circles."[8] Thus, instead of approaching the concept of border as a univocal, homogeneous notion, a purely legalistic or geopolitical term, Balibar emphasizes diverging ways of living the moment of border-crossing, and the central question of how human subjects are shaped by borders. Different people in different social contexts do not experience borders in the same way; there are many differences and inequalities around borders. This explains the fact that borders are perceived differently and can acquire multiple meanings and connotations. In particular, Balibar's phenomenology of the border is based on a main dichotomy: on the one hand, the subject of border-crossing is presented as a "rich person from a rich country." He writes: "For a rich person from a rich country, a person who tends towards the cosmopolitan ... the border has become an embarkation formality, a point of symbolic acknowledgement of his social status."[9] On the other hand, Balibar presents the perspective of a "poor person from a poor country": "For a poor person from a poor country, however, the border tends to be something quite different: not only is it an obstacle which is very difficult to surmount, but it is a place he runs up against repeatedly ... it becomes, in the end, a place where he *resides.*"[10]

[8] Balibar, *Politics,* 76.

[9] Ibid., 83.

[10] Balibar, *Politics,* 83.

Balibar's description is based, of course, on a quite broad example and a generalization. The divide between "rich people from rich countries" and "poor people from poor countries" should not be taken for a precise ethnographic or sociological category. However, this division captures an important aspect of borders in an age of globalization. Firstly, Balibar's phenomenological sketch emphasizes the important factor of inequality and asymmetry in the experience of borders. Instead of grounding research on borders on the empty and disembodied subject of globalization as "freedom of movement," Balibar points out a key issue concerning the concept of border. Borders are not mere territorial or geopolitical entities, passive sites of crossing or partition. The key question is that borders produce subjects; they entail a constituent, world-making power. Most importantly, the fact of being allowed to traverse a border is a privilege that only citizens of some selected countries can experience. For "poor people from poor countries," Balibar explains, the border is not a site of crossing, or an embarkation formality. For the poor, borders are not obstacles to be surmounted or legal procedures. The border can become permanent, a "viscous spatio-temporal zone,"[11] a place of residence. Balibar continues by proposing a substantial demarcation between the fact of having a border and the fact of being a border. Drawing on a pivotal essay by psychoanalyst André Green on the concept of borderline personalities, Balibar writes that "it is difficult enough to live *on* a border, but that is as nothing compared with *being* a border oneself. [Green] meant this in the sense of the splitting of multiple identities – migrant identities – but we must look at the material bases of the phenomenon."[12] Balibar's reflections resonate with other materialist critiques of the ideology of a 'borderless world' at the heart of capitalist globalization, such as Masao Miyoshi's analysis of the uneven freedom of movement produced by the global hegemony of transnational corporations, and Guillermo Gomez-Pena's rejection of the concept of a borderless world for a world made up instead of endless borderlands.

Philosophies of the border need to address this "material base" of the phenomenon of border-crossing. This process needs to take Balibar's concept of "being a border" as a point of departure. In an age of globalization, people from countries from Africa, Asia, Eastern Europe and Latin America

[11] Ibid., 83.

[12] Balibar, *Politics*, 83.

are constantly defined by borders as inescapable places of residence and ontological conditions. For many people on the move, from refugees to migrant workers, the border is neither an embarkation formality nor an obstacle to be overcome once for all. Borders can be a constant state of being, a central element of one's life and social position. This means that many disadvantaged people are today constantly facing the experience of a border—at the same time a break and a crossing, a separation and a potential movement, an inclusion and an exclusion—as the most important part of their life and sense of belonging. Indeed, for many people the very possibility of survival is tied to the logic of the border, in the form of holding the right documentation or work permit, of being allowed into a place or joining relatives living on the other side. Many refugees and subaltern migrants today do not have borders; they *are* borders. A discourse on place shifts into a crucial debate about the kind of subjectivities produced in an age of neoliberal globalization, alleged "freedom of movement" and what Arjun Appadurai calls the "world of flows"[13] of capital and commodities. Borders reveal that globalization implies growing technologies of control of human movement and immobility. As spaces of enclosure, borders produce subjects. The standpoint of being a border leads us to explore the materiality of subjectivity in an era of neoliberal globalization. Borders are not mere geographical entities, divisions of space or sites of territorial dispute. The border is a central element in defining how people inhabit their own surroundings and communities, who they are and how they are perceived. It is a way of being and a constituent aspect of the everyday life of people on the move, especially people escaping from poverty, war and violence. The border becomes the expression of processes of exclusion, recognition, crossing, immobility, trespass and selective inclusion. Borders define subjects as legitimate citizens or workers, allowing entry or denying status within a globalized labor market and the international division of labor.

Balibar's insights have been developed in subsequent works on the concept of the border, especially Sandro Mezzadra and Brett Neilson's pivotal volume *Border as Method*. In their volume Mezzadra and Neilson address the role of borders in a world dominated by global capitalism in its current, neoliberal phase. They show that the border is a key means of capitalist exploitation but also, at the same time, a tool of possible resistance.

[13] Appadurai, "Grassroots," 5.

Accordingly, Mezzadra and Neilson build on the idea of the border as the center of "the formation and regulation of labor markets ... Every struggle played out along a border intervenes in the complex assemblages that sustain labor markets and the related production of subjectivity."[14] Borders are the core of contemporary forms of class struggle and, as Mezzadra and Neilson write, "a crucial factor in producing hierarchies and fragmentation within the composition of living labor."[15] Being a border means being entangled in a process of fragmentation, division and exploitation that enables the reproduction of capitalism as an economic system. According to Mezzadra and Neilson, borders should not be seen as devices "serving merely to block or obstruct global passages of people, money, or objects."[16] Rather, the border "plays a decisive role in the production of labor power as a commodity";[17] it constitutes a process of "filtering and differentiation"[18] inscribed into the living bodies of migrant workers, the bearers of labor power.

In the context of neoliberal capitalism, being a border means being caught in processes of regulation and production of subjectivity within a global accumulation of capital. Accordingly, a politics and a philosophy of the border need to see border-production as a central aspect of capitalism and what Mezzadra and Neilson call "differential inclusion"[19] of labor-power. Differential inclusion means "the stratification and multiplication of systems of entry, status, residence, and legitimacy,"[20] which underlie "tensions, encounters, and clashes between the practices and movements of migrants and the workings of the various apparatuses of governance and governmentality that target them."[21] Mezzadra and Neilson's remarks resonate with Nicholas De Genova's concept of the "obscene of inclusion" that underlies the "scene of exclusion" of border controls. De Genova observes that the inclusion of migrants "is finally devoted to the

[14] Sandro Mezzadra and Brett Neilson, *Border as Method, or the Multiplication of Labour* (Durham NC: Duke University Press, 2013), 266.

[15] Mezzadra, *Border as Method*, 266.

[16] Ibid., ix.

[17] Ibid., 20.

[18] Ibid., 19.

[19] Ibid., 157.

[20] Ibid., 164.

[21] Ibid., 165.

subordination of their labor, which can be best accomplished only to the extent that their incorporation is permanently beleaguered with the kinds of exclusionary and commonly racist campaigns that ensure that this inclusion is itself, precisely, a form of subjugation."[22]

Neoliberal globalization does not entail a "borderless world" but rather an increased regulation of the strategies of inclusion and exclusion in order to ensure the reproduction of inequality. For this reason, the struggle for the rights of impoverished migrants, refugees and asylum-seekers should not be merely a fight for inclusion. The fetish of inclusion should be questioned too, because "differential" and "obscene" inclusion means exploitation and appropriation of migrant labor power. Protest against expulsion needs to be complemented by a struggle for economic and social equality, human and civil rights of those who are included, international solidarity and the reclamation of a common interest of workers against the accumulation of capital and the violence of financial capitalism. In the context of neoliberal globalization, borders are not mere devices for exclusion and partition, or a scene of deportation. Borders regulate the exploitation of labor-power and the possibilities of resistance and political opposition. They define a "multiplication" of labor that challenges stable distinctions between center and periphery, North and South, or—to refer once more to Balibar's essay—"rich" and "poor." The concept of being a border emphasizes the living experience of differential inclusion as central site of domination and resistance.

Mezzadra and Neilson challenge the notion of the border as a system of exclusion in order to stress "the hierarchizing and stratifying capacity of borders, examining their articulation to capital and political power."[23] Borders are pervasive; they complicate the figure of the citizen and the worker. Instead of a unified subject—for example, "the poor" in Balibar's account—borders determine a multiplicity of subject-positions that are connected by a global mechanism of regulation and exploitation, "inclusion through exclusion"[24] and production of forms of illegality useful to the maximum exploitation of labor. Borders define subjects in a multitude of contexts and sites of struggle. The position of the border at the heart of a

[22] Nicholas De Genova, "Spectacles of migrant 'illegality': the scene of exclusion, the obscene of inclusion," *Ethnic and Racial Studies* 36, no. 7 (2013): 5.

[23] Mezzandra and Nielson, *Border as Method*, 7.

[24] De Genova, "Spectacle of Migrant," 5.

spatio-temporal continuum defined by neoliberal globalization moves away from the concept of exclusion and exteriority at the core of much postcolonial theory. Thus, Mezzadra and Neilson question Walter Mignolo's "epistemology of the exteriority," and Mignolo's seminal work on "colonial difference" and "border-thinking." Mignolo focuses on the "exteriority of capitalism, that moment in which 'living labor' is transformed into 'capitalist labor,' the exploitation of the [sur]plus-value."[25] Mignolo explains that, by exteriority, he does not mean simply "the outside," but "the space where tensions emerge once capitalism becomes the dominant economic system and eliminates all the possibilities of anything outside it, but not its exteriority."[26] Exteriority is not so much a physical space—a somewhere—as an epistemological standpoint, a position-taking located at the margins of the global system produced by Western capitalist modernity. Through exteriority, Mignolo's reflections assume what he calls "the standpoint of the colonial difference"[27] as a way of questioning Eurocentric critiques of Eurocentrism. He emphasizes the politics of the locus of enunciation in order to displace deconstructions of global modernity pursued from within the European philosophical legacy. Mignolo hence stresses the position of exteriority, of speaking from the standpoint of the excluded from Western modernity, as a crucial element for an effective critique of the violence of coloniality. In contrast with Mignolo's philosophy of exteriority, that is, a location of knowledge-production that is not encompassed by Western modernity, Mezzadra and Neilson's concept of "differential inclusion" reframes the global discourse on borders by challenging the dichotomy between inside and outside, interior and exterior, included and excluded. Borders become devices for capital accumulation, differential technologies for regulating the flow of labor power and the making of profit. Global subjects of the twenty-first century need to be placed within a logic of bordering that is not based on radical break or partition but on interconnected forms of power and control. Borders ensure the relative mobility and immobility of labor power in the service of financial capitalism and a global economic order.

[25] Walter Mignolo, "The Geopolitics of Knowledge and the Colonial Difference," *The South Atlantic Quarterly* 101, no. 1 (2002): 75.

[26] Ibid.

[27] Ibid., 65.

The Body and the Border

Thinking from the border means re-discussing the concept of subjectivity: borders do not presuppose but rather produce subjects. The experience of living on a border is constituent and productive: neither the citizen nor the excluded, the position of the subject becomes a way of witnessing to borderline conditions of simultaneous inclusion and exclusion. The ethical subject defined by the experience of the border is caught between possibility and impossibility of speaking; it goes beyond the rhetoric of identity and otherness. Being a border hence means acknowledging the entanglement of subjectivities within the continuum of capital accumulation on an international scale. It also means assuming the concept of the border as a cognitive standpoint for reimagining ideas of the subject in the twenty-first century. In addition, it reframes the concept of a global class struggle into a multiplicity of border struggles where lines of demarcation, inclusion and exploitation are constantly redefined. *Under the Sky of Lampedusa* provides a poetic description of what it means to be (on) a border today. By speaking from an unstable position on Europe's borderlines, the authors of the anthology do not simply protest against the indifference of European governments regarding the suffering of migrants. The poems are explorations of the border as an ontological state; they offer images of textual space as ways to inhabit the border location and transmitting other voices through the text. They give voice to the experience of living on borderlines.[28]

Interestingly, some of the poems in the collection go beyond the mechanism of "compassionate repression" which, according to anthropologist Didier Fassin, involves "a compassionate attention to individual suffering in which the search for a common humanity resides in the recognition of bare life, that of the physical alterations of the body."[29] Against the spectacle of suffering bodies in need of salvation and compassion, migrant bodies become, in *Under the Sky of Lampedusa*, a poetic location from which subjectivity is being repositioned and reimagined. Poetry enables writers to inhabit, figuratively, the body of the migrant as a space for transmitting

[28] Jacques Derrida explores the aporia of the term "living on borderlines" in an important essay where he remarks how texts "overrun" their borders and limits "not by submerging or drowning them in an undifferentiated homogeneity, but rather making them more complex, dividing and multiplying strokes and lines" (69).

[29] Didier Fassin, "Compassion and Repression: The Moral Economy of Immigration Policies in France," *Cultural Anthropology* 20, no. 3 (2005): 372.

experiences within a liminal temporality. In this regard, a poem included in *Under the Sky of Lampedusa* is significantly titled “Confini” (“Borders”). The author, Benedetta Davalli, is an Italian poet and a psychologist. The poem she contributed to the anthology speaks to the general question about borders as ontological condition. The poem starts with a question, which also suggests an important parallel. Davalli writes

> I confini del mondo somigliano
> Forse alla pelle umana?
> La mia pelle e’ confine
> Fra l’interno del mio corpo
> E l’esterno mondo[30]

The central image focuses on a parallel between the human body and the outside world. Interestingly, the first image proposed in the first line already presents an ambiguity and a proliferation of meaning. Davalli adopts the expression “the borders of the world,” which could mean, at the same time, the borders that exist in the world—that is, the borders of nation-states, regions and countries, the borders that belong to the world—and the borders *of* the world—that is the borders between the world and something else, in this case the interior part of the human body. The double genitive “of” creates this ambivalence, which remains as a central motif in the poem. The borders that divide nations, regions and peoples can be connected to a more substantial border, the border that divide the human body from external reality. The human body becomes a sort of envelope and a barrier. Psychoanalyst André Green notes that the “skin envelope or container”[31] of the human body is, in a sense, the first border that each human being encounters. The skin is, as Davalli notes in her poem, a border between inside and outside. Yet, the first border of the human body is already marked by processes of exclusion and inclusion, or differential inclusion. The bodily border belongs to the world as its point of differentiation, the membrane out of which the subject recognizes a separate existence. The border emerges as the standpoint from which the world can be inhabited, yet it simultaneously signals a partial exclusion or differentiation from the

[30] “Do the borders of the world /perhaps, resemble human skin? /My skin is a border Between the inside of my body/ And the outside world” (my translation); Benedetta Davali, “Confini,” in. *Sotto il Cielo di Lampedusa*. Vol. 2 (Milan: Rayuela, 2015), 105.

[31] André Green, *On Private Madness* (London: Karnac, 1996), 62.

ambient world. Davalli's intriguing poem expands on the parallel between the body and the world by suggesting that her body *is* the world, and her borders, so to speak, are the borders of the world. This poetic image strongly resonates with Gloria Anzaldúa's focus on the bodily in *La Frontera / Borderlands*, in which Anzaldúa describes the US–Mexican border as "*una herida abierda* where the Third World grates against the First and bleeds."[32] In a similar exploration of a bodily metaphor, Davalli continues her poem by suggesting a parallel between the body and the world. The human body is in the world, at its border, but it also extends to the whole world as a guiding metaphor for designating outside reality:

La mia pelle respira
Il mare e' il respiro del mondo
La mia pelle suda
La pioggia e' il sudore del mondo
. . .
I nostri respiri migranti
Dalle viscere al cuore
Dai mari alle acque amniotiche
Della parola partorita altrove.[33]

The parallel between the body and the world—the borders of the human skin and the borders of the real world—extends and deepens. Breathing is reimagined as a migrant movement, a transit from the most visceral parts of the body to the center—the heart. The sea is compared to amniotic liquid, a place of birth, which gives birth to a "word," which however comes from afar, born elsewhere. The poem provides a captivating parallel between bodily acts and the movement of migrants across the sea, refiguring the Mediterranean as a space of life rather than mere death. The poem itself—the "word"—is said to be born from the sea, in a continuum with the deaths and losses of the migrants dying during the transit. The poem is an emanation of the outside world, it defines the textual space as a territory for mediating the folding of the self and the world and their continual differentiation. The representation of the border in Davalli's poem captures the instability of the

[32] Anzaldúa, *Borderlands*, 3.

[33] "my skin breaths /the sea is the breath of the world / my skin sweats /rain is the sweat of the world . . . Our migrant breaths /from the bowels to the heart /from the seas to amniotic waters /of a word born elsewhere" (my translation); Davalli, "Confini," 105.

border, the ongoing connection between the poet's bodily existence—her flesh, breath and skin—and the presence of the migrants. Most importantly, the experience of being a border is expressed on a phenomenological level, as an intimate condition that re-enacts the tragedy of migrants and refugees in every instant of one's life, every breath, every tactile sensation. The poem translates the experience of migrants into a reimagining of the human body as a border that constantly resonates with the movement of migrants, echoing the outside world within the interior body. Being a border here assumes the task of responding to the suffering of the migrants from the other side of Europe's geopolitical borderlines. The poetic response to the experience of the migrant is always at risk of becoming a form of appropriation, misinterpretation and a new-found kind of authority to speak on behalf of the migrant. However, this risk is the counterpart of an ethical imperative, a necessary registration of how contemporary events affect subjects on both sides of the European borderland. These poems do not exclude or avoid running the risk of "speaking" and of responding by creating a potential channel of communication to address the stories of migrants. However, this is only a beginning, which should be followed by a more sustained ability to listen to the migrant. For this reason, these poems do not "solve" the tragedy of migrants nor do they offer a conclusive stance on how the suffering of migrants should be represented. Rather, these works emphasize the ethical and aesthetic double binds at the heart of what Mariangela Palladino has recently called "trans-coastal narratives" in the Mediterranean: narratives that reimagine the Mediterranean as an element of continuity between North and South, and a site of encounters and exchanges deeply signed by colonial and postcolonial legacies and diasporas.

The poem "La Pelle" ("The Skin") is composed by Italo-Brazilian poet Reginaldo Cerolini, a migrant who declares his passion and love for his country of residence, Italy, as central element of his biographical note. The poem builds on the parallel between human body and borders. The poem begins as follows:

> Un giorno io
> Ti faro' entrare nella mia pelle
> E incontrerai il sangue vivo dei
> Naufraghi di cinque continenti[34]

[34] "One day /I will let you inside my skin /And you will meet the living blood /Of five continents' shipwrecked" (my translation); Reginaldo Cerolini, "La Pelle," in *Sotto il Cielo di Lampedusa*. Vol. 2. (Milan: Rayuela, 2015), 128.

Dead migrants are said to survive, and to come alive, inside the skin of the poet. Whereas Davalli's poem stretched the image of her own body, making it into a border in order to encompass the borders of the world, Cerolini's work performs a specular movement by introjecting and incorporating the bodies of migrants inside his own body. The poem provides a more explicit political statement by listing, in a vivid and evocative language, all the things that migrants could end up doing once in Italy, if they survive the transit across the Mediterranean. The poet denounces the life-conditions of those who entered Europe and survive there, going through experiences such as doing odd jobs and sharing rooms, becoming drug dealers, prostitutes and outcasts, slaves and servants, warehousemen, dishwashers, caregivers or beggars. In the concluding stanza, Cerolini affirms that "la mia pelle non e' un confine, ma un inizio senza fine."[35] His skin is not a border, yet by keeping all lost lives within his own body, his own skin, the poet allows the reader to become a foreigner. The body of the poet becomes the starting point for seeing thing from the standpoint of the migrant and refugee. "The Skin" moves from the idea of the human body as a border to the possibility of traversing the border, of building a space of transit—a transitional space—through the writing of the poem. Poetry becomes a means for border-crossing, and the poem concludes with an exhortation to free all the desires, hopes and struggles for survival of migrants. The appeal to the reader sounds like an invitation, an invite to access the inside of the poet's skin, where all the "errand souls"[36] of dead migrants and shipwrecked survive.

The image of the border shifts into a reflection on the role of poetry as the creation of a transitional space where the experience of migrants could be heard and their life acknowledged. The poems do not forget the economic dimension of migrants' conditions, or the processes of "differential inclusion" whereby borders assume the role of regulating the exploitation of migrant labor power. Being a border implies, as psychoanalyst André Green points out, "a loss of distinction between space *and* time."[37] Borders are not

[35] "my skin is not a border, but a beginning without end" (my translation); Cerolini, "La Pelle," 130.

[36] Cerolini, "La Pelle," 130.

[37] Green, *On Private Madness*, 63.

stable lines or points in space: being a border involves experiencing the border as central part of one's own life story and memory. The border reappears, constantly, as capture and regulation of transitions. In *Under the Sky of Lampedusa,* poetic expression aims to place the reader in the position of the migrant. Poetry becomes a space aimed at challenging borders' differential inclusion, shaping a new subject from border struggles, a new political and poetic subject that does not merely claim the right of inclusion, but rather the making of international solidarities. The experience of the border as poetic location involves a rethinking of the subject of ethics beyond identity and otherness.

Transitional Space and the Ethic of Transmission

The politics and poetics of borders hence result in a rethinking of subjectivity. Neither self nor other, the ethical locus of the subject becomes transitional and borderline. Building on psychoanalyst D.W. Winnicott's definition of transitionality as "the union of two now separate things ... at the point in time and space of the initiation of their state of separateness," Homi K. Bhabha describes the experience of a transitional space as location "where space is conjoined and time separate, and then ... vice versa, back and forth, the confluence of time in a contradiction of space."[38] Transitional spaces and times are better seen as movements of contraction and dilatation that affect the very idea of difference. The border, grasped as transitional space, operates as a process of alternate enclosure and aperture in which subjectivities are constantly reshaped. It means experiencing multiple positions at the same time, that is, a division of space in a moment of standstill or, on the other hand, the same space at different moments, in a repetition of the same through differential temporal exclusions. A subject can inhabit the border as the same space, a bodily, material space that encapsulates foreign experiences, or a specific time, in which the coexistence of multiple spaces interconnected is suddenly realized. A poem included in *Under the Sky of Lampedusa* with the title "Ode Marittima (fantasma)," (Ghostly Ode to the Sea) by Austrian-Italian poet Barbara Pumhösel, expresses the shift in subjectivity that poetry can signify. While written by an Austrian poet and accomplished children fiction writer now living near Florence, the poem

[38] Homi K. Bhabha, "Making Emptiness." Anish Kapoor, 1998, Accessed 15.01.2016. http://anishkapoor.com/185/making-emptiness-by-homi-k-bhabha

assumes the standpoint of the migrant. The speaking subject of the poem is an unnamed male migrant, who laments his inability to write his own ode to the sea, having died too early during the crossing. The poem represents a space for inhabiting other subjectivities and speaking not on behalf, but rather from the absent point of view of dead migrants. The poem indicates this shift:

> i miei occhi coscienti
> hanno smesso di esserlo
> prima di poter arrivare
> alle parole
> non ho potuto nemmeno dettarle
> a mio figlio perché non lo vedrò
> lui non si ricorderà di me
> non gli insegnerò versi
> nella lingua verso cui andavo
> quando sono stato fermato
> da una morte senza permesso
> di soggiorno i miei compagni
> portati indietro tutti insieme
> fantasmi vivi o morti
> con una firma che dice soltanto
> uno senza diritti senza il diritto
> alla parola alla sua
> Ode marittima[39]

This extract from the poem indicates that space between the experience of the migrant and the words that will be able to transmit his experience. The dead, absent speaker is forever trapped into this interval, this transitional space that becomes a permanent location. The poem gives voice to the interstice in which the subject writing the poem imagines herself traversing the gap between a lost life and its echoes and traces in the text. The ode to the sea becomes a juncture, a way to reconnect subjects divided by multiple

[39] "my conscious eyes /Have stopped being so /Before being able to arrive /At words /I couldn't even dictate them /To my son because I will not see him /He will not remember me / I will not teach him verse /Into the language I was going towards /When I was stopped /By a death without leave /To remain my companions /All sent back /Ghosts dead or alive /With a signature only stating /One without rights without the right /To speech, to his own /Ode to the sea" (my translation); Barbara Pumhösel, "Ode Marittima (fantasma)," in *Sotto il Cielo di Lampedusa*. Vol. 2. (Milan: Rayuela, 2015), 83.

spatial and temporal borders. The poem becomes itself a border, a space that signals both a division and a connection that are constantly redefined through the act of reading and imagining the experience that writing attempts to represent. Poems included in *Under the Sky of Lampedusa* propose a transition across the borders of Europe, yet they also testify to the impossibility of fully representing the position of the migrant from within Europe. The constant shift in subjective experiences that are not being directly lived by the authors of these poems do not merely witness the suffering and death of migrants. They also create a subject-position able to transmit a trace of lost, silenced experiences. The poems reclaim a border subjectivity that falls neither into the secure place of the citizen gazing at the migrant—its other—nor into the political appropriation of migrant lives, who are not, properly speaking, "represented" into these poems. In its refusal to make the body of the migrant a mere spectacle of compassion, but rather assuming the impossible position of border-crossing through the act of poetic creation, *Under the Sky of Lampedusa* is an intense exploration of this impasse and this act of transmission. By inhabiting the position of the border as a space redefining the position of the subject and the text, poetry becomes a form of custodianship of migrant experiences that are neither entirely lost, nor completely recovered. Rather, it is the process of constant loss and the imperative of retrieval that these poems indicate, with urgency. Even before any political discourse on the closure of Europe, the human experience of migrants needs to find a voice, and these poems offer a transitional starting point, a borderline location from which future writers will be able to listen to migrants' voices, including them into the political space of Europe but also challenging any ideology of differential inclusion that is not based on economic and social equality.

Bibliography

Adorno, Theodor. 1980. "Commitment." In *Aesthetics and Politics.* Trans. Ronald Taylor, 177–195. London: Verso.

Agamben, Giorgio. 2002. *Remnants of Auschwitz.* Trans. Daniel Heller-Roazen. New York: Zone.

Andrijasevic, Rutvica. 2010. From Exception to Excess: Detention and Deportations Across the Mediterranean Space. In *The Deportation Regime: Sovereignty, Space, and the Freedom of Movement*, ed. Nicholas de Genova and Nathalie Peutz, 147–165. Durham: Duke UP.

Anzaldúa, Gloria. 1981. *Borderlands/La Frontera.* San Francisco: Aunt Lute.

Appadurai, Arjun. 2000. Grassroots Globalisation and the Research Imagination. *Public Culture* 12 (1): 1–19.
Balibar, Etienne. 2002. *Politics and the Other Scene*. Trans. Christine Jones, James Swenson, and Chris Turner. London: Verso.
Bhabha, Homi K. 1998. "Making Emptiness." *Anish Kapoor*. http://anishkapoor.com/185/making-emptiness-by-homi-k-bhabha. Accessed 15 Jan 2016.
De Genova, Nicholas. 2013. Spectacles of Migrant 'Illegality': The Scene of Exclusion, the Obscene of Inclusion. *Ethnic and Racial Studies* 36 (7): 1–19.
Derrida, Jacques. 1979. Living On. In *Deconstruction and Criticism*, ed. Harold Bloom et al., 62–142. London: Continuum.
Fassin, Didier. 2005. Compassion and Repression: The Moral Economy of Immigration Policies in France. *Cultural Anthropology* 20 (3): 362–387.
Friese, Heidrun. 2012. Border Economies. Lampedusa and the Nascent Migration Industry. *Shima: The International Journal of Research into Island Cultures* 6 (2): 66–84.
Ginzburg, Carlo. 2000. *No Island Is an Island*. New York: Columbia UP.
Gomez-Pena, Guillermo. 1996. *The New World Border*. San Francisco: City Lights.
Green, André. 1996. *On Private Madness*. London: Karnac.
Menozzi, Filippo. 2014. *Postcolonial Custodianship: Cultural and Literary Inheritance*. New York: Routledge.
Mezzadra, Sandro, and Brett Neilson. 2013. *Border as Method, or the Multiplication of Labour*. Durham: Duke UP.
Mignolo, Walter. 2002. The Geopolitics of Knowledge and the Colonial Difference. *The South Atlantic Quarterly* 101 (1): 57–96.
Miyoshi, Masao. 1993. A Borderless World? From Colonialism to Transnationalism and the Decline of the Nation-State. *Critical Inquiry* 19 (4): 726–751.
MultiVERSI. 2015. *Sotto il Cielo di Lampedusa*. Vol. 2. Milan: Rayuela.
Palladino, Mariangela. 2014. From Roots to Routes… to Borders: Trans-Coastal Narratives Across the Mediterranean. *Comparative Critical Studies* 11 (2–3): 219–234.

Land, Territory and Border: Liminality in Contemporary Israeli Literature

Adia Mendelson-Maoz

Borders and national identity are considered the foundation of the modern nation-state. Nevertheless, as Adriana Kamp points out, studies have not examined the relationship between these two concepts. Creating a border is generally considered part of physical nation-building, whereas constituting one's identity is thought of as a psychological facet of nation-building. Kamp suggests a difference in terms of hardware (the border) and software (the identity), and emphasizes the cultural and ideological importance of borders which diverges from the formal role of the land.[1]

In the Israeli context, the land is both a motherland and a historical home.[2] After the 1948 war, Israel applied the principle of territorial sovereignty to its land and employed rhetorical and institutional mechanisms to generate commitment to guarding the border and tightening bonds with the land.[3] Spatial language drawing on patriotism glorified the territory of

---

[1] Adriana Kamp, "Ha-gvul ki'fney yanus – Merhav ve'toda'a leumit be-israel," [Borders, Space and National Identity in Israel] *Teoria u'bikoret* 16 (2000): 13–43.

[2] Zeli Gurevitz and Gideon Aranne, "Al ha-maqom," [On the Place] Alpayim 4 (1993): 9–44.

[3] Kamp, "Ha-gvul ki'fney yanus," 19.

A. Mendelson-Maoz (✉)
Open University of Israel, Ra'anana, Israel

J. Elbert Decker, D. Winchock (eds.), *Borderlands and Liminal Subjects*, https://doi.org/10.1007/978-3-319-67813-9_3

Israel, encouraging Israelis to visit and learn about the country.[4] The Six Day War in 1967 introduced a new concept—the Green Line—the borderline between the State of Israel and the Occupied Territories. A border presumably signifies the separation between the "here" and the "there," between "my country" and a foreign country, which can be hostile. However the context of the Occupied Territories blurred this notion of borders and created a twilight zone, which is simultaneously internal and external, apparently temporary but in fact permanent.[5] Whereas previously territory justified a national struggle that elicited solidarity, the Occupied Territories appear to violate a clear connection between the nation and the territory, which thus implicates and complicates the national Jewish identity.

Ariella Azoulay and Adi Ophir discuss the symbolic nature and psychological implications of borders and argue that the Territories are not "external" or akin to some remote continent that can easily be ignored. Rather, they are "external" in the sense of a looming shadow since for individuals to feel normal and for society to see itself as free and democratic, huge efforts need to be made to repress the "external" and prevent it from reaching consciousness. Parenthesized, ignored and denied, the Territories are nevertheless part of the Israeli identity.[6] The shaky balance is upset and demons are unleashed when the external manifests itself.

The occupation of the West Bank that began in 1967 did not overly affect most Israelis for the next two decades. It burst onto the broader Israeli scene during the First Intifada in 1987. This popular uprising, but in particular the role played by civilians and the fact that this was perhaps the first time that Israelis had heard the voice of Palestinians, was a clear indication that the notion of the Territories could no longer be repressed. The ambiguous concept of the border, its professed temporary status and the undefined twilight zone it created undermined the Israeli sense of

[4] Oz Almog, *The Sabra: The Creation of the New Jew*, trans. Haim Watzman. (Berkeley: University of California Press, 2000).

[5] This is an ostensibly temporary situation, but the rhetoric that promises "calm" and "security" actually defines the occupation as an interim situation that can continue ad infinitum and thus represses the fact that it creates occupation. Hannan Hever, "Ten lo badranim – v'yanuach be-shalom," [Give him Entertainers, and he will rest in Peace] in: *Canoni v'populari* [Canonic and Popular] (Tel Aviv: Resling, 2007), 193–208. See also: Adi Ophir and Ariella Azoulay, *Mishtar zeh she-eino ehad* [This Regime Which Is Not One] (Tel Aviv: Resling, 2008).

[6] Ophir and Azoulay, *Mishtar zeh she-eino ehad*, 26–27.

control and normality. The border became symbolic of the unease associated with a lack of hierarchy or linear order.

In literary works dealing with the Intifada, whether they focus primarily on the experiences of Israeli soldiers over the Green Line (such as works by Ben-Ner, Polity, Ron-Furer and Kravitz)[7] or concentrate on Israeli society in Israel's big cities (such as works by Iczkovits, Yehoshua, Matatlon and Nevo),[8] the theme of space is related to the concept of borders. Although they differ in terms of poetics and ethics, in most of these texts the borders stand for a transition from one moral and psychological existence to another that creates a physical, psychological and moral rift which adversely impacts the soldier's identity. In this liminal zone, civil identity is suspended and another identity is subsumed that obeys laws aligned with male stereotypes of roughness and aggression.[9] For some protagonists leaving one reality for another leads to emotional dissonance and at times psychological breakdown. These descriptions of a reality that unfolds according to other rules often criticize the Israeli situation, but they do not challenge the basic assumption of a border between Israel and the Territories. Hannan Hever noted that the two juxtaposed spaces create a dichotomy between the

[7] Yitzhak Ben-Ner, *Ta'atuon* [Delusion] (Jerusalem: Am Oved, 1989); Roy Polity, *Arnavonei gagot*, [Roof Rabbits] (Tel Aviv: Am Oved, 2001); Asher Kravitz, *Ani Mustafa Rabinovitch* [I, Mustafa Rabinovitch] (Bnei Brak: Sifriat Poalim -- Ha-kibbuts Ha-meuhad, 2004); Liran Ron-Furer, *Tismonet* ha-*mahsom* [Checkpoint Syndrome] (Tel Aviv: Gvanim, 2003).

[8] Yaniv Iczkovits, *Dofek*, [Pulse] (Tel Aviv: Ha-kibbuts ha-meuhad, 2007); A.B. Yehoshua, *Friendly Fire*, trans. Stuart Schoffman (New York: Harcourt Inc., 2008), first published in Hebrew: *Esh yedidutit* (Tel Aviv: Ha-kibbuts ha-meuhad, 2007); Ronit Matalon, *Bliss*, trans. Jessica Cohen (New York: Metropolitan Books, 2003). first published in Hebrew: *Sarah, Sarah* (Tel Aviv: Am-Oved, 2000); Eshkol Nevo, *World Cup Wishes* (London, Chatto & Windus, 2010), first published in Hebrew: *Misha'la a'hat yemina* (Tel Aviv: Kinneret/Zmora-Bitan/Dvir, 2007).

[9] Ofra Meisels, "Likrat gius," [Before Enlisting], in: *Mitbagrim be'israel -- hebetim ishiyim. mishpahtiyim ve'hevratiyi* [Adolescents in Israel – Personal, Family and Social Aspects], ed. H. Plum, (Even Yehuda: Rekhes, 1995), 177–200; Liora Sion, *Dimoyei gavriut etzel lohamim: ha-sherut be-hativot heil raglim ke-teckes ma'avar mi-na'arut le-bagrut* [Images of Manhood among Combat Soldiers: Military Service in Israeli infantry as a Rite of Passage from Youth to Adulthood] (Jerusalem: The Dayan Center for Social Science Research, The Hebrew University, 1997).

declared national, supposedly enlightened morality and Israel's oppression of the Palestinian people in the Occupied Territories.[10]

This chapter analyzes the concept of borders and sovereignty in the Hebrew literature of the Intifada era and discusses the powerful thematic and poetic strategies writers have employed to confront these issues. In particular three works will be discussed: Yitzhak Ben-Ner's *Delusion* published in 1989, Orly Castel-Bloom's *Dolly City* published in 1992 and Michal Govrin's *Snapshots* published in 2002.[11]

Something Is Rotten in the State of Israel

Ben-Ner's *Delusion* was one of the first novels published on the Intifada. It presents a portrait of the Israel soldier and uses allegorical elements to probe ethical issues. The novel is made up of four parts, each of which is narrated by a different character. Each part explores the evasiveness of the concept of border that fails to differentiate between the "here" and the "there" in terms of behavior and ideological beliefs.

The first part narrated by Holly (a man) describes the gradual moral decline of an Israeli soldier. Raised and educated in a family that believes in the liberal values of justice and eschews violence, Holly gradually learns to be violent and cruel while serving in the Territories and enjoys torturing Palestinians. After these torture incidents, he is arrested and incarcerated in a military jail, where he begins to smell. The terrible stench emanating from his body is clearly a metaphor for the moral turpitude of the army and the state. Because of his bodily decrepitude, he is sent to a mental institution. But not everyone thinks that Holly stinks. A group of extreme right-wing settlers interpret his stench as a wondrous perfume or a kind of sacred symbol, and spirit him out of the institution amid a celebration of song and dance to draw spiritual inspiration from him. The odor in the text is an

[10] According to Hever, acceptance of this basic assumption is a major attribute of popular literature on the Intifada. He contends that critical literature must remove itself from national moral framework, which he believes is based on dual morality (Hever, "Ten lo badranim," 196).

[11] Ben-Ner, *Ta'atuon*; Orly Castel-Bloom, *Dolly City*, trans. Dalya Bilu (London: Loki Books, 1997), first published in Hebrew (Tel Aviv: Zmora-Bitan, 1992); Michal Govrin, *Snapshots*, trans. Barbara Harshav (New York: Riverhead Books, 2007), first published in Hebrew: *Hevzekim* (Tel Aviv: Am-Oved, 2002).

incurable illness, and is contagious as well, since even the psychiatrist expresses messianic enthusiasm, and the madness spreads like a disease.

The second part is narrated by Holly's father, Oded Tzidon, a doctor whose wife was killed in a shooting attack; he describes himself as a warrior for peace. Holly's father collapses upon learning that he has now lost his son as well. He cannot get over the putrid smell that emanates from his son. Oded is in the throes of an inner struggle that tests his beliefs to the utmost. As a former peace activist, he has already faced his wife's death in a terror attack and must now come to terms with the behavior of his son who deviates from the family's moral code.

Charul, a secret service agent assigned to capture wanted Palestinians, narrates the third part. It also presents a clash between beliefs, ideology and the situation on the ground. Charul causes a military operation to fail when he decides, without consulting his commander, to kill a Palestinian who is later revealed to be a double agent employed by the Israelis. His eagerness to undertake an extraordinary operation ruins him and destroys his career.

The final part is narrated by Michel Sachtout, an Israeli soldier institutionalized in a psychiatric hospital. Sachtout is a kind of mirror image of Holly, but he does not attract the same attention as Holly and his odor; rather, he is unable to reach out to people or speak clearly.

Ben-Ner's novel confronts ideologies, values and military norms in a realm with no boundaries. Each monologue shows how difficult it is to remain true to a belief or ideology. No one seems immune and no one can maintain attitudes that they once considered right and humane. Holly develops an emotional and mental distancing mechanism that helps him survive in the military world. The world "across the border" unravels the borders of his identity, transforming him into a puppet. He gradually suppresses his gentleness and morality, and represses others' civilian and personal lives instead. Sucked into the realm of violence, he is robotically unaware of his behavior. Torture and violence become neutral, normative behavior for him. The text illustrates the dissonance between the author's graphic descriptions of horror, and the mindless, amused way the soldiers perceive their acts. The radicalized situations and the soldiers' lack of self-criticism are embedded in a chaotic and incoherent text. David Fishelov commented that this attitude toward horror "constitutes a continuation and an indirect collaboration with the horror itself"[12] since there is no reflective criticism of the situation.

Holly's first name hints at sanctity (holy), but his surname is Tzidon (Sidon), a Lebanese city that has been the site of many battles. He exemplifies the split between the Zionist warrior who believes in protecting the lives of the nation's citizens and feels solidarity and agreement with the borders as a consensual territory, and the soldier of the Intifada who crosses the border into a region where he is both here and there, where the rules are ambiguous and where the task of safeguarding the nation morphs into violent attempts to quell an occupied population. This situation generates a liminal area between the civilian world and the military world and between the soldier's normative personal life and army life.[13] His alienation from his former self brings him to the edge of insanity. As Holly phrases it during a violent operation, "...just to keep my sanity. Only to keep my sanity. They can all go insane, I don't care. I'll stay normal, I must stay normal."[14]

However, not only Holly breaches the border of normative behavior. Oded, his father, feels confused after losing his former beliefs. Christine Korsgaard noted: "It is the conceptions of ourselves that are most important to us that give rise to unconditional obligations. For to violate them is to lose your integrity and so your identity, and to no longer be who you are."[15] Following the death of his wife and the smell of his son, Oded is unable to repress the injustice, incapable of re-crossing the border and forced to remain in the twilight zone, while not knowing what he is doing and what he is fighting for. He walks the streets wearing a sign reading "No one is guilty"[16] and mourns the loss of his son.

Charul's mistake of killing the wrong person is another source of confusion. Here as well the dividing line between "we" and "the enemy" is fuzzy. The Palestinian he kills belongs to the category of "the enemy," and Charul believed this would be a feather in his cap until he discovers that he was a double agent. The book concludes with insanity, a final stage where people

[12] David Fishelov, "*Megamot ba-shira bi'shnot ha-shmonim*" [Trends in the Poetry of the 80's,] *Achshav* 67/68 (Fall-Winter 2002–2003): 184–5.

[13] See also: Adia Mendelson-Maoz, "Hurled into the Heart of Darkness – Moral Luck and the Hebrew Literature of the Intifada." *Hebrew Studies* 52 (2011): 315–339.

[14] Ben-Ner, *Ta'atuon*, 53–4.

[15] Christine M. Korsgaard, *The Source of Normativity* (Cambridge: Cambridge University Press, 1996), 102.

[16] Ben-Ner, *Ta'atuon*, 156.

cannot cope with harsh situations, their deeds or with the deeds of others. Suddenly it is impossible to decide who is right and who is to blame.

Madness and cruelty are also evidenced in the second literary example presented below. Here too the concept of border is allegorical although very different from the first.

The Anatomy of the Map

Castel-Bloom's *Dolly City* is a difficult text which takes place in a world made up of bits of cultural images, pieces of modern myths and shards of decontextualized signs. *Dolly City* does not reflect some real city but rather a Western urban-grotesque experience that alludes to locations in Tel Aviv such as the Carmel market or Hilton beach but also to other places including the Thames River, water fountains that pee in an arc and a memorial called Dachau.

The character of Dolly, the main protagonist of the work and a physician, is based on an inverted myth of motherhood. Dolly finds a newborn in a garbage bag in a car and decides to adopt him. She tries to protect the tiny creature from the harmful ways of the world by desperate measures of motherly care and sacrifices herself daily, like in the fairy tales, to insure the baby's survival in a crazed city and a hostile world. But anxiety and aggression toward herself, the baby and other family members, dead and alive, cause her to perform scientific experiments on him, and in particular cut him up to examine his internal organs, dissect him, give him medication for diseases he does not suffer from and even to score his skin and flesh here and there, for kicks. The son survives this torture, grows up big and strong and enrolls in the Brutal Seamanship Military Academy.

Dolly City opens with a description of a goldfish's demise. Dolly picks it out of the tank, slices it in strips (though it keeps slipping from her fingers onto the kitchen counter), cooks it slightly and eats the pieces. The cooking and eating of the fish take on symbolic significance as of the second paragraph.

> Then I looked at the pieces. In very ancient times, in the land of Canaan, righteous men would sacrifice bigger animals than these to god. When they cut up a lamb, they would be left with big, bloody, significant pieces in their hands, and their covenant would mean something.[17]

[17] Castel-Bloom, *Dolly City*, 11.

The opening scene makes the first association between the fish, Jewish history and the covenant with the Lord. In ancient times, the founding fathers of Judaism made sacrifices. Whereas the sacrifices of antiquity were full of meaning, in the reality of *Dolly City*, a sacrifice becomes small, fake, distorted. The death and sacrifice of the goldfish are the foundation for the entire novel, which to a large extent has a cyclical structure. After the fish dies Dolly looks at her dying dog and finally decides to give her a lethal injection. She has a similar reaction to the baby she finds in the dog undertaker's car. She decides not to kill the baby only because she is sure that the baby is so weak that he will die before the day is over. Even after Dolly begins to develop maternal instincts, she continues to endanger the baby's life, either through the scientific experiments she conducts on him or through her fear of what she might do to him, for instance throw him out the window.[18] Thus the description of the fish on the first page of the work symbolizing a sacrifice to God is transformed into a parallel image of the blood bond between a child and his mother, his god, his country. This theme emerges later in the book in the context of borders. The inversion of the image of mother and physician from life-saver to life-ender is echoed in the shift from life giver in the name of God, to life sacrificer in the name of God and country.

Dolly City embodies the history of the Jewish people—"I wandered from field to field ... like the Israelites wandering from place to place throughout the long years of exile."[19] Her world is committed to history and this commitment is part of Dolly the mother, and grotesquely, becomes part of her son's anatomy. Thus, in a scene suggestive of the covenant and perhaps the binding of Isaac, Dolly defines her son's calling on his body:

> The baby was still lying on his stomach. I put him to sleep, even though I still didn't know where I was going to cut ... I took a knife and began cutting here and there. I drew a map of the Land of Israel – as I remembered it from the biblical period – on his back, and marked in all those Philistine towns like Gath and Ashkelon, and with the blade of the knife I etched the Sea of Galilee and the Jordan River which empties out into the Dead Sea ... drops of blood began willing up in the river beds cutting across the country. The sight of the map of the Land of Israel amateurishly sketched on my son's back gave me a

[18] "There was a moment when I almost threw? the baby down. Ten times over, I checked that I was still holding him" (Ibid., 38–39).

[19] Ibid., 109.

> frisson of delight ... my baby screamed in pain but I stood firm ... I contemplated the carved-up back: it was a map of the Land of Israel: nobody could mistake it.[20]

The etching of the map of Eretz Yisrael from the Mediterranean to the Jordan River on the baby's back is not only an act of extreme cruelty. By carving the map Dolly transforms the covenant of circumcision undergone by every Jewish male infant and God into a covenant between himself and the map, himself and national destiny. From Dolly's point of view, this captures her full identification with the idea that the Jewish mother raises her son so that his body can serve military national aims and primarily the defense of the borders of the Land of Israel. This act is in fact the ultimate proclamation that all the mother's acts are directed toward the moment of her bereavement. Carving a bloody map of the entire Land of Israel on the boy's back is subversive on two narrative levels: it presents the image of the map and its violent context, and establishes the long pre-occupation with the founding myth of Isaac's binding.[21]

After several years during which Dolly's son is raised by her sister, Dolly meets him again and is amazed to find that the map of the whole of Eretz Yisrael on his back has "returned" to the '67 borders[22]:

> I saw the map of the Land of Israel which I had etched on his back so many years ago. The map was amazingly accurate and up-to-date; someone had gone over all the lines and expanded them according to the child's growth. I examined the map. One thing stood out – he had returned to the '67 borders. It was beyond belief! Yes. That's the generation gap for you, I reflected. My mother spits on the Arabs, I look them straight in the eye, and one day my son will lick their asses.[23]

[20] Ibid., 44.

[21] Adia Mendelson-Maoz, "On Human Parts – Orly Castel-Bloom and the Israeli Contemporary Extreme," *Novels of the Contemporary Extreme*, eds. Naomi Mandel and Alain-Philippe-Durand (London and New York: Continuum, 2006), 163–173.

[22] The reference is to the borders of Israel on June 4, 1967, on the eve of the Six Day War. According to these borders Judea, Samaria and the Gaza Strip, as well as East Jerusalem, are not part of Israel. A whole or partial Israeli return to the '67 borders has been discussed in talks between Israelis and Palestinians, and still comes up in any context of the founding of a Palestinian state alongside Israel.

[23] Castel-Bloom, *Dolly City*, 132.

Dolly is surprised at the change undergone by the map carved on her son's back. This change is tantamount to a rebellion by the son against his mother, who represents heritage and nation. Dolly is even alarmed by the "return" to the '67 borders, when her son joins a military academy:

> He had returned to the '67 borders. And that's nothing to brag about in a military academy, because it endangers the security of the state.[24]

Dolly, trying to save *Dolly City* from a cancer epidemic that has affected everyone, is aware of her mental infirmity and defines her disease as "the disease of infinite possibilities, of doubt determining reality,"[25] and in political terms:

> I might as well take the opportunity to say a couple of things about madness here. Madness is a predator. Its food is the soul. It takes over the soul as rapidly as our armies occupied Judea, Samaria and the Gaza Strip in 1967 ... and if a state like the State of Israel can't control the Arabs in the territories, how can anybody expect me, a private individual, to control the occupied territory inside me?[26]

Hannan Hever argued that the map informs the collective as in the literature of 1948, but whereas in the 1948 literature the military map subordinated the individual to an outer, objective orientation imposed by the collective to instill the national allegory, in Castel-Bloom's novel reality is determined by the individual body.[27] Thus a liminal concept of border is shifted to a place with no supervision and no control. As in Ben-Ner's text, madness spreads like an epidemic.

Castel-Bloom's act thus breaches the borders, shatters the national narrative and reveals the violence inherent in the story of the domination of national space. She inscribes a political situation on an individual's body, thereby ridiculing the political solution and exposing the deceit of nationalistic historiography.

[24] Ibid., 171.
[25] Ibid., 59.
[26] Ibid., 110.
[27] Hannan Hever, "Mapa shel hol" [map of sand] *Teoria u'bikoret* 20 (2002): 165–190.

Deterritorialization and Nomadism

Govrin's *Snapshots* proposes another perspective on the concept of territory by dismantling borders and creating deterritorialization of not just the liminal space of the Occupied Territories but also the entire national space and sovereignty. She offers spatial and ethical alternative to get out of the situation and its madness. *Snapshots* tells the story of Ilana Tsuriel, known as Lana, who is killed in a road accident on the Strasbourg-Munich autobahn on her way to lecture about the peace monument that she plans to build in Jerusalem. Among the possessions she leaves behind is a notebook of "snapshots" that is handed over to Tirtsa, her childhood friend from Haifa. Typographically, the notes appear in separate sections, in different styles and fonts, and they interweave various stories, times and spaces, thus revealing Lana's relationships with the three men in her life. The first relationship is with her father, Aaron Tsuriel, whose life story mirrors the history of Zionism, including immigration to pre-state Israel, and the nation-building project; the snapshots are addressed to her father and are written during the year after his death. The two other men in Lana's life are her husband, Alain Greenberg, a French Jew with anti-Zionist opinions, a Holocaust survivor whose life is devoted to archival endeavors to save memorabilia from the Second World War, and her lover Sayyid Ashabi, an actor and director in the Palestinian Theater in East Jerusalem whose story reveals the Palestinian narrative. The novel is set in the early 1990s against the backdrop of the First Intifada and the First Gulf War. During these events, Lana and her two sons David and Jonathan wander between New York, Paris and Jerusalem.

Views from the window on her journey and the anonymity of an individual roaming through spaces are the basis for Lana's written snapshots. Her notes are packed with descriptions of nature and human landscapes, with scenes of forests, huge billboards and people waiting at stations. They are distinctive in terms of their color and language and document the airports and cafés, and the hotels where she meets her lovers. In her movements through space, Lana removes borders, builds new bridges and creates lines of flight from the territorial system.

Lana leaves Israel after college in a sort of reaction to her father's generation of pioneers who set out on a journey toward their ancestral land spurred by a dream of settlement. Lana gives up the Zionist dream of "place" as a home and prefers to substitute nomadic journeys. Lana's abandonment of Israel is nurtured by ideological (left-wing) beliefs prompted by a sense of disappointment with the Israeli state. However when she explains it to herself, she paradoxically perceives herself as continuing the wandering that was part of her father's life story. His tales of emigration and wandering may have infiltrated his daughter's persona. She cannot be satisfied with a ready-made home and prefers to reconstruct his trajectories. As she comments: "Anything just to get as far away as possible from your story, Father. To live on the other side of the century, the story of *our own* wanderings."[28]

Lana divides her time between New Jersey and Paris, crisscrossing the world to give lectures in New York, Amsterdam and Copenhagen. In Paris, she lives with Alain, her husband, but spends very little time there: he too is away from home much of the time. Alain—"this professional wandering Jew"[29]—believes that only wandering can ensure the continued existence of the Jewish people.

The wanderings of Lana's father to the Promised Land and Alain's search for archival data are also elements in the life of Sayyid, the third party in the romantic triangle, who constantly competes with Alain and the figure of Lana's father in trying to reconstruct the old maps of Palestine. Against the backdrop of Zionist territorial historiography, Sayyid, who was born in Silwan in Jerusalem, feels foreign in his birthplace and wanders through Amsterdam, Paris, New York, Beirut, Tunis and Jerusalem. Sayyid stages a play about the Nakba and the expulsion of 1948 that presents a generation of pioneers that may be parallels, but also contrasts with Lana's father's generation.[30] Lana and Sayyid meet in places that are inevitably transient, a hotel, a car, and they form ties with territories viewed as neutral both in Jerusalem and outside Israel: "The hallucinatory driving from one side of Jerusalem to the other. The night before we leave. Outlining a secret map with the turns of the steering-wheel, in a last attempt to explain something to Sayyid."[31]

The concept of nomadism that dismantles territory and borders derives not only from Lena's lifestyle but also because she is an architect involved in building projects for the homeless. For Lana, the twentieth century is

[28] Govrin, *Snapshots*, 18, my italics.

[29] Ibid., 45.

[30] Lana is surrounded by refugees made up of Holocaust survivors, Palestinians and the refugees Lana devotes her architectural work to.

[31] Ibid., 284.

defined by refugees, and she decides to dedicate herself professionally to the problem.[32] Her dissertation is entitled "Refugee Settlement in Early Statehood." She also designs residential complexes for refugees in Europe. At the same time she is planning an anti-monument to peace in Jerusalem to be built around the Jewish concepts of *shmitta* (literally "release"—the sabbatical year when the land is left fallow), and *sukkot*—(temporary huts observant Jews live in every year during the weeklong holiday of Sukkot). Her professional decisions reflect the tension between building a home and possessing a land, and releasing it.

Traditionally architecture creates shape as well as borders and is directly related to territory. However, in Govrin's text, Lena pores over her anti-monument to peace, which embodies a utopian attitude toward the land. The anti-monument is the antithesis of monuments that have physical presence, are attached to the land and remind us of the past. Instead, Lana aims to create an anti-monument made of huts whose physical presence will be unstable, located in a liminal region looking toward the future and whose primary message projects the notion of *shmitta*. Rather than looking at the monument, her idea is to ask people to build a hut and live in it for a short time. She plans to build a kitchen, library and meeting rooms constructed midway between the temporary and the permanent, with roofs open to the sky. These will include a colony of huts with a restricted life-cycle; it will be built on the edge of the desert, with a moat around it.

Her anti-monument expropriates, creates a people-art, a temporary art that frees the territory instead of clinging to it, and allows every guest to construct his/her own hut on foundations that lack sovereignty. They adhere to a nomadic ideal; as Rosi Braidotti noted: "the nomad has a sharpened sense of territory but no possessiveness about it."[33]

Rimmon-Kenan stresses that Lana's anti-monument bridges between religious, ethnic and national territorial frameworks, and removes their boundaries. Its location is liminal, and the notion of the sabbatical year and the huts underscores the deterritorialization and the annulment of sovereignty over land. By the same token, Lana's life of wandering and love affairs are also equally associated with that notion and may concretize

[32] Ibid., 40.

[33] Rosi Braidotti, *Nomadic subjects: embodiment and sexual difference in contemporary feminist theory* (New York: Columbia University Press, 1994), 36.

the transformation of boundaries into thresholds.[34] Lana thinks of Jerusalem as a woman: "Jerusalem the woman. Loyal, unfaithful, saint and whore, the city of God's lust, the city that maddens all those who yearn to own her, to demand an exclusive claim to her."[35] For this reason, she wants to turn the city into a state that will belong to no one: "Untouched. Not the homeland of any tribe."

In their writing on nomadism and rhizomatic thought, Deleuze and Guattari ascribe a pivotal place to *Becoming* as a way of escaping the territorial system of power (Oedipal, binary, genealogical). By replacing the aspiration for a stable, unchanging identity, *becoming* is associated with an identity that develops ad infinitum. Braidotti deals with nomadism from a feminist point of view and links nomadism and the notion of identity: "This figuration [becoming] expresses the desire for an identity made of transitions, successive shifts, and coordinated changes, without and against an essential unity."[36] This perception abandons aspirations for unity and instead stimulates the desire for a process of infinite becoming that results from the rhizomatic outlook where there is no center or boundary, and the lines extend everywhere. Nomadic movement is also connected to the notion that things are subject to a process-based continuing context, with no place for fixation. The absence of the fixation of the home, and the temporality of borders, generates an unending process of becoming.[37]

Becoming is only possible in the context of a minority; "there is no becoming majoritarian; majority is never becoming. All becoming is minoritarian."[38] For Deleuze and Guattari, "all becomings begin with and pass through becoming-woman. It is the key to all other becomings."[39] The connection between nomadism and the endless becoming of the subject's identity and the links between them and the notion of *becoming-woman* (as a minority) formed the crux of feminist criticism of Deleuze and Guattari. While Deleuze and Guattari describe becoming as

[34] Shlomit Rimmon-Kenan, "Place, Space, and Michal Govrin's 'Snapshots'." *Narrative* 17.2 (May 2009): 222.

[35] Govrin, *Snapshots*, 114.

[36] Braidotti, *Nomadic Subjects*, 22.

[37] See also Rosi Braidotti, "Affirming the Affirmative," *Rhizomes* 11/12 (Fall 2005/Spring 2006).

[38] Gilles Deleuze and Félix Guattari, *A Thousand Plateaus* (Minnesota: Continuum, 1987), 106.

[39] Ibid., 277.

becoming-woman, they continue the philosophical tradition in which Woman is the philosopher's Other. Luce Irigaray, for instance, identified this as a male implication, again based on a metaphysical axis of difference between masculinity and femininity, because only those who maintain the stable position of a subject (i.e., white males) can suggest conceding it. She argues that "The metaphor of becoming-woman is a male appropriation and recuperation of the positions and struggles of woman. As such, it risks depoliticizing, possibly even aestheticizing, struggles and political challenges crucial to the survival and self-definition of women."[40] It is worth recalling that while becoming is intended toward a specific stable essence, in the Deleuzian model the becoming project is infinite and directionless. Braidotti[41] and Grosz[42] view rhizomatic thought as an immensely powerful tool, a vital resource that can be used for the feminist struggle. In Govrin's text, these ties between the nomadic lives and art and the constantly forming identity and femininity take on further ethical and political significance.

The female protagonist's choice to abandon the concept of home and to opt for nomadism appears as a choice made by women, characterized by her contrast with the prevalent image of women as located in the home, that is, as subject who is supervised by boundaries. For women in general, and for the woman character in the novel, the home—which can symbolize intimacy and security—is a locus that is ruled, supervised and restricted. It is a political space, which positions a binary division and does not permit the boundaries to be crossed. Confronting that space are the nomads, who indeed are subject to inherent uncertainty and hazards, but also enable the borders to be crossed, breaking through the subject's fixated identity, allowing her to replace binary, genealogical relations with rhizomatic, temporary and multi-shaded contexts.

Lana's version is one of total deterritorialization as reflected in the concept of *shmitta*. However, while Lana dreams of eliminating the borders and redeeming territory from any form of ownership, she discovers that

[40] Luce Irigaray, *This Sex which is not One* (Ithaca, N.Y: Cornell University Press, 1985), 140–141.

[41] Rosi Braidotti, "Nomadism with Difference: Deleuze's legacy in a feminist perspective," *Man and World* 29 (1996): 305–309.

[42] Elizabeth Grosz, "A Thousand Tiny Sexes: Feminism and Rhizomatics," In *Gilles Deleuze and the theater of philosophy*, edited by Dorothea Olkowski and Costantin V. Boundas (NY: Routledge, 1994), 188.

everyone who seemed to support her is aiming for reterritorialization.[43] Later in the novel it emerges that for the men in her life and for the other people involved in her project, removing the borders is only one chapter in the chronicle of building new borders and declaring a different sovereignty over the disputed territory. Thus, while Govrin presents an unusual idea for dismantling borders, she shows how the revolutionary nature of her protagonist, and its implications which threaten the core of political and gendered power, is doomed to failure. Alongside this radical solution, she also depicts a more realistic view that portrays how a woman's ethical alternative is crushed and threatened by violence. Ultimately, the end of sovereignty and possession cannot succeed[44] in a place where men thirst for war, a place where weapons continue to assault Jerusalem rather than let the land heal itself.

Conclusion

In the political reality of Israel, maps and the borders marked on them are an authoritative way of establishing facts on the ground. Borders supply a direction, a description and a presentation, but they are abstract entities—a remote enactment of ideology that often sparks intellectual and political debates among politicians, whereas the average Israeli usually tries to simply ignore their problematic implications. The novels discussed here propose different poetic interpretations of the concept of borders and liminality: odor and insanity that spread like a disease in Ben-Ner's novel, the grotesque anatomy of the border in Castel-Bloom's novel and the artistic project of annulling borders in Govrin's novel.

Nonetheless, the works examined here all attempt to show that the state of occupation is not only a political issue of sole interest to politicians but rather a sickness that invades the lives of all Israelis and challenges their beliefs and values. The novels use symbolic strategies to show how the state of occupation elicits aggression and violence, nourishes harsh stereotypes and hatred and threatens to destroy humanism. A state without stable

[43] Deleuze and Guattari, *A Thousand Plateaus*, 508.

[44] Levitan suggested examining "the Prozbul Writ, which was instigated by the Jewish Sages against financial *shmitta*, in sense of "*tikkun olam*" (repairing the world) because the shmitta is unrealistic." And hence indeed "the utopia that her book [Govrin's] proposes, despite its beautiful idea, is unrealistic, and there is no other alternative than to release it." Amos Levitan, "Mah lishmot, mah le'ehoz?" [What to keep what to release] *Iton 77* 269 (2002): 34.

borders turns into a realm and a metaphor for confusion, contradiction, fear, aggression and madness. Castel-Bloom and Ben-Ner's novels show how this malaise invades the self and harms the psyche. In Govrin's text, the protagonist finds "lines of flights" by choosing deterritorialization and nomadism. In a sense, Govrin's text is more optimistic, as it explores an esthetical and ethical alternative, and yet it also reveals the gap between the theoretical path, generally supported by the left wing in Israeli politics, and its realization, which is unattainable in a place ruled by men.

In all three novels, the issue of borders and humanity is linked to intergenerational relationships between parents and children, as well as the historical context and the humanist legacy of Zionism. While the fathers built the country, their sons (in Ben-Ner) and their daughters (in Castel-Bloom and Govrin) deviate from their path in a sad reflection on how things have changed. The notion of corruption is central to all these texts, and the protagonists' inability to change this condition is devastating.

The literary community in Israel has always been an important part of the cultural arena, either by supporting hegemonic stances or by criticizing them, openly or indirectly. Each of these works tries to challenge the concept of borders and liminality, to criticize the occupation, to show the corruption and its implications. They not only demonstrate the richness of the Hebrew literature that confronts the political situation in Israel but also reveal a cultural and political debate that is not always well known outside Israel.

Bibliography

Primary Resources

Ben-Ner, Yitzhak. 1989. *Ta'atuon* (Delusion). Jerusalem: Am oved.

Castel-Bloom, Orly. 1992. *Dolly City*. Tel-Aviv: Zmora bitan. Trans. Dalya Bilu. London: Loki Books, 1997.

Govrin, Michal. 2002. *Hevzekim* (*Snapshots*). Tel Aviv: Am-oved. Trans. Barbara Harshav. New York: Riverhead Books, 2007.

Iczkovits, Yaniv. 2007. *Dofek* (Pulse). Tel-Aviv: Ha-kibbuts ha-meuhad.

Kravitz, Asher. 2008. *Ani Mustafa Rabinovitch* (I, Mustafa Rabinovitch). 2nd ed. Bnei Brak: Sifriat poalim and Ha-kibbuts ha-meuhad, 2004.

Matalon, Ronit. 2000. *Sarah, Sarah* (*Bliss*). Tel Aviv: Am oved. Trans. Jessica Cohen. New York: Metropolitan Books, 2003.

Nevo, Eshkol. 2007. *Mish'ala a'hat yemina* (*World Cup Wishes*). Or Yehudah: Zemorah-Bitan. Trans. Sondra Silverston. London: Chatto & Windus, 2010.

Polity, Roy. 2001. *Arnavonei gagot* (Roof Rabbits). Tel-Aviv: Am oved.

Rabinyan, Dorit. 2015. *Gader hayah* (Borderlife). Tel-Aviv: Am oved.

Ron-Furer, Liran. 2003. *Tismonet ha-mahsom* (Checkpoint Syndrome). Tel-Aviv: Gvanim.

Yehoshua, Abraham B. 2007. *Esh yedidutit* (*Friendly Fire*). Tel-Aviv: Ha-kibbuts ha-meuhad. Trans. Stuart Schoffman. New York: Harcourt Inc, 2008.

Secondary Resources

Almog, Oz. 2000. *The Sabra: The Creation of the New Jew*. Trans. Haim Watzman. Berkeley: University of California Press.

Braidotti, Rosi. 1994. *Nomadic subjects: Embodiment and Sexual Difference in Contemporary Feminist Theory*. New York: Columbia University Press.

———. 1996. Nomadism with Difference: Deleuze's Legacy in a Feminist Perspective. *Man and World* 29: 305–309.

———. 2005/2006. Affirming the Affirmative: On Nomadic Affectivity. *Rhizomes 11/12*. http://www.rhizomes.net/issue11/braidotti.html

Deleuze, Gilles, and Félix Guattari. 1987. *A Thousand Plateaus*. Trans. Brian Massumi. Minneapolis: Continuum.

Fishelov, David. 2002–2003. Megamot ba-shira bi-shnot ha-shmonim (Trends in the Poetry of the 80's). Achshav 67/68 (Fall-Winter): 184–185.

Grosz, Elizabeth. 1994. A Thousand Tiny Sexes: Feminism and Rhizomatics. In *Gilles Deleuze and the Theater of Philosophy*, ed. Dorothea Olkowski and Costantin V. Boundas, 187–210. New York: Routledge.

Gurevitz, Zeli, and Gideon Aranne. 1993. "Al ha-makom" (On the Place). *Alpayim* 4: 9–44.

Hever, Hannan. 2002. "Mapa shel hol mi-sifrut ivrit le-sifrut israelit" (Map of Sand – From Hebrew Literature to Israeli Literature). *Teoria u'bikoret* 20: 165–190.

Hever, Hannan. 2007. "Ten lo badranim – v'yanuach be'shalom" (Give him Entertainers, and he will rest in Peace). *Canoni v'populari* (Canonic and Popular), 193–208. Tel Aviv: Resling.

Irigaray, Luce. 1985. *This Sex Which Is Not One*. Trans. Catherine Porter with Carolyn Burke. Ithaca: Cornell University Press.

Kamp, Adriana. 2000. "Ha-gvul ki'fney yanus – merhav ve-toda'a leumit be-israel" (The Border as a Janus Face – Space and National Identity in Israel). *Teoria u'bikoret* 16: 13–43. http://theory-and-criticism.vanleer.org.il//NetisUtils/srvrutil_getPDF.aspx/2g3dXy/%2F%2F16-2.pdf

Korsgaard, Christine M. 1996. *The Source of Normativity*. Cambridge: Cambridge University Press.

Levitan, Amos. 2002. Ma lishmot, ma le'ehoz? (What to Drop What to Keep). *Iton* 77 (269): 33–35.

Meisels, Ofra. 1995. Likrat gius (Before Enlisting). In *Mitbagrim be'israel – hebetim ishiyim. mishpahtiyim ve'hevratiyi* (Adolescents in Israel – Individual, Family and Social Characteristics), ed. H. Plum, 177–200. Even Yehuda: Rekhes.

Mendelson-Maoz, Adia. 2006. On Human Parts – Orly Castel-Bloom and the Israeli Contemporary Extreme. In *Novels of the Contemporary Extreme*, ed. Naomi Mandel and Alain-Philippe -Durand, 163–173. London/New York: Continuum.

———. 2011. Hurled into the Heart of Darkness – Moral Luck and the Hebrew Literature of the Intifada. *Hebrew Studies* 52: 315–339. http://www.jstor.org.ezp-prod1.hul.harvard.edu/stable/pdf/23343593.pdf?acceptTC=true

Ophir, Adi, and Ariella Azoulay. 2008. *Mishtar zeh she-eino ehad* (This Regime Which Is Not One). Tel-Aviv: Resling.

Rimmon-Kenan, Shlomit. 2009. Place, Space, and Michal Govrin's 'Snapshots'. *Narrative* 17 (2): 220–234. https://muse.jhu.edu/login?auth=0&type=summary&url=/journals/narrative/v017/17.2.rimmon-kenan.pdf

Sion, Liora. 1997. *Dimoyei gavriut etzel lohamim: ha-sherut be-hativot heil raglim ke-teckes ma'avar mi-na'arut le-bagrut* (Images of Manhood Among Combat Soldiers: Military Service in the Israeli Infantry as a Rite of Passage from Youth to Adulthood). Jerusalem: The Dayan Center for Social Science Research, the Hebrew University.

Zones of Maximal Translatability: Borderspace and Women's Time

Heather H. Yeung

but every signifying practice does not encompass the infinite totality of that process. Multiple constraints – which are ultimately socio-political – stop the signifying process at one or another of the theses that it traverses; they knot it and lock it into a given surface or structure; they discard practice under fixed, fragmentary, symbolic matrices, the tracings of various social constraints that obliterate the infinity of the process. . .[1]

(Julia Kristeva)

How is it understood, or misunderstood, but also, what future, what prospects does it have? If, as we believe, it is true that women will awaken in the coming millennium, what can the profound meaning of that awakening, that civilization, be?[2]

(Julia Kristeva and Catherine Clément)

---

[1] Julia Kristeva, *Revolution in Poetic Language*. Trans. Margaret Waller (New York: Columbia UP, 1984), 88. The "infinity of the process", Kristeva writes, is the "semiotic chora" (88).

[2] Julia Kristeva and Catherine Clément. *The Feminine and the Sacred*. Trans. Jane Marie Todd. (New York: Columbia UP, 2001), 2. On this page, too, Kristeva defines the project of *The Feminine and the Sacred* as contrapuntal—a "book in two voices".

H.H. Yeung (✉)
University of Dundee, Dundee, UK

J. Elbert Decker, D. Winchock (eds.), *Borderlands and Liminal Subjects*, https://doi.org/10.1007/978-3-319-67813-9_4

There is then a 'becoming-feminist' of time theory itself...[3]
(Emily Apter)

1: The Now

I write this from a hill at the East of Ankara, in a week in early June 2016. In this week Britain gears up for an EU membership referendum; the US presidency race is well underway; the question of Turkish EU membership continues to be raised, as does the idea, reiterated, of what exactly it is that comprises a citizen of this and many other countries, where their centres of power and their borders lie, when nationhood and national identity is no longer (or, has never been) simply a question of singularity of language, ethnicity, culture, or belief. This week, as is the same for any week, the news shows a series of particularities and general models, attitudes of investigation and protectionism; identity politics of all sorts collide and combine, spanning the globe, opposites nullifying each other: the "trending topics" on the *Foreign Affairs* website are currently "NATO", "China", "ISIS", and "Environment"[4]; *Jane* notes that NATO has recognized "Cyberspace" as an operational domain, and reports from Konya on a joint training exercise between Italy, Turkey, Pakistan, and Saudi Arabia[5]; *Hurriyet* notes the Venice Commission's review of Turkey's legal policies on the internet, and Erdoğan is criticized for attendance at Muhammed Ali's funeral and warned against travel to the US[6]; *Al Jazeera* features the violent identitarian event of the Orlando shooting, the continued war in Syria, an attack in Paris....[7]

In an interview with Ross Guberman conducted two decades ago, Julia Kristeva speaks from Paris after a period spent in the United States. She speaks against nation-phobias, for hospitality across borders, for

[3] Emily Apter, "Women's Time' in Theory', *differences: a Journal of Feminist Cultural Studies* 21.1 (2010), 17.

[4] The magazine of the Council on Foreign Relations, http://www.foreignaffairs.com, accessed June 10–15, 2016.

[5] *IHS Jane's Defense Daily*: http://www.janes.com/article/61396/nato-recognises-cyber-as-operational-domain-in-move-to-adapt, and http://www.janes.com/article/61318/air-forces-hone-real-world-combat-skills-at-anatolian-eagle-exercise-in-turkey, accessed June 14, 2016.

[6] *Hürriyet Daily News English*: http://hurriyetdailynews.com, accessed June 14–15, 2016.

[7] *Al Jazeera English*: http://www.aljazeera.com, accessed June 14, 2016.

foreignness, and notes how this global world makes us "the inheritors of all traditions".[8] Two decades on, we ought to be more capable of sitting at these crossroads, of acknowledging the simultaneous violence and porosity of the borderspace, and contemplating the nexus. On the news this week as much as a decade ago, global collectives of powers dominate and intrigue, enigmatic nations decentralized from the dominant point of view are investigated, as is the deep-time subject of our peripheral vision as *homo sapiens sapiens.* This deep-time subject is the world stage itself, which surrounds us, provides us with life, and is netted by communications technologies of our own invention.[9] Language, language gaps or slippages, and mistranslation is a constant theme in these performances. On this stage which we necessarily cannot perceive in its totality,[10] state actors continue to play out ancient games, mirrored on smaller levels at the limits of their sovereign domains; constant acts of translation and reinterpretation occur, and with these, moments of violence and rupture (sometimes physical, always affective) when a sovereign or legal demand for singular definition comes face to face with an opposing request or demand which cannot be parsed into its own matrix (*sapientia* become *loquans* become *affectus*). This is the basic situation of the checkpoint; the activity where incompatible systems of power and definition are exercised in the act of border-control which mobilizes an at times unspeakable condition of affect. These checkpoints, these interactions, are marked by moments of constitution and effacement. The many facts or facets of the multiply identifying self are turned around to face the absolute other, the perverse mirror, against which it refracts and redefines itself, in which its *process* across borders which are physical (land and body) and is faced with a series of constraints is placed under trial.[11]

[8] Julia Kristeva interview with Ross Guberman, trans. Ross Guberman *Julia Kristeva Interviews* (New York: Columbia UP, 2006), 264–5.

[9] On the subject of the contemporary concern with our environment *as peripheral surroundings*, see in particular Timothy Morton, *Ecology Without Nature* (Harvard: Harvard UP, 2009). For the intersection of these concerns with sovereign power and contemporary communications systems in actor network theory, Bruno Latour's *Reassembling the Social* (Oxford: OUP, 2005) and *Politics of Nature* (Harvard: Harvard UP, 2009).

[10] Again, see Morton, *Ecology Without Nature*, 175: "the environment is that which cannot be indicated directly".

[11] This sentence written with all resonance of Julia Kristeva's *sujet en procès* as the subject in process/under trial (see Kristeva, *Revolution*: 37, and the epigraph to this essay), where subjectivity in the face of sovereign control/definition is inherently affective, social, legal, and above all, mutable.

At the borders of this essay sit a triptych of epigraphs which mirror, distilled, the trajectory of this work, also calling into question the situation, the borders, and the origin-points of the essay itself. They indicate, before the essay "proper" has begun, the signifying form of the paratext and the difficulty of the readerly encounter with a complex textual border zone, where the "now" of reading clashes not only with the dominant time of the writing to come (in the body of the essay), but the time and expanse of each textual and philosophical moment excerpted, re-contextualized, in the epigraphs. Thus, this essay begins not with a singular voice, but with a polyphony, set in an intentionally complex series of overlapping, intersecting, juxtaposing, temporalities, which are simultaneously self-constituting and self-effacing. The essay begins multiple times, each time a different "now"; each time gesturing towards quite a different origin-point for thought, moving in different directions in time and space, opening up a different set of borders or points of trial. In so doing I call to the formal aspect of the paratextual-textual enactment of the border zone encounter, a major aspect of the analysis which ensues, mirroring the significant intersection of the form of a work with its subject matter(s). The epigraph-paratexts are also a chronology of the writing of previous, similar points of encounter; the first, the staging of constraint and rupture, of the "subject in process"—the subject at, and/or breaking through, the border zone—and the infinity and infinite mutability of the "process", of Julia Kristeva's *Revolution in Poetic Language*; the second, a playing out of polyphonic future-thought, of projective encounters in languages and beliefs, and, specifically, feminine language and belief, as co-written in Julia Kristeva and Catherine Clément's *The Feminine and the Sacred*; the third, the present/future, the possibilities of the feminine in an essay by Emily Apter which thinks through and updates the work done in Julia Kristeva's seminal "Women's Time" essay. Each epigraph was written out of a very different original context (in time, in place, in language) and thus exists discretely within itself, but each epigraph also now converses within the time of this essay, is tacitly oriented towards, even translated into, the current work of exploration in clashing and polyphonic spatio-temporal encounters; the conversations and aporias, the multiplicities, and violences of misunderstanding that are thrown up in the encounter between forms of sovereignty and those subjects who resist singular, empirical, definition.

My orientation, as I type, is Eastward. I enact a true meaning of "orientation" as linguistic and real "turn" towards the east. I write this across cultures and linguistic memories in a single (sovereign?) language resonant with the violence and appropriation of past and current Empires, real and imagined. This language is, in this moment, decentred, foreign to its place of composition, resonant with the effects of translation, the "irremediable collapse" that Guy Scarpetta reads in Roland Barthes as essential to the encounter with the orient (or, what is East to us).[12] My Orientation is physical (the direction of my face, of my desk) but also plumbs other depths: I sit at the nexus point between my two countries of origin (Scotland, China), and, facing Eastwards, I type in a language radically other from both the nation I face and the nation in which I currently orientate myself. As I type this I stage myself as well as my subject matter in a zone of multiple potential mistranslations. For Barthes, this Orientation also involves cultural identification through signs and through language, and the essential mis-interpretation of all acts of translation. Yet for there to be these slippages, these moments of violence, these gaps, we must also have form, and we also must bear witness to the play on the stage of the world of the text (or the text *as* this staging, as this play).[13]

Language, itself the medium of this performance of identity quest/questioning in multiple forms (oral, written, electronic, physical, live, recorded...), is itself placed under question; form and medium become simultaneously the stage and the subject of Barthes's affective fragmenting in derision and dissociation of the subject on trial or at the crossroads. We must, he writes, seek to renew our metaphors, find in this all the "emptiness [...that is] the self-consistence of the world"[14]; here, Barthes takes up the stance in "the gaping utopia" of the *neuter*. Yet, tellingly, this final stance in this interview is spoken under the subheading "WEAPONS", and "war" has been defined as the "very structure of meaning".[15] I write this in essay form, gesturing towards a multiplicity of different genres of the written (and spoken) word. I perform, here, a series of crossing places and points of view; each writer/thinker I address in this essay—Julia Kristeva, Marina Warner, and Emily Apter—represents at once a given perspective and a universal, a multiplicity, and its necessarily fluid, singular origins in being.

[12] Roland Barthes interview with Guy Scarpetta, "Digressions", *The Grain of the Voice: Interviews 1962–1980*, Trans. Linda Coverdale (Berkeley: U California P, 1991), 115.

[13] Barthes writes "Today I propose this metaphor: the stage of the world (the world as stage) is occupied by a play of 'decors' (texts); if you raise one backdrop, another appears behind it, and so on [...] a complete *mise-en-scène* of the plural which derides and dissociates the subject" ("Digressions", 116).

[14] Barthes, "Digressions", 118.

[15] Barthes, "Digressions", 127.

Our intersection, our crossroads, becomes an enigmatic, embattled one, circling around a productive aporia (paradox?), which is something we can never quite reach—bounded in the particularities of space and time.[16] Yet this environmental paradox will eventually lead us to turn towards the manner in which translation, border-crossing, rupture, and space intersect in Emily Apter, Julia Kristeva, and Marina Warner, particularly in these texts—*The Translation Zone*, *Murder in Byzantium*, and *The Leto Bundle*—born out of a concern with moments of disruption and violent mistranslation, where these crossing places, real and fictional, are so often those, in some ways, of the Orient. But at our current point, we are simply setting the stage, fashioning the spaces in which these encounters will occur, demonstrating the overall texture of this "planetary era".[17] A Catalpa tree flowers outside my window next to an Ash; the air is heavy with the pollen of the Norway Spruce; thunder clouds roll in and commingle with traffic noise and the dust and pollution which collects above the city I face away from.

0: Points of Origin/Disappearance

Alice Jardine's introductory essay to the first English translation of Julia Kristeva's "Women's Time" places as its epigraphs quotations from Kristeva's *Revolution in Poetic Language* (1974)[18] and A.J. Thompson and A.V. Martinet's *Practical English Grammar* (1969).[19] The first of these epigraphs reads "[t]hat this rupture can be in complicity with the law, or, rather can constitute a point of departure for even deeper changes: that is the major problem".[20] The epigraph is in part a translator's need to concisely situate Kristeva's thought for an American audience for whom, at this point, the work of Kristeva has not been readily available in English, but

[16] Morton, *Ecology Without Nature*, 52: "... you will never be able to find some 'thing' in between, however close to the boundary line you get".

[17] Julia Kristeva, *This Incredible Need to Believe*, trans. Beverley Brie Brahic (New York: Columbia UP, 2009), 98.

[18] The date given here is for the first French publication of this text by Seuil, which, although published as a partial English translation in 1984 by Margaret Waller for Columbia University Press, has never been fully translated into English. Jardine, for this epigraph, gives her own translation of the French text.

[19] Alice Jardine, "Introduction to Julia Kristeva's 'Women's Time'", *Signs: A Journal of Women in Culture and Society* 7.1 (1981), 5–12.

[20] Jardine, "Introduction", 5.

it also gestures towards the open, aporetic, essential centrepoint around which Kristeva's text revolves: the *chôra*,[21] and the "plural, contradictory, heterogenous" processes of signification (drives, maternal discontinuity, political struggle, "pulverization of language") that complicate and lead us towards a sensation of this point of origin; the modality, or "strange temporality", of the "future perfect" as the state of being simultaneously past and future in which we, thus faced with struggle and rupture, find ourselves.[22] Our present is figured in the gap between the two points of the composition of the future perfect as verb, and is configured in the action of the verb, which *in itself* crosses boundaries, translates, and corrupts senses of time.[23] The hendyadic resonance of the *chora* itself, as it sits linguistically at its own crossroads, contains its own double action, a double signification. *Chora* is at once the originary feminine third-space, applied in different ways and across centuries and languages by different thinkers, and it is also, quite literally, a political *outside*: *chora* is the noun used for the space (wasteland and minor municipality alike) that is outside of the main polis—outside of the immediate space of sovereign articulation and control. It is a space outside any singularity of time, outside of space itself, but in and through which any temporal or spatial system is called to account, is opened to itself. And so we return to the Future Perfect: before this has been read, it will have already happened; these boundaries still facing us will have already been crossed, ruptured....

Let us not, however, get ahead of ourselves. The condensed matrix of paratextual reference that Jardine's epigraphs, as well as the nature of her own "introduction" as epigraph, mobilize—past, present, and future readings of Kristeva which are moments of definition outside of the nominal "primary text" and in turn redefine our encounter with that text—and enact

[21] Many notes to Kristeva's work here (including her own) trace the *chora* ($\chi\omega\rho\alpha$) back to Plato's *Timaeus* as an "essentially mobile", "extremely provisional" concept which exists in a zone of radical uncertainty between object-status and being as a mode of language, which defies belief—is at the limits (see Kristeva, *Revolution*, 25 and 239 n.12). Tellingly, the *Timaeus* also configures the chora problem *outside* of the dialectic of "model form" and "model's copy": it is a "third kind of form" which disrupts any sovereign binary—thus, it destroys borders and boundaries, is "baffling and obscure [...] the nurse of all Becoming"—so feminized—and is "ever-existing"—thus always-already—an eternal feminine. Plato, *Timaeus*, trans. R.G. Bury (Loeb 234), 113 and 528.

[22] Kristeva, *Revolution*, 88, 85.

[23] Jardine, "Introduction", 5; Julia Kristeva, "Women's Time", trans. Alice Jardine, *Signs* 7.1 (1981), 14.

the complexities of the border zone as strange temporality of reading and reference that Kristeva's work (in this case "Women's Time") also seeks to encounter, expose, and navigate. The notes and the footnotes to the epigraphs are themselves references to a complicity with and point of departure from laws and boundaries (of grammar; of nation-states…). The paratext provides a formal enactment of the encounter at the cross-roads, and it is a "zone without any hard and fast boundary on either the inward side (turned towards the text) or the outward side (turned towards the worlds discourse on the text)".[24] The paratext proves that this border- or translation-zone encounter opens up and circles around a gap, a space, a *chora*, and also proves the polyvalence of the encounter: it is at once in warring tongues (particularly if the paratext(s) and text(s) are written in different languages and by different writers, but even when they are quite simply different texts) and warring genres (very often the paratext will gesture towards a type of writing that the text in question absolutely *is not*), and is in itself a radically different form from the text (a fragment). How do these paratexts communicate except out of a space of violent translation? What is the operation of the paratext if it is not to effect some form of violent manipulation of the essential identity of the text and of our reading process? The choraic structure of the gap between that the paratext-text creates forces us, too, to read as the paratext does across borders, across the bounds of generic expectation and the identity politics of the sovereign state, whose totality in itself is placed in question by the very existence of the paratext in relation to the text, and of its dispossessive gap.

The paratext is before, after, and paradoxically (we cannot read paracoustically) simultaneous to the text itself. It is in and outside of itself a point of impossible encounter and possible longing—an enactment of the future perfect. The "full" text *forms* the violent encounter or staged translations it also enacts and takes as its subject matter, it *forces the acts of translation and of orientation*. The paratext becomes subject to *xenophobia* in its fullest sense: as Emily Apter remarks on how *xenos* means that which is both foreign and "guest-friend"[25]—*xenophobia* as an affective act of coded repulsion and invitation, a point whose complete translation is impossible,

[24] Gérard Genette, *Paratexts: Thresholds of Interpretation*, trans. Jane E. Lewin (Cambridge: Cambridge UP, 1997), 2.

[25] Emily Apter, *The Translation Zone: A New Comparative Literature* (Princeton: Princeton UP, 2006), 179.

whose invitation *in spite and because of* difference is also an enactment of the "contrapuntal consciousness" that Marina Warner sees as essential to productive anti-violent correspondence across border zones.[26] In this sense, the choice to approach in this essay Kristeva, Warner, and Apter via *Murder in Byzantium*, *The Leto Bundle*, and *The Translation Zone* is much less than arbitrary. Each text faces the Near East. Each text is written out of a sense of violent encounter and cultural disruption, particularly catalysed by the global affective resonance of the WTC attacks of September 11, 2001.[27] Each text works globally, transhistorically, and across borders and nation-states, configuring multiple possibilities of perspective. Each text exposes formally and thematically the violent encounters which are its subject matter, and seeks to mobilize a potentially choraic or feminine third-space and time of encounter in order to work productively against the affective violence of sovereign control in the exercise of soft power—naming at the city limits or border zone as possession/dispossession of identity. Each text uses city-states and conflicted border zones of the real, historic, mythic, and/or fictional Near East through which to illuminate moments at the limits of sovereign control which cut across these perspectives. Each text establishes a space of discourse which is polyphonic, which combats formal expectation, and tells us stories "of a *subject*, if you like [...], that includes the ego, displaces it, traverses it, hollows it out, recomposes it, revives it"[28]—in effect, *translates* it, *irrationalizes* it—stories which are written "to invite reflection—to give the princes and sultans of this world pause",[29] where "a strong feminine component [...] offsets [...] the sovereign",[30] whose "prophetic time signatures" are written through breaks,

[26] Marina Warner, "In the Time of Not Yet: On the Imaginary of Edward Said" in *Conflicting Humanities*, ed. Rosi Braidotti and Paul Gilroy (London: Bloomsbury, 2016), 270. Here, Warner is writing against violence out of Edward Said's concept of contrapuntalism. The primary example she reflects upon is the nation-spanning conflict-dispelling post-identitarian post-generic musical project of Daniel Barenboim and Edward Said—the *Western-Eastern Divan Orchestra*.

[27] For an expansion of Kristeva's and Warner's writing out of these events in relation to *Murder in Byzantium* and *The Leto Bundle*, see my 'Against Spectacle: International Terror and the Crisis of the Feminine Subject' in Peter Childs, Sebastian Groes and Claire Colebrook (eds) *Women's Fiction and Post-9/11 Contexts* (New York: Lexington, 2015), 51–64. The Preface to Apter's *The Translation Zone* opens "This book was shaped by the traumatic experience of September 11, 2001 [... and] the surreal aftermath of that fateful day" (vii).

[28] Kristeva, *Hatred and Forgiveness*, 275.

[29] Warner, *Stranger Magic*, 436.

[30] Julia Kristeva, *Interviews*, 267.

duration, endurance, “pastness and futurity”.[31] Each text now sits at a remove to our “now” of reading—a cacophony of noise and silence, of warring tongues and identities....

The encounter, translation, and rupture in each of these texts which mark and perform this translation zone on a generic level are immediately apparent. Apter’s *The Translation Zone* opens with a prose introduction which gives, amongst other things, the contexts of the book’s production, but between this and the chapters proper there exists a manifesto—“20 Theses on Translation”—written as a list of statements which resonate, complement, and contradict each other. The structure Apter’s text then takes on contradicts any astringent sense of linearity of design—the nominal first chapter (which is bookended by the book’s epilogue) is placed after the preface and the theses, but before the title page for the “first part” of the book; *The Translation Zone* has multiple beginnings and endings, enacts its own theses, is placed internationally and at points of crisis, conflict, and redefinition—America, Istanbul, Algeria, the Balkans... in Englishes, Turkishes, Creoles.... Languages, literatures, theories, and thoughts migrate and are translated and mistranslated globally, mirroring lost mother tongues and diplomatic states, gesturing towards a global Babel.... Constant gaps and mistakes giving rise to a trans[ ]ation zone (substitute in an *l* and/or an *n*)[32]: an enactment of the chora’s existence as disruptive moment at the crossroads and unreachable centrepoint, as aporia, as “cultural caesura”.[33]

In Warner’s *The Leto Bundle*, generic disruption begins early on, but not before the prologue situates us momentarily in a very familiar present and very familiar space where non-place meets checkpoint zone: the customs department of an international airport. Further to this, the novel ventriloquises different forms of textual expression—archaeologist’s and archivist’s notes, e-mail correspondences and online fora, lullabies and letters, interweave with more conventional prose narrative expression in speech and description. The novel’s prologue is bookended with an epilogue and the novel’s table of contents with a chronology. Like Apter’s *Translation Zone* it presents us with a muddled chronology and complexifies the act of readerly encounter through paratextual accompaniment. But perhaps the most interesting moment in *The Leto Bundle*’s zones of transgeneric encounter is the threnody

[31] Apter, “‘Women’s Time’ In Theory”, 17.

[32] Apter, *The Translation Zone*, 5.

[33] Apter, *The Translation Zone*, 5.

which hovers in the zone between the end of the novel proper and its epilogue. This threnody is the most intense moment of non-translated communication by the transhistorical, or even mythic, character around whom the novel revolves (at different times and in different places called Leto, Ella, Nellie, Lettice, Helen, even "Outis"), at the point at which she disappears from the text, and, indeed, disappears at the point at which the text has almost completed itself. The threnody marks itself by its own name as something which exists outside of the generic bounds of the novel form—its roots in the Ode, but its real generic marker being its existence outside of the bound of language in *threnos*—wailing, just as "Leto's" being, compromised, lacking linguistic expression, and made increasingly mythic by her passage across multiple embattled national and symbolic borders from myth to a novelistic present, and the use, here, of an ancient form of poetic expression translated not only into English, but also into a fragmentary prose. Yet this moment is telling also since it marks a point where "Leto" is finally able to narrate some sort of a story through the lament pock marked by the silence of the space of the page—finally existing/disappearing with minimal mediation—becoming wholly untranslatable. The threnody itself is *spaced* rather than punctuated: blanks on the page mark pregnant interruptions even of this interrupting genre by something radically different.

Kristeva's *Murder in Byzantium*, in turn, exists across border zones in the space of encounter between real and fictional cities (Paris, "Santa Varvara", the Byzantium of the Komnenos dynasty as told in the *Alexiad* and imagined in the novel through the lens of, first, an historian and second, a journalist, Istanbul now...) and languages (French, "Santa Varvarian", Byzantine Greek, Chinese...), mobilizing ancient and contemporary frames of temporality, as well as effecting a crossing point between philosophical, mathematical, and Oriental ideas of the infinite ("the infinite", ∞, and 無 限 are at different times used to emphasize ultimately untranslatable nature of this concept/affect).[34] Echoing her own critical preoccupations with avant-garde writing and intertextuality, Kristeva invites us to read her recent works, including *Murder in Byzantium*, against the grain of genre.[35] Enacting these ruptures of genre signification within the text itself, *Murder in Byzantium* uses epigraph,

[34] See my "Reading Kristeva with Kristeva", *Studies in the Literary Imagination* 47.1 (2014) for a fuller exploration of the contact zone between these conflicting representations (117), and, more broadly, the effects of translinguistic naming and mistranslation in Kristeva's *Murder in Byzantium*.

[35] See Kristeva, *Hatred and Forgiveness*, 6; *This Incredible Need to Believe*, 47.

preface, intertext, e-mail, hymn, and even images from maps to disrupt the linear, or sovereign, process of reading. Its narrative is written out of the global traumatic experience of the WTC attacks; it closes with a fictionalized dream-narrative of a series of bombings in Paris. And just as *The Leto Bundle* and *The Translation Zone* open in a very specific liminal zone and swiftly shift to another embattled, international, sovereign domain, so too does *Murder in Byzantium*. Where for *The Translation Zone* this was New York City after the WTC attacks (with a subsequent shift to Istanbul in 1933). *The Leto Bundle* opens in airport at Shiloh (a city in this novel), shifting then to the state museum at Albion (the mythic Capital of the novel)—a movement too from identity to cultural translation and encounter. *Murder in Byzantium* opens (in its preface) at a liminal-space extraordinaire: on a coastline, at a lighthouse, on the outskirts of Santa Varvara—Kristeva's fictional megalopolis—and shifts, with the main body of the novel, to Paris where a journalist is about to be sent to report across the globe in Santa Varvara, eventually making an affective journey to Byzantium (the medieval double to Santa Varvara's contemporary city-state), Along with this, the novel opens with the challenge which makes Santa Varvara immediately the ultimate, mythic, city-state "and so good luck if you are able to identify the particular Santa Varvara that I am speaking about right now!".[36]

All three texts speak out of the human condition globally, contemporarily, mythically. All three stage many different versions of encounters across borders, and in these encounters demonstrate the way in which language fails to translate across borders, how the checkpoint is marked, ultimately, by fragility and aporia—form is never a solid totality. In writing, this fragility of speech at the translation zone is explored in counterpoint to the monolithic, singular, identity requirements and allegiances of the sovereign state.[37] The ancient associations of present violence are at their most visible, Denise Riley reminds us, when language, politics, and questions of identity and belonging intersect.[38] Is it telling that in these three texts these

[36] Julia Kristeva, *Murder In Byzantium*, 1.

[37] See Kristeva, *Interviews*, 203: "the human condition, insofar as it involves the use of speech, is very fragile [. . .] writing explores that fragility". In a lecture at the British Academy in 2010, Kristeva updates this vision of the kaleidoscopic, transnational self as "simultaneously itself and infinitely open to otherness: *ego affectus est*" ("Is there such a thing as European Culture?", British Academy, London. (24 May 2010), n.p.).

[38] See Denise Riley, *Impersonal Passion: Language as Affect* (Durham NC: Duke UP, 2005), "The impact of violence in the present may indeed revive far older associations in its target" (11).

intersections are often marked not by voice but by silence? That these moments of silence, or spacing, are then countered with a voice, or form, or genre different to that which has preceded the silence? These embattled operations of multiplicity and translation are not only radical in the sense that they mark an uprooting and reconfiguration of the relationship between subject and sovereign when face-to-face encounter occurs in a violent zone of translation, but also inasmuch as these myths and political realities are mirrored in the very manner our own neuroplasticity operates: Catherine Malabou writes that our central nervous system (CNS) negotiates its ever-shifting perceptual boundaries through "the constitution and effacement of forms"[39]; recent studies in neuroscience, too, show us that conflict adaptation (the ability to change concepts at will, to synthesize in ambiguity "warring" information/perceptions) is not solely subject to the sovereign control of consciousness; that the execution of complex behaviour does not have to be a product of a reduction of the irrelevant or the unconscious.[40] Conscious, unconscious, mythic, literary, political... as Emily Apter writes in one of her 20 theses on translation: "the translation zone is a war zone".[41] All in all, it proves the simultaneous need for and impossibility of translation, also mobilizing, through the operations of metaphor, the profoundly affective dimension of the translating, border-crossing genre-bending act—the constant and necessary disruption of sovereignty as *translatio imperii.*

3: The Monsters of the Crossroads

What, then, takes place at these crossroads, in these zones of translation where it is not only language that is under trial? How do structures of sovereignty work when even the city-state is figured as peripheral? When it is not only citizenship/identity but also the mythic, the neurological, and language/silence that is mobilized, active, and questioned in these self-reconstructing and affective encounters? Emily Apter demonstrates that the zone of maximal translation is at any checkpoint where sovereign legitimacy

[39] Catherine Malabou, *What Should We Do with Our Brain?* trans. Sebastian Rand (New York: Fordham UP, 2008), 77.

[40] See in particular Kobe Desender and Eva Van den Bussche, "Is Consciousness Necessary for Conflict Adaptation? A State of the Art", in *Frontiers in Human Neuroscience* 6 (2012), 3.1–13.

[41] Emily Apter, *The Translation Zone: A New Comparative Literature* (Princeton: Princeton UP, 2006): xi.

(geopolitical or artistic, or both) is put to the test.[42] Dawid Kołoszyc notes that there are many points in the work of Julia Kristeva where she declares herself a "monster of the crossroads"[43] (Kristeva here echoes at once Kafka and Greek myth); transnationally, transgenerically, translinguistically the crossroads encounter is enacted in Kristeva's work. Warner, too, reflecting literary and geopolitical histories at her work, is interested in zones "between East and West" of mythic and contemporary cultural "cross-fertilization [...] which have been deemed irrational or unenlightened", in whose stories we "[encounter] much that is revealing about ourselves", stories which also illuminate "the current state of conflict and flux, [of] domestic tensions, foreign wars, and also possibilities for change".[44] In the light of this, it is to the Near East again and to the figures of the Sphinx and Oedipus—that ancient encounter of un-Kinged King and Monster at a crossroads outside of a city-state—that we now turn for a model. Let us begin again with a, or many, myth(s) which, like those of the *chora*, deal with questions of being, of language, of the polis, and of the space of mistranslation...

There are many versions of Oedipus's encounter with the Sphinx. The tale has multiple topographies, multiple beginnings, multiple endings. Topographies that are made further complex by the shifting borders of the Near East: antiquity's zones of encounter now multiplied and also erased by today's events. Not to mention the many variations of the encounter itself told across time, and, indeed, even the variations of physical description and of naming in terms of the subjects involved: there is more than one version of the Sphinx[45,46]; there is more than one version of Oedipus (*τυραννος*? *Rex*? *King*? *Roi*? *Re*? *Alcade*? Sophocles? Ovid? Dryden? Voltaire? Freud? Pasolini? García Márquez? You decide...). In

[42] Emily Apter, "Translation at the Checkpoint", *Journal of Postcolonial Writing* 50.1 (2014), 56.

[43] Dawid Kołoszyc, "The Monstrous Crossroads of Kristeva's Textual Practice", *Studies in the Literary Imagination* 47.1 (2014), 1.

[44] Warner, *Stranger Magic*, 26, 25, 26.

[45] As early as *Cratylus*, the fragile changeability and violent mistranslation of the Sphinx's textual and sonorous identity is acknowledged and used as an example of the danger of combining sovereign textual power and what Harold Bloom would call poetic misprision. In conversation with Hermogenes, Sophocles complains: "...the Sphinx, for instance, is called Sphinx, instead of phix, and there are many other examples". Plato, *Cratylus*, trans. Harold North Fowler (Loeb 167), 107.

[46] Willis Goth Regier's *Book of the Sphinx* (Nebraska: U Nebraska P, 2004) catalogues versions and versionings of this profoundly liminal, violent, enigmatic, "nimble symbol" (xviii).

Sophocles's tale of Oedipus's fated accounting, the riddle of the Sphinx is presumed so well known it is only alluded to; conversation between Oedipus and Creon about the Sphinx revolve around the role of intellectual illumination and self-definition which occurs in the moment of encounter with the "riddling song".[47] Nothing in this encounter, it seems, is stable, even sovereign power. Everything in this encounter, it seems, is born from and leads to monstrosity and violence—at its simplest, the encounter implicates both the many versions of the tragic redefinition of Oedipus *and* the death or mythic dissolution of this particular Sphinx.

Versions of this myth, whatever they do not share, do possess a similarity in terms of the geometry of the crossroads—the space of encounter—itself. That it, in fact, is not a crossroads at all but a point of encounter between *three* roads. That our emplacement in this encounter is at the city limits of Thebes. As we know, the *chora* is not only a spacing and immanence of production, but it is also what is *outside of* the *polis*, outside of sovereign control. And the encounter between the Sphinx and Oedipus, tellingly, takes place on the road from Corinth *before the city limits* of Thebes. Oedipus, king dispossessed of the kingdom of his birth, then the kingdom of his upbringing, returning unknowingly to the former city-state, undergoes this sovereign test, setting a mythic, aporetic, fluid, model for many border zone encounters to come. At this point, regardless of where he has been or where he is going, in the moment of this encounter Oedipus has entered the Sphinx's sovereign domain. The riddle, or "riddling song", itself is as obscure and multiple as Oedipus's answer is singular (note how Oedipus's answer is man *anthropos* rather than man gender). The Sphinx represents non-anthropic being, untranslatable speech, and mythic time[48]; Oedipus takes on the sovereign role of anthropocentric man.

Sphinx reigns amidst rubble, riddles, dead bodies, orientation—nowhere; everywhere in language in space and in time. The riddle and its

[47] Sophocles, *Oedipus Tyrannus*, trans. Hugh Lloyd-Jones (Loeb 20), 339. Tellingly, where Creon situates the centre of power with the Sphinx and speaks of how the Sphinx's song "forced us to let go what was obscure and attend to what lay before our feet", Oedipus misunderstands, replying how, as sovereign, he "shall begin again and light up obscurity" (339), or, does Oedipus here cast himself in the Sphinx's role?

[48] The conversation between Euripides and Dionysus in Aristophanes's (2002) *Frogs* makes the foreignness (strange music? barbaric language? hybrid being?) that surrounds the Sphinx, the case of its non-translatability and its obscure origins in mythic time, abundantly clear—see Loeb 180, 200–201.

answer is the ultimate moment where the translation zone is configured as radical violence. It is an inscrutable encounter. The riddle posed by the absolute other reflects in itself and its answer the process/progress/position of the self, and in this exchange the inevitable rupture of all state sovereignty (that of the Sphinx, that of Oedipus) is implied. Oedipus, sovereign extraordinaire, replies not for himself, but takes on the voice of *all man*: the role of the border police. In the face of his monolithic reply (*anthropos*, which may as well translate to a state of national belonging) the Sphinx cannot but throw herself to her death—not only her being, but her place of being, is dissolved, becomes foreign: within the anthropocene as established in a single word by Oedipus, the hybrid Sphinx must redefine herself and/or cease to exist. The Sphinx, lest we forget, is also the mythic monument at Giza which in itself is *orientated*,[49] and whose oriental otherness ensures Sphinx reflects that of many other mythic shes, and "dies repeatedly [...] watches empires fall".[50]

Over and again we find examples of this pattern of border zone encounter and dissolution in Apter, Kristeva, and Warner. We have seen how it occurs on a formal, generic, level; it is this macrocosmic level which supports the microcosmic narratives of encounter and rupture and change, and even the manners in which the texts shift between different forms of expression, different (real and imagined) topographies. On this narrative level, the naming-function in the novels is significant. A name—a word—an identity—refuses translation and exerts its sovereign power to damn anything outside of itself. In this zone of maximal translation, in the service of definition of anything outside of the progress of the *translatio imperii*, the naming-function becomes a describing function: deixis disappears and language takes its place in the manner of an adjective, or epithet. The subject becomes foreign to itself even in language, is estranged from its own being in terms of place, time, and multiplicity in an eternal feedback loop of foreignness.[51]

[49] Regier writes at the crossroads of Egyptian and Greek myth how the Egyptian sphinx represents also Horemakhet—the orient—"Sun on the Horizon" (*Book of the Sphinx*, 3), and also notes how sphinxes permeate Levantine cultures (note here how the naming reflects itself, as *levantine* etymologically also implicates a rising of the sun from the east), their influential origin myths including Christianity.

[50] Regier, *Book of the Sphinx*, 5.

[51] See Anne Carson on the adjective/*epithethon*, where adjective "is in itself and adjective meaning 'placed on top', 'imported', 'foreign'". *The Autobiography of Red* (London: Cape, 1998), 4.

Kristeva writes her variation of the Y-junction of Oedipus's encounter as an X, or crux (in a medieval sense as cross, mark (indication and deletion), centrepoint, and riddle). Her crossroads thus admits further possibilities of movement towards and away from the city-state; or, even, genomically, poetically, in adding a leg, or foot, this encounter becomes feminine—the traveller is no longer possessed of an oedipal limpness, rather, of physical, rhythmic excess! *Murder in Byzantium*'s "metaphysical" detective plot and "historical" quest narrative[52] hinges on these points of convergence. Sebastian Chrest-Jones, university professor-murderer-obsessive, journeys towards a real and imagined Byzantium by way of affective identification (a transhistorical love affair!) with Anna Comnena and an etymological search for his own origins via his own crux: the centrepoint of his name. *Chrest* leads us at once towards the history of the crusades in the Near East, as it underwent a series of metonymic shifts to become a nominative marker of crusader ancestry, and to the present of writing of the novel—the etymology of naming is shared with the novelist herself *Krist*eva. Genetically, too, there are links: Sebastian is figured as the dark double of another Chrest in the novel—his cousin and pursuer the detective-inspector Northrop Rilsky. And, finally, these links prove violent and symbolic: the "cross" of the Chrest marking the two murderers of the novel: Sebastian and Xiao Chang. The cross marks and negates, is a point of rupture and encounter with the infinite (Xiao Chang is also styled as "the infinite") at the crossroads of languages and histories—French, Bulgarian, Ancient Greek, Latin, Chinese, and Maths collide; the symbol is at once excessive and radically empty, sign at once of patriotic zeal and murder, and of multiplicity and continuation.

In the preface to Warner's *Leto Bundle*, the custom's room at Shiloh airport sees a strange visitor: a mummy cartonnage. This is our first encounter with Leto (/Ella/Nellie/Lettice...). Tellingly, this physical object is empty but multiply resonant. The curator explains "The Leto Bundle": "we've always called her 'Helen' because of the cartonnage – the face mask – is very beautiful. We don't really know – there are other stories [...] She's just a bundle of bandages. But Greek".[53] Everything and nothing, subject of obstructed borders and violent incursion and debate, "Outis" becomes Leto's surname in the c.21st narrative of *The Leto Bundle*. Like the

[52] Kristeva, *Hatred and Forgiveness*, 275.

[53] Marina Warner, *The Leto Bundle*, 4.

chora, Barthes's neuter, and the infinite gap at Kristeva's X-roads, "Outis", although absolutely other, is also absolutely *not* "synonymous with emptiness",[54] even as the cartonnage simply contains a bundle of bandages and no body. In gesturing towards this no-body, as she travels through time and space in the novel, Warner takes a Greek word transliterated into English to form this name resonant with encounter and riddle (Odysseus's trickery of Polyphemus), with the self being translated.[55] "Outis" is marked by and in her own speech—the speech of the novel's Threnody—by gaps and mistranslations; this resonates in her names, produces in her disappearance from any singular context the title, the form, and the first and final moments of the novel—the description of the "Leto Bundle"; the "missing persons" advertisement for "Ella Outis".

Warner's Leto or Outis, and the cruxes of Kristeva's novel, are nothing, are at once infinitely present and mythic, impossible to distil into a singular identity or temporality, impossible to find anywhere but in the zone of translation through which they disappear. They, and the texts in which they exist, challenge the perceived operations, times, and spaces of sovereign statehood. Language adjectives itself: meaning is placed on top of moments of significance, the function of signification is disrupted from its basic deictic tendencies into something which dispossesses the original moment or thing of itself. Identities and questions of belonging are shifting, kaleidoscopic. The relationship between the individual, its self-expression, the substitutions of the self in the face of the operations of state sovereignty, articulation, the work of writing, its form, and the operations of genre, are placed in and revolve around the gap, show us—in trans[ ]ation—the way towards thinking across borders and identities, in women's time, the future perfect's hidden present, the chora. We bear witness to a writing of the crossroads, writing that lays bare the operations of sovereign power and calls it into question, which is profoundly abstract and personal, mythic and

[54] Emily Apter, "En-Chôra", *Grey Room* 20 (2005), 80. Here Apter is writing of the chora in the shadow of Derrida's *Chora L Works.*

[55] I refer here to Book IX of the *Odyssey*. When the drunken Polyphemus asks for the name of his interlocutor, Odysseus does not respond with his own name, rather, tricks the cyclops, by momentarily divesting himself of nominative identity and answering 'οὔτις'. This ensures that, after Odysseus blinds him, Polyphemus is only able to give a name which is not a name in his complaint; Odysseus's identity is protected. *Οὔ τις* (and the subjunctive μή τίς) is rendered in several ways in translation (variously as No-one/Noman/Nobody) and is pronounced, roughly, as Warner renders Ella/Leto's name: 'outis'.

contemporary, "oblique, cubist, plural, an intermingled intimacy at the crossroads of my encounters, the languages I speak and write, the various times inhabiting them and inhabiting me, and my irreconcilable identities".[56]

Bibliography

Apter, Emily. 2005. En-Chôra. *Grey Room* 20: 80–83.

———. 2006. *The Translation Zone: A New Comparative Literature*. Princeton: Princeton University Press.

———. 2010. 'Women's Time' in Theory. *Differences: A Journal of Feminist Cultural Studies* 21 (1): 1–18.

———. 2014. Translation at the Checkpoint. *Journal of Postcolonial Writing* 50 (1): 56–74.

Aristophanes. 2002. *Frogs*. Trans. Jeffrey Henderson. Cambridge, MA: Harvard University Press. Loeb Classical Library 180. https://doi.org/10.4159/DLCL.aristophanes-frogs.2002

Barthes, Roland, and Guy Scarpetta. 1991. Digressions. In *The Grain of the Voice: Interviews 1962–1980*. Trans. Linda Coverdale. Berkeley: University of California Press (*Promesse*, 1971/Seuil, 1981).

Carson, Anne. 2010. *Autobiography of Red: A Novel in Verse*. London: Jonathan Cape.

Derrida, Jacques, and Peter Eisenmann. 1997. *Chora L Works,* ed. Jeffrey Kupnis and Thomas Leeser. New York: The Monacelli Press.

Desender, Kobe, and Eva Van den Bussche. 2012. Is Consciousness Necessary for Conflict Adaptation? A State of the Art. *Frontiers in Human Neuroscience* 6 (3): 1–13. https://doi.org/10.3389/fnhum.2012.00003

Genette, Gérard. 1997. *Paratexts: Thresholds of Interpretation*. Trans. Jane E. Lewin. Cambridge: Cambridge University Press (Seuil, 1987).

http://www.aljazeera.com. Accessed 14 June 2016.

http://www.foreignaffairs.com. Accessed 10, 13, 15 June 2016.

http://www.janes.com. Accessed 14 June 2016.

Jardine, Alice. 1981. Introduction to Julia Kristeva's 'Women's Time'. *Signs: A Journal of Women in Culture and Society* 7 (1): 5–12.

Kołoszyc, Dawid. 2014. The Monstrous Crossroads of Kristeva's Textual Practice. *Studies in the Literary Imagination* 47 (1): 1–26.

Kristeva, Julia. 1974. *La révolution du langage poétique: l'avant garde à la fin du XIXe siècle: Lautréamont et Mallarmé.* Paris: Éditions du Seuil.

[56] Kristeva, *Hatred and Forgiveness*, 247.

———. 1981. Women's Time. Trans. Alice Jardine and Harry Blake. *Signs: A Journal of Women in Culture and Society* 7(1): 13–35 (*34/44: cahiers de recherché de sciences des texts et documents* 5, 1979).
———. 1984. *Revolution in Poetic Language*. Trans. Margaret Waller. New York: Columbia University Press.
———. 1996. *Interviews*, ed. Ross Mitchell Guberman. New York: Columbia University Press.
———. 2002. *Intimate Revolt: The Powers of Psychoanalysis 2*. Trans. Jeanine Herman. New York: Columbia University Press (Fayard, 1996/1997).
———. 2006. *Murder in Byzantium: A Novel*. Trans. C. Jon Delogu. New York: Columbia University Press (Fayard, 2004).
———. 2009. *This Incredible Need to Believe*. Trans. Beverly Brie Brahic. New York: Columbia University Press (Donzelli Editore, 2006).
———. 2010a. *Hatred and Forgiveness*. Trans. Jeanine Herman. New York: Columbia University Press, (Fayard, 2005).
———. 2010b. *Is There Such a Thing as European Culture?* British Academy, London. Lecture, May 24.
Kristeva, Julia, and Catherine Clément. 2001. *The Feminine and the Sacred*. Trans. Jane Marie Todd. New York: Columbia University Press (Éditions Stock, 1999).
Latour, Bruno. 2005. *Reassembling the Social: An Introduction to Actor-Network-Theory*. Oxford: Oxford University Press.
———. 2009. *Politics of Nature: How to Bring the Sciences into Democracy*. Trans. Catherine Porter. Harvard: Harvard University Press (Éd. La Découverte, 1999).
Malabou, Catherine. 2008. *What Should We Do with Our Brain?* Trans. Sebastian Rand. New York: Fordham University Press (Bayard, 2004).
Morton, Timothy. 2009. *Ecology Without Nature: Rethinking Environmental Aesthetics*. Harvard: Harvard University Press.
Plato. 1926. *Cratylus*. Trans. Harold North Fowler. Cambridge, MA: Harvard University Press. Loeb Classical Library 167. https://doi.org/10.4159/DLCL.plato_philosopher-cratylus.1926
———. 1929. *Timaeus*. Trans. R.G. Bury. Cambridge, MA: Harvard University Press. Loeb Classical Library 234. https://doi.org/10.4159/DLCL.plato-philosopher_timaeus.1929
Regier, Willis Goth. 2004. *Book of the Sphinx*. Nebraska: University of Nebraska Press.
Riley, Denise. 2005. *Impersonal Passion: Language as Affect*. Durham: Duke University Press.
Sophocles. 1994. *Oedipus Tyrannus*. Trans. Hugh Lloyd-Jones. Cambridge, MA: Harvard University Press. Loeb Classical Library 20. https://doi.org/10.4159/DLCL.sophocles-oedipus_tyrannus.1994
Warner, Marina. 2002. *The Leto Bundle*. London: Vintage.

———. 2011. *Stranger Magic: Charmed States and the Arabian Nights*. London: Vintage.

———. 2016. In the Time of Not Yet: On the Imaginary of Edward Said. In *Conflicting Humanities*, ed. Rosi Braidotti and Paul Gilroy, 267–276. London: Bloomsbury.

Yeung, Heather H. 2014. Reading Kristeva with Kristeva. *Studies in the Literary Imagination* 47 (1): 111–127.

———. 2015. Against Spectacle: International Terror and the Crisis of the Feminine Subject. In *Women's Fiction and Post-9/11 Contexts*, ed. Peter Childs, Sebastian Groes, and Claire Colebrook, 51–64. New York: Lexington.

PART II

Racial and Ethnic Borderlands

A Search for Colonial Histories: The Conquest by Yxta Maya Murray

Salvador C. Fernández

The arrival of the Spaniards to the Americas produces marvelous narratives that document the lives, histories, and travelling experiences of natives and foreigners, constructing literary tropes of departures, journeys, and arrivals.[1] Such tropes are used to develop stories that describe fantastic literary characters that become desirable subjects and objects to possess. For example, Fray Bernardino de Sahagún's *Historia general de las cosas de la Nueva España* not only constructs a taxonomy of *nigrománticos* (necromantic), *hechiceros* (enchanter), and *trampistas* (impostor) but also provides a description of *magos* (magicians) and *saltimbanquis* (mountebanks). The presence of nigrománticos, hechiceros, trampistas, magos, and saltimbanquis provides a supernatural texture to the narratives of the encounter between the Europeans and indigenous communities as these magical figures acquire polyphonic meanings that oscillate from an affirmation of pre-Hispanic mythology (e.g. the return of Quetzalcoatl) to a nonviolent attempt to deter the journeys of the conquistadores. Consequently, the colonial narratives depicting the encounter between the Americas and Europe produce a historical archive that Chican@ and Latin@ writers explore to construct fictional and fantastical stories that

[1] I would like to thank Anna Palmer, Lilianna Henkel, and Aracely Ruvalcaba for their superb editing and critical input in this chapter.

S.C. Fernández (✉)
Department of Spanish, Occidental College, Los Angeles, CA, USA

J. Elbert Decker, D. Winchock (eds.), *Borderlands and Liminal Subjects*, https://doi.org/10.1007/978-3-319-67813-9_5

examine the colonial and postcolonial socio-cultural subjectivities.[2] In fact, in her historical novel *The Conquest* (2002), Yxta Maya Murray narrates the personal and social story of Sara Rosario González, a Chicana scholar who restores manuscripts at the Getty Museum in Los Angeles, California.[3] Sara, who comes from a working-class family and lives in South Pasadena, restores a sixteenth-century manuscript titled *The Conquest.* In the novel scholars attributed the text to Padre Miguel Santiago de Pasamonte, an apocryphal, gifted pre-Cervantes writer who allegedly penned three erotic novels entitled *Las tres furias*, *La noche triste*, and *El santo de España* between 1560 and 1568. In *The Conquest*, De Pasamonte recounts the story of Helen, a female Aztec juggler who Hernán Cortés brings to Europe dressed as a man. While living a forced exiled life in Europe Helen plans to assassinate Charles V and the Pope as vengeance for the killing of her family and community as a result of the Conquest of New Spain. The historical disjuncture and the central stories that Yxta Maya Murray highlight in the novel symbolically represent the border expressions that identify social and cultural issues of deterritorialized and displaced communities.

Structurally, Murray's novel, *The Conquest*, alternates between narrating a historical story associated with Helen's personal experiences and telling a contemporary tale linked to Sara as a Chicana who struggles to balance her professional, social, and personal life, illustrated by her troubled relationship with Karl and the loss of her mother. Murray juxtaposes a contemporary and a historical story to examine the concept of historical hegemony in order to question the narrative concepts of authorship, authenticity, and authoritative voice. Additionally, she highlights a personal and collective historical consciousness associated with the construction of colonial and decolonial histories that form border cultures like the Chicana/o community. Thus, Murray's novel, *The Conquest,* exemplifies the importance of using textual

[2] I am using the term "archive" in reference to Michel Foucault's use in his text *The Archeology of Knowledge and the Discourse of Language*, (New York: Vintage Books, 2010). For a study of this concept, see Gilles Deleuze, *Foucault*, (Minneapolis: University of Minnesota Press, 1986), 1–22.

[3] Yxta Maya Murray's novel was well received by the national press. For example, see Salvador Carrasco's review "The Mestiza Scheherazade," *Los Angeles Times Book Review*, October 27, 2002. Salvador Carrasco is director and writer of the film *La otra conquista*.

affinities to establish a correlation between historical narratives and contemporary socio-cultural explorations in a literary work.[4]

As a result of the juxtaposition between a historical and a contemporary story in the novel, the reader notices that Murray constructs a work that emphasizes narrative and thematic ambiguities, especially as the story explores the genesis of the historical text *The Conquest*. Indeed, as Sara restores de Pasamonte's manuscript, she informs the reader that because de Pasamonte's text seemingly lacks any record of origin, literary historians face difficulty tracking its publication, readership, and critical reception. In the search for its origin, she finds that it is not until 1813, during the Peninsular War, that the text emerges in Madrid. This uncertain origin of the text allows the protagonist to speculate about its authorship. Specifically, Sara informs the reader that most of the scholars familiar with *The Conquest* attribute the manuscript to Miguel Santiago de Pasamonte, but she and her supervisor at the Getty Museum, Teresa Shaugnnessey, suppose that an Aztec woman penned the work. Sara expresses the text's authorial ambiguities in the following way: "We believe it was composed in Cáceres, Spain, circa 1570, and because of the stylographics similarities to the other text most scholars agree that it was authored by one Padre Miguel Santiago de Pasamonte"[5]; however, Teresa declares, "a woman wrote this folio, and an Aztec woman at that."[6] The question of authorship, publication, and distribution of de Pasamonte's text become a critical narrative strategy that Yxta Maya Murray uses not only to emplot the story of her novel, but also to question the construction and hegemony of gender, racial, and ideological representations of a colonial history. In this case, Murray not only alters the authorship of text from a male to a female author, but also displaces the nationality of the author from Spanish to Aztec. Indeed, it is a twofold socio-literary transgression that displaces the traditional Spanish colonial empire's cultural and political relations. In this context, the novelist transforms the importance of the origins of a historical text into a narrative device to critique a literary discourse that produces a prescribed historical

[4] In reference to Tony Morrison's *Beloved*, in an interview entitled "On the Borderlands of U.S. Empire: The Limitations of Geography, Ideology, and Disciplinarity" done by Mónica González García, José David Saldívar speaks of the importance of this type of writings as examples of a language and a discourse that is "uniquely figural expression that would explain its ineffable subaltern mysteries" (195).

[5] Yxta Maya Murray, *The Conquest* (New York: Rayo, 2002), 5.

[6] Ibid.

hegemony used to represent exotic or magical colonial and neo-colonial subjects as represented by Helen, Aztec juggler, and Sara, manuscript curator at the Getty. Helen and Sara in this context demonstrate the deterritorialized subject that metaphorically occupies "a vague and undetermined place created by the emotional residue of an unnatural boundary" as Gloria Anzaldúa shows in *Borderlands/La frontera: The New Mestiza.*[7]

The critique of a colonial hegemony associated with the Spanish Empire in the Americas also provides a historical subtext to contextualize cultural inquiries dealing with the representation of artistic artifacts and the establishment of a contemporary cultural heritage of the Chicano/a community in Los Angeles.[8] When the protagonist's mother, Beatrice, takes Sara to see a Pre-Hispanic art exhibit at a local museum, she views the displayed artifacts as stolen autochthonous products that should be returned to what is now Mexico. Such is her conviction that Beatrice steals an *amoxtli*, a sixteenth-century Mesoamerican book which was part of the display. As a result of the removal of the *amoxtli,* the authorities charge Beatrice with grand theft, a criminal act that the novelist uses to establish a contrast between a colonial and postcolonial collective and personal symbolic act of resistance.[9] Moreover, Beatrice's act serves to highlight a form of cultural colonialism and establishes an ironic parallelism in the narrative between the stealing of the *amoxtli*, a symbolic action representing the liberation of colonial possessions and the museum's acquisition of such artifacts.[10] This narrative's emphasis echoes with Gloria Anzaldúa's reference to emotional residual of a natural boundary. In addition, when Beatrice steals the *amoxtli,* she symbolically recaptures and reappropriates a conquered object.

[7] Gloria Anzaldúa, *Borderlands/La frontera* (Spinsters/Aunt Lute Books, San Francisco, 1987), 3.

[8] The symbolic actions by the narrator's mother exemplify the studies by James Clifford in *The Predicament of Culture: Twentieth-Century Ethnography, Literature, and Art* (Cambridge: Harvard University Press, 1988) where he analyzes the history and exotic values that Western modern art institutions contract with tribal cultural signifiers.

[9] I must note that the reappropriation of the *amoxtli* takes place by a Mexican woman in a territory that was once part of Mexico.

[10] For a study on the role that *amoxtli* play in the formation of a cultural literacy in the Americas, see Walter D. Mignolo, "Signs and Their Transmission: The Question of the Book in the New World," in *A Book of the Book: Some Works and Projections about the Book and Writing*, Edited by Jerome Rothenberg and Steven Clay (New York City: Granary Book, 2000), 351–371.

This resonates with the performative text titled *Codex Espangliensis: from Columbus to the Border Patrol* by Guillermo Gómez Peña, Enrique Chagoya, and Felicia Rice.[11] Both cases manifest the importance of counter narratives and actions that defy the notions of cultural and historical authorities that misplace and de-figure autochthonous cultural representations in the process of colonization.

In addition, Sara's mother, Beatrice, utilizes the exhibit of pre-Hispanic artifacts as a teaching device to instruct her daughter on an alternative reading of the conquest of the Americas. This narrative episode questions critical cultural representational practices that Karen Mary Dávalos studies in her work *Exhibiting Mestizaje: Mexican (American) Museums in the Diaspora* wherein she delineates how museums de-contextualize colonial artifacts to establish a narrative that identifies who creates and contributes national capital. To establish a comparison with the exhibit of the *amoxtli* and the museum's curatorial practices, Murray refers to canonical Spanish American crónicas, such as *Historia verdadera de la conquista de la Nueva España* by Bernal Díaz del Castillo and *Cartas de relación* by Hernán Cortés. In doing so, she presents documentation of the violence associated with the colonization of New Spain. In this context, Beatrice views the art exhibit as a cultural act that demonstrates five hundred years of stealing art, constructing colonial histories, reconstructing memories, and dominating Mesoamerican cultures. Beatrice's interpretation of the colonial art exhibit deconstructs the traditional cultural values associated with colonial art as it appears in a museum. Moreover, Beatrice's act of forcefully repossessing an *amoxtli* from the museum liberates this artifact as a colonial possession and restores the noble and majestic values that the *amoxtli* represents for the protagonist's mother. From Beatrice's point of view, the *amoxtli* at the museum artificially presents an idealization of the pre-Hispanic period and the museum's curatorial practices erase the history of violence, performed by the Spanish Empire's violent acts and histories that, ironically, the *amoxtli* itself narrates in its pictorial representations. These actions that Beatrice performs symbolically and historically represent the effects of deterritorialized border subjectivities.

[11] Guillermo Gómez Peña, Enrique Chagoya, and Felicia Rice, *Codex Espangliensis: from Columbus to the Border Patrol* (Santa Cruz, Calif.: Moving Parts Press, 1998); Please see the study by Damián Baca, "The Chicano Codex: Writing against Historical and Pedagogical Colonization," *College English* 71.6 (2009), 564–583.

To document Beatrice's exaltation of the *amoxtli*, Murray alludes to Spanish American cronistas who narrate the Conquest of New Spain, such as Bernal Díaz del Castillo. Murray's use of the cronistas documents the cultural literary heritage of the pre-Hispanic indigenous communities and functions as a cultural sign that constructs a Chicano/a literary heritage. In this case, Murray appropriates the cronistas' colonial discourse to recount vivid descriptions of Aztec locations that provide literary value. More specifically, replicating the language that Bernal Díaz del Castillo employs in his *Historia verdadera de la conquista de la Nueva España*, Murray establishes the exaltation of an Aztec library that the indigenous empire built prior to the arrival of the Spaniards. Bernal Díaz de Castillo describes in his crónica the cultural legacy that the conquistadores found in Tenochtitlán. He recounts how in the Universal College the Aztecs study grammar, theology, logic, philosophy, and other arts; he also saw how they printed books.[12] It is not surprising that Bernal Díaz del Castillo highlights the classical cultural development of the American communities. According to Tzvetan Todorov in his seminal study of colonial discourse, *The Conquest of America* (1984), the Aztecs possessed a long educational tradition of mastering the study of language, rhetoric, and philosophy at schools named *calmecac*. Todorov states, "The *calmecac* is in fact a school of interpretation, and speech, of rhetoric and hermeneutics."[13] In this context, Beatrice's repossession of an *amoxtli* from the museum acquires a new meaning. Her act also represents the recovery of a valuable literary history and knowledge that becomes integral for the cultural formation and the personal identity of her transnational culture as a Mexican and Chicana. Her repossession of the artifact illustrates the reconstruction of history and the cultural capital that deterritorialized and border cultures possess.

Furthermore, Murray underscores the significance of the *amoxtli* and its artistic role in the formation of Aztec culture as she compares this pictorial text to the great Florileguim of Alexandria. The comparison between an *amoxtli* and the great Florilegium of Alexandria establishes a corresponding cultural and capital value between a work critical for a non-Western literary formation and a book, with a classical status, associated with the formation

[12] Bernal Díaz del Castillo, *Historia verdadera de la conquista de la Nueva España*. (México, Editorial Porrúa, 1986), 583.

[13] Tzvetan Todorov, *The Conquest of America*. Translated by Richard Howard (New York, Harper Torchbooks, 1984), 78.

of a cultural paradigm in Western civilization. Murray appropriates Bernal Díaz del Castillo's crónica, *Historia verdadera de la conquista de La Nueva España*, to displace the hegemonic historical and literary value that colonial crónicas acquired after the Conquest. The narration of epic stories, as exemplified by Díaz del Castillo's crónica, functioned as an economic request from their authors to Spanish Royal Court, so that they could obtain financial remuneration for the material wealth that these cronistas found for and brought to Spain. In contrast with the original intentions of some of these written histories, Murray not only recreates but also recuperates a literary cultural sign and a symbolic space that challenge the dominant colonial discourse. Consequently, the importance given to the crónicas because of their focus on the Aztec literary and educational traditions represents another questioning of historical hegemony. It also functions as a critique of authoritative discourses that acquire both individual and collective values to continue the inquiries and exploration of the relationship between colonial and postcolonial cultural domains.

The protagonist's mother, Beatrice, embodies a Chicana/o historical consciousness, which underlines the important correlation between indigenous historical representations and the contemporary social reality of her daughter, Sara. Moreover, through the character of Beatrice, the novelist establishes a historical analogy between Helen, a resistant pre-Hispanic character in de Pasamonte's manuscript, and Sara Rosario González, as a contemporary Chicana intellectual who challenges the authority of authorship in de Pasamonte's work, *The Conquest.* Indeed, the historical and literary relationship that the novelist forms between Sara and Helen constructs a narrative structure pivotal for the characterization of Sara and Helen. For example, the latter character, an Aztec rebel, sees herself as a social transgressor and as an individual who explores cultural and ideological practices to recover and restore personal and symbolic stories that accentuate community values for colonized subjects.

In a similar way, as Sara restores de Pasamonte's manuscript, *The Conquest*, she recuperates the lost history of the text, creates a historical genealogy for the protagonists and the authors, and details how the fall of the Aztec Empire affects Helen's life. Both female figures exemplify displaced characters whose tasks search for the reconstruction of a lost social center and community. Moreover, the novelist's conceptual play with the notions of restoring and recovering become applicable to the importance of orality and its cultural ramifications for the formation of transnational literary histories linked to postcolonial subjectivities, such as Chicano/a cultures.

Specifically, Sara's mother possesses unique oral skills that prove her to be a gifted storyteller. Thus, Beatrice transforms herself into a literary figure, who recreates and retells historical fables that bring back memories that the distance of time and space has displaced in favor of other hegemonic narratives. I interpret the artistic talent and her orality in the context of Gloria Anzaldúa's notion of a border woman who possesses the facultad (the gift or talent); as "the capacity to see in surface phenomena the meaning of deeper realities, to see the deep structure below the surface."[14]

As a storyteller, Beatrice not only recovers and recounts historical fables, but her act of speaking also reenacts cultural performances that recall historical parallels, where autochthonous fables and stories acquire the function of didactic narratives to exemplify the problematic relationship between the colonized and the colonizer.[15] For example, one time Beatrice tells Sara the story of Tzotzil, a lonely and hopeless Aztec alchemist who anticipates the dark and apocalyptic future of the Aztec Empire, indicating the destruction of the empire with the arrival of the Europeans. As recounted by Beatrice, in this fable Tzotzil visits a fortune-teller, who informs him that his love, Anactorra, will be born five thousand years later. Anactorra, a cantankerous woman known for her culinary skills, dies as an old woman in love with Tzotzil. The symbolic relationship between Tzotzil and Anactorra produces a tragic-comic historical vision that I read as a cultural paradigm often associated with the conquest of the Americas. This tragic and common vision of a cultural paradigm I often associate with the ambiguity of deterritorialized and border cultures. Murray reworks this tragic-comic vision to characterize her Chicana protagonist Sara, who sees herself as both Tzotzil and Anactorra because the protagonist in Murray's novel experiences a form of psychological trauma in which she fuses real and imaginary acts. In Homi K. Bhabha's terms, Beatrice's story in a certain way demonstrates "a split in the discursive ambivalence that emerges in the

[14] Anzaldúa, *Borderlands*, 38.

[15] The characterization of Beatrice in certain terms illustrates Gayatri Chakravorty Spivak's term of the "effects of the real," that she postulates in her work *In Other Worlds: Essays in the Cultural Politics* (New York; Routledge, 1988), where there is a play "between fact (historical event) and fiction (literary event)," 243–244.

contestation of narrative authority between the pedagogical and the performative."[16]

In *The Conquest* the typification of storytellers, as represented by Beatrice and her daughter, illustrates the discursive ambivalence that Homi K. Bhabha identifies to challenge the colonial narrative authority. For example, Sara casts a spell on her lover Karl in order to steal him from an Anglo-American woman, Claire O'Connell. To accomplish her desires Sara recounts to Karl Sullivan the story of Helen, an Aztec performer taken by Hernán Cortés to Europe. Sara, who inherits her mother's capacity as a storyteller, romances Karl with Aztec historical fables which acquire magical powers.[17] The cultural reproduction of Sara as storyteller follows a very conventional narrative device to trace alternative modes of cultural representations that often typify postcolonial artifacts. However, Sara's use of orality serves as a pivotal discursive mode to challenge the traditional parameters of writing colonial histories. Using orality as a discursive method, Sara transforms personal and communal fables and stories into forms of historical and literary narration as she textualizes the life of Helen.[18] For these two Chicana characters, Sara and Beatrice, as representations of postcolonial artifacts, this conventional rhetorical tool becomes a literary innovation to recuperate and recreate both historical and literary figures, and they use it to open up new subjectivities to ground and expand the construction of Chicana/o literary culture. As Gloria Anzaldúa states, the borderwoman is in a constant state of "mental nepantilism. . .a product of the transfer of the cultural and spiritual values of one group to another."[19]

The relationship between Sara and Karl resembles Malintzin and Cortés, whose personal encounter serves as a catalyst to establish the traumatic formation of a new nation, Mexico. In a similar way, the romantic struggles between Sara and Karl illustrate how historical romances function as cultural

[16] Homi K. Bhabha, "DissemiNation: Time, Narrative, and the Margins of the Modern Nation." *Nation and Narration*, Edited by Homi K. Bhabha, (New York: Routledge, 1990), 299.

[17] The use of indigenous subjects to create postcolonial subjects as political allegories also appears in Chicano poetry, such as Juan Felipe Herrera's text *Mayan Drifter: Chicano Poet in the Lowlands of America* (Philadelphia: Temple University Press, 1997).

[18] Laura Esquivel's novel *Malinche* (New York: Atria Books, 2006) also exemplifies the importance of orality to contextualize female historical figures.

[19] Anzaldúa, *Borderlands*, 78.

and political allegories to represent the political relationship between the colonized and the colonizer.[20] Moreover, with the incorporation of these trans-generational traditional fables, stories, and the intertextual references to Chicana/o texts Murray dramatizes the personal and collective traumas of colonialized subjects. More importantly, the novelist problematizes Chicana cultural transactions that Gloria Anzaldúa foregrounds in her canonical work *Borderlands/La frontera: The New Mestiza.*[21]

In addition, the narration of these fables and stories accentuates a prominent colonial narrative trope, textual hybridity, used to emplot histories of the conquest of America, as best exemplified by the Miguel León Portilla's classical collection of narratives, *Visión de los vencidos* (*Broken Spears*). In this case, León Portilla's work reconstructs the Conquest of New Spain using oral, pictorial, and written texts from Spanish, Mestizo, and Native cultures to show the textual diversity and narrative complexity of constructing well-known historical events. However, in the reconstruction of this known history, León Portilla also problematizes the structural, linguistic, and semantic manner of representing histories of colonized subjects. Moreover, some contemporary Mexican novelists, such as Ignacio Solares in *Nen, la inútil*, Carmen Boullosa in *Duerme*, and Laura Esquivel in *Malinche*, have also appropriated this narrative device to interpret historical traumas that demonstrate the colonial cultural heritage in the Americas. Thus, contemporary Mexican and Chicano/a novelists and historians continue to struggle with the colonial historical heritage that marks national and transnational, as well as personal and collective traumas in both sides of the US–Mexican border.

From another point of view, the emphasis that Murray puts on the trans-generational cultural function of orality to typify Sara's personal and symbolic psychological trauma parallels Arjun Appadurai's analysis of diasporic communities that he studies in his work "Disjuncture and Difference in the

[20] For studies on this colonial relationship see Jean Wyatt, "On Not Being La Malinche: Border Negotiations of Gender in Sandra Cisneros's 'Never Marry A Mexican' and 'Woman Hollering Creek,'" *Tulsa Studies in Women's Literature* 14 (1995): 243–71; and Martha J. Cutter, "Malinche's Legacy: Translation, Betrayal, and Interlingualism in Chicano/a Literature," *The Arizona Quarterly* 66 (2010): 1–33.

[21] More recently, the use of intergenerational stories and fables has been read as examples of the contested spaces between the United States and the Americas, as examined by José David Saldívar in *Trans-Americanity: Subaltern Modernities, Global Coloniality, and the Cultures of Greater Mexico* (Durham: Duke University Press, 2012).

Global Economy." Specifically, he states that "The task of cultural reproduction, even in its most intimate arenas, such as husband-wife and parent-child relations, becomes both politicized and exposed to the traumas of deterritorialization as family members pool and negotiate their mutual understanding and aspirations in sometimes fractured spatial arrangements."[22] Thus, as Sara tells her lover, Karl, Helen's tale, she not only puts a spell on him, but also performs traditional cultural acts that stress the personal and collective characterization of a Chicana protagonist. The novelist, in recounting Helen's story and casting the spell on Karl, employs heterogeneous textual references to critique the cultural politics and hegemonic representation of the relationship between the colonized and the colonizer in a way that reminds the reader of Miguel León Portilla's critique of hegemonic histories dealing with the Conquest of New Spain.

Moreover, Sara's recounting of Helen's life as a spell also acquires political symbolism because her story demonstrates the personal and collective traumas of deterritorialization and border cultures.[23] In the novel, after the Conquest of New Spain, Hernán Cortés takes a troupe of Aztec performers (including a young woman dressed as a man, Helen) to Europe as presents for the Pope and the King of Spain. From a literary point of view, the forced exile of Helen and the Aztec troupers not only critiques the concept of marvelous positions, associated with the colonization of the Americas, but it also deconstructs a hegemonic narrative typical of colonial subjectivities. Yxta Maya Murray plays with the literary parameters between historical accounts of the Conquest of New Spain and the literary tropes of departures, journeys, and arrivals that describe deterritorialized and fantastic literary characters. Examining colonial subjectivities, I read Helen as an exiled Aztec woman who embodies the burden of bringing to justice those who were responsible for the destruction of her family and the Aztec empire, mainly the Spanish King Charles V and Pope Clement VII.

In the recounting of Helen's life, the novelist marks and enacts personal and collective traumas of deterritorialization in specific geographical

[22] Arjun Appaduria "Disjuncture and Difference in the Global Economy," in *Theorizing Diaspora: A Reader*, 25–48. Edited by Jana Evans Braziel and Anita Mannur (Malden: Blackwell Publishing, 2003), 42.

[23] The use of the spell parallels the tradition of cultural identifiers that other Chicana/o novelists use to create autochthonous social representations. José David Saldívar in *Tans-Americanity* reads these uses of cultural identifiers as "decolonial text of métissage, a repository of memory, of colonial semiosis, and Americanity, like the Anden Inca *quipu*" (171).

locations where Helen lives. The first stage of Helen's life takes place in Tenochtitlán. In this location the novel depicts how the process of military colonization affect Helen and her family and demonstrates her cultural development as she experiences the rapid process of cultural domination and transformation as a colonized subject that becomes aware of physical and cultural deterritorialization. Indeed, the narrative in this stage emphasizes the social and personal metamorphosis of Helen's identity, from a woman who belongs to an elite Aztec family to a woman who becomes Cortés' slave. As the daughter of Tlakaelel, a pivotal leader and philosopher who played an important role in the metamorphosis of Aztec mythology, Helen is raised to be a future wife of the Aztec King Moctezuma.[24] Helen's genealogical background, linked to the historical figure of Tlakaelel, follows a Chicana/o literary tradition, where the texts affirm or critique the cultural value attributed to this important Aztec philosopher. In this case, Murray exalts his personal, cultural, and political importance when she identifies him not only as a patriotic figure, but also as a prince full of wealth and political power. Helen, as a narrator, states: "My beloved father Tlakaelel, when he lived had been a prince of a great and wealthy province, and a fierce patriot who knew the power of his ancestors."[25] Murray's exaltation of Tlakaelel differs from Gloria Anzaldúa's reading of him. Anzaldúa critiques Tlakaelel's historical importance and the role that he plays in the historiography of the Aztec empire because he transforms the Aztec philosophy and culture, displacing female deities in order to cement the construction of a militaristic state.

The cultural and philosophical metamorphosis and the displacement of female deities lead to the loss of a cultural prestige and religious significance, creating a gender social imbalance between male and female religious figures. In *Borderland/La frontera* Anzaldúa affirms, "Before the Aztecs became a militaristic, bureaucratic state male predatory warfare and conquest were based on patrilineal nobility, the principle of balanced opposition between the sexes existed."[26] Anzaldúa's and Murray's readings of Tlakaelel display the multiple historical and cultural possibilities to interpret Aztec

[24] Miguel León Portilla in his "Apéndice" to *Visión de los vencidos* credits Tlakaelel as the thinker and leader who establishes the worship of Huichilopochti as the Aztec main deity (202–203).

[25] Murray, *The Conquest*, 56.

[26] Anzaldúa, *Borderlands*, 31.

mythology for Chicano/a scholars. On the one hand, Murray employs Tlakaelel to trace a well-established literary value and history of Chicano/a culture while, Anzaldúa scrutinizes the traditional role of an Aztec patriarchal lineage that still impacts its ideology and development of cultural expressions. In this context, Murray's cultural appropriation of Tlakaelel exemplifies a textual and cultural heterogeneity that defines Chicana/o narratives, texts that recover and rework an Aztec mythology to trace a cultural historiography linked to a colonized experience.

Moreover, Murray reframes the exaltation of an Aztec masculine figure to emphasize a genealogical cultural capital that she employs to characterize Helen as a figure of social transgression. Interestingly, Murray's typification of Helen as a female transgressor in *The Conquest* evokes Anzaldúa's vision of Chicanas as resistant female figures.[27] For example, Anzaldúa sees herself in the following way, "My Chicana identity is grounded in the Indian woman's history of resistance. The Aztec rites of mourning were rites of defiance protesting the cultural changes which disrupted the equality and balance between female and male, and protesting their demotion to a lesser status, their denigration."[28] Murray incorporates Anzaldúa's act of defiance and resistance to recreate a cultural literary paradigm to cast Helen as an Aztec female who enacts personal and collective resistance.[29] Here, Helen defies the familial and social expectation of becoming Moctezuma's wife. Helen rebels not only against the familial expectations, but also against the traditional gender roles assigned to women when she aspires to be a juggler. The Aztecs, renowned for their school for jugglers and magicians, prohibited women from formally studying this royal profession. However, the gender barriers that she encounters do not stop her from teaching

[27] This reading reflects the notion of transnational feminism as seen in some works by Chicana novelists, for example, Ana Castillo. In her work *Chicano Nations: The Hemispheric Origins of Mexican American Literature*, (New York: New York University Press, 2011) Marissa K. López states that Castillo's works "*Sapogonia* and *The Guardians* explore the multiplicity of U.S. Latina/o identity while developing a model of chicanismo as global consciousness, a politics that retains geopolitical specificity while also remaining attuned to the world" (170).

[28] Anzaldúa, *Borderlands*, 21.

[29] The characterization of Helen exemplifies Judith Butler's philosophical concerns in *Gender Trouble: Feminism and the Subversion of Identity* (New York: Routledge, 1990). She explores issues dealing with "the articulation of a temporal trope of a subversive sexuality that flourishes prior to the imposition of a law, after its overthrow, or during the reign as a constant challenge to its authority" (29).

herself the art of juggling by emulating a fictional character named Maxixa, identified in the novel as one of the greatest jugglers of the Aztec Empire. Helen's personal growth and passion for juggling distances her from her prearranged personal future and symbolically represents a subversion of gender roles and identity to typify Helen as a woman who transgresses the prescribed social norms.

In this reading, Yxta Maya Murray establishes a parallelism between Helen and Sara as two female characters who transgress the assigned gender and cultural roles. Helen's characterization demonstrates the actions of a female transgressor linked to an Aztec society who limits the role of women. In addition, Helen's actions in Europe symbolically identify her as a cultural transgressor who passes as a European writer and male performer. Helen's action parallels Sara's work at the Getty Museum because she plays the role of a Chicana translator, who deciphers the colonized histories of her contemporary community. Moreover, she embodies the transgressive possibilities of Gloria Anzaldúa's mestiza, or borderland identity who "puts history through a sieve, winnows out the lies, looks at the forces that we as a race, as women, have been part of."[30]

Ironically, upon the arrival of Cortés, and specifically after a battle between the Aztecs and the Spaniards where all the members of her family die, Helen foresees her future as a concubine and slave of the Conquistador. Helen survives the violent encounter because she hides her identity by donning the uniform of a male juggling performer. I read the representation of Helen as a cross-dresser as a symbol of the postcolonial subject who appropriates and subverts cultural and social codes to manipulate authoritarian social practices of a colonial state. Indeed, her ability to survive the Conquest of New Spain as well as her journey to Europe illustrates the symbolism of Helen as an act of resistance. The typification of Helen as a cross-dresser follows a very well-established cultural practice of colonial women who see themselves as mujeres varoniles who fight and transgress the closed public space that the hermetic colonial social parameters offer them. In the narratives associated with the conquest of the Americas and its colonial heritage, there are many literary examples that employ the trope of

[30] Anzaldúa, *Borderlands*, 82.

cross-dressing.[31] Indeed, Helen, as a cross-dresser and as juggler fuses an external reality with what Anzaldúa calls "The other mode of consciousness [that] facilitates images from the soul and the unconscious through dreams and the imagination."[32] As a result of the conquest of New Spain, Helen's performative acts not only challenge the gender and social expectations of Aztec society, but they also question her personal and cultural experiences as a new colonized subject which influence the emergence of a new consciousness as a forced exile in Europe.

Helen's typification as a cross-dresser and its ideological implications as an act of social and cultural resistance contrasts with the objectification that she experiences as an exiled subject when Hernán Cortés takes her to Spain and Italy as a slave. Helen's life in Europe constitutes another specific example of the experiences of deterritorialization. In the novel, after conquering the Aztec Empire in 1528, Cortés brings a group of Aztec performers as gifts for Pope Clement VII and for Charles V, among them are Helen and her Master Maxixa. Cortés presents them to the Pope, but he is not interested in possessing them. Consequently, Cortés houses them in an apartment, where the Europeans stare at them, reconstructing a performative social spectacle that objectifies Helen, Maxixa, and other members of the juggling troupe. The public viewing of the Aztec troupe by Europeans reveals a social hierarchy that marks the colonial political relations between Europe and the Americas.

In addition to exploring Helen's character as a deterritorialized subject, Yxta Maya Murray also incorporates psychological aspects that border characters experience as members of a dislocated community to document the protagonist's life in Rome. Consequently, Helen in her new setting, experiences a sense of nostalgia for her place of origin, as exemplified by her remembrance of a memorable historical past of her family and community. In her memories, Helen exalts her own community and personal history resembling nostalgic narratives often associated with fragmented subjects

[31] For example, Catalina de Erauso (La Monja Alférez, 1592–1650) dressed as a man and fought in the colonization of the Americans in Chile; Sor Juana Inés de la Cruz also exemplifies the theme of cross-dresser; as a man she attends the university in Mexico City. Sor Juana also explores the theme of cross-dressing in her play *Los empeños de una casa*, when her main character Doña Leonor disguises herself as a man to critic men's intellectual and cognitive abilities. For a study in Catalina de Erauso, see Sherry M. Velasco, *Lieutenant Nun: Transgenderism, Lesbian Desire, & Catalina de Erauso.* (Austin: University of Texas Press, 2000).

[32] Anzaldúa, *Borderlands*, 37.

who have been forcefully displaced or have left their local communities. The dislocation and the distance from their geographical place and space trigger individual and collective memories that recuperate a glorious past often ignoring, conflicting social and psychological traits that the people felt in their own native community.[33] From this point of view, the presence in *The Conquest* of a personal nostalgic narrative conveys a twofold purpose. On the one hand, Helen's feelings of nostalgia for a magnificent past contribute to the erasure of the history of violence between the Aztec Empire and other indigenous communities.

At the same time, these nostalgic feelings also ignore the physical and psychological traumas that dominate her life in Tenochtitlán as she experiences the encounter between the Aztecs and the Spaniards. From this latter point of view, Helen's memories of the past signify a mechanism of personal survival as she remembers her ancestral, honorable blood lineage and forgets a problematic past. Thus, she is able to reframe the Mexicans as morally superior to Spaniards. On the other hand, her life in Europe also produces an imaginary of a new culture and setting, a space and place, belonging to a new city and an Empire that is artificially framed by a new utopian setting, in which she occupies and participates as a performer. Helen sees her artistic participation, originally forbidden by her own community, as an integral producer of culture and an addition to the societal glamor of Europe. Helen's view of her performance contrasts with the troubling memories as an aspiring woman juggler in a closed and restricted Aztec society prior to the arrival of the Spaniards. However, I interpret Helen's actions as an erasure of a historical past linked to temporal and geographical dislocation of deterritorialized communities that strive for acceptance and integration into a new social and cultural milieu. Indeed, I read that she desires acceptance into these communities, but in her own personal and social terms.

The use and appropriation of place and space that the Empire gives Helen and her fellow jugglers as deterritorialized figures in Europe determine the personal and social functionality of each character. For instance, Helen's attention to her physical and psychological state allows her to work and personally develop within the constrained social space that the Empire

[33] Rajagopalan Radhakrishnan in "Ethnicity in an Age of Diaspora," published in *Theorizing Diaspora: A Reader*, edited by Jana Evans Braziel and Anita Mannur (Malden: Backwell Publishing, 2003): 120–131, explores these personal and cultural questions "our diasporan gaze" and gives importance to understanding the historical and political crises of the homeland (128).

provides her to practice their art, an activity that provides happiness in her life. However, Helen's personal and psychological assimilation contrasts with her fellow Aztec companions who prefer to die or commit suicide instead of liberating themselves from the closed place and space where they live. For Helen, her fellow Aztec jugglers' unstable mental and personal sentiments about their lives remind her of the feelings of alienation and rejection that she felt in her own community when she was destined to be a wife for Moctezuma. Murray's description of the psychological instability of the Aztec performers in contrast with Helen's positive mental outlook as a woman juggler exemplifies the hierarchical levels of personal adoptability and assimilation for deterritorialized communities. As a functional and adoptable subject living in the Empire, Helen appropriates the spaces given to her to practice and present an art that later becomes a form of resistance against the Empire.

Yxta Maya Murray constructs a historical story that employs distinctive geographical settings in the Americas and Europe to capture multiple social realities that are fused to create a personal and collective quest for a search of personal legitimacy, cultural authenticity, and historical authorship. In *The Conquest* Sara's construction and retelling of Helen's story embodies a socio-cultural reading of the first half of the sixteenth-century from a comparative perspective to examine key geo-political conflicts that marked the colonial relationship between Spain and the Americas. Among the key socio-political events that defined the historiography of the period are the political influence and growth of the Spanish Empire under Charles V. Murray's novel, then, contextualizes the socio-cultural relationship between the Spanish and Aztecs in order to identify and critique hegemonic social parallelism that defines her characters. For example, at the time of the Spanish arrival, the novel reconstructs Moctezuma's recreational setting full of intellect and pleasures, where women were tutored and educated to serve the king—an act similar to life in European courts where some of the women have hidden talents and become poets and others study astronomy. Her talents are always hidden, except when the Emperor needs them symbolically illustrating the stories of deterritorialized communities. Murray emplots a symbolic narrative with a unique historical complexity that amplifies the traditional cultural literary traditions associated with Chican@ cultural heritage. Indeed, Murray's historical context expands the dominant historical paradigm of the formation of the Chican@ identity as presented by the canonical texts, including Gloria Anzaldúa's work. Finally, from the theoretical perspective postulated by Hayden White,

The Conquest epitomizes a narrative characterized by meta-historical attributes, a work aware of its historical consciousness and its epistemological implications, given that the reader becomes aware of the importance of cultural transactions that historically influences the identity of Chican@ culture.

Bibliography

Anzaldúa, Gloria. 1987. *Borderlands/La frontera: The New Mestiza.* San Francisco: Spinsters/Aunt Lute.

Appaduria, Arjun. 2003. Disjuncture and Difference in the Global Economy. In *Theorizing Diaspora: A Reader*, ed. Jana Evans Braziel and Anita Mannur, 25–48. Malden: Blackwell Publishing.

Baca, Damián. 2009. The Chicano Codex: Writing Against Historical and Pedagogical Colonization. *College English* 71 (6): 564–583.

Bhabha, Homi K. 1990. DissemiNation: Time, Narrative, and the Margins of the Modern Nation. In *Nation and Narration*, ed. Homi K. Bhabha, 291–322. New York: Routledge.

Boullosa, Carmen. 1994. *Duerme.* Madrid: Alfaguara.

Butler, Judith. 1990. *Gender Trouble: Feminism and the Subversion of Identity.* New York: Routledge.

Carrasco, Salvador. 2002. The Mestiza Scheherazade. *Los Angeles Times Book Review*, October 27.

Clifford, James. 1988. *The Predicament of Culture: Twentieth-Century Ethnography, Literature, and Art.* Cambridge: Harvard University Press.

Cortés, Hernán. 1985. *Cartas de relación.* México: Editorial Porrúa.

Cutter, Martha J. 2010. Malinche's Legacy: Translation, Betrayal, and Interlingualism in Chicano/a Literature. *The Arizona Quarterly* 66: 1–33.

Dávalos, Karen Mary. 2001. *Exhibiting Mestizaje: Mexican (American) Museums in the Diaspora.* Albuquerque: University of New Mexico.

De la Cruz, Sor Juana Inés. 1985. Los empeños de una casa. In *Obras completas*, ed. Francisco Monterde, 627–704. México: Editorial Porrúa.

Deleuze, Gilles. 1986. *Foucault.* Trans. Séan Hand. Minneapolis: University of Minnesota Press.

De Sahagún, Fray Bernardino. 1989. *Historia general de las cosas de la Nueva España.* México: Editorial Porrúa.

Díaz del Castillo, Bernal. 1986. *Historia verdadera de la conquista de la Nueva España.* México: Editorial Porrúa.

Esquivel, Laura. 2006. *Malinche.* New York: Atria Books.

Foucault, Michel. 2010. *The Archeology of Knowledge and the Discourse of Language.* New York: Vintage Books.

Gómez Peña, Guillermo, Enrique Chagoya, and Felicia Rice. 1998. *Codex Espangliensis: From Columbus to the Border Patrol.* Santa Cruz: Moving Parts Press.

González García, Mónica. 2012. On the Borderlands of U.S. Empire: The Limitations of Geography, Ideology, and Disciplinarity. In *Trans-Americanity: Subaltern Modernities, Global Coloniality, and the Cultures of Greater Mexico*, 183–211. Durham: Duke University Press.

Herrera, Juan Felipe. 1997. *Mayan Drifter: Chicano Poet in the Lowlands of America.* Philadelphia: Temple University Press.

León-Portilla, Miguel. 1992a. *Visión de los vencidos: Relaciones indígenas de la Conquista.* México: UNAM.

———. 1992b. Apéndice. In *Vision de los vencidos*, ed. Miguel León Portilla, 171–205. México: UNAM.

López, Marissa K. 2011. *Chicano Nations: The Hemispheric Origins of Mexican American Literature.* New York: New York University Press.

Murray, Yxta Maya. 2002. *The Conquest.* New York: Rayo.

Mignolo, Walter D. 2000. Signs and Their Transmission: The Question of the Book in the New World. In *A Book of the Book: Some Works and Projections About the Book and Writing*, ed. Jerome Rothenberg and Steven Clay, 351–371. New York: Granary Book.

Radhakrishnan, Rajagopalan. 2003. Ethnicity in an Age of Diaspora. In *Theorizing Diaspora: A Reader*, ed. Jana Evans Braziel and Anita Mannur, 120–131. Malden: Backwell Publishing.

Saldívar, José David. 2012. *Trans-Americanity: Subaltern Modernities, Global Coloniality, and the Cultures of Greater Mexico.* Durham: Duke University Press.

Spivak, Gayatri Chakravorty. 1988. *In Other Worlds: Essays in the Cultural Politics.* New York: Routledge.

Solares, Ignacio. 1994. *Nen, la inútil.* México: Alfaguara.

Todorov, Tzvetan. 1984. *The Conquest of America.* Trans. Richard Howard. New York: Harper Torchbooks.

Velasco, Sherry M. 2000. *Lieutenant Nun: Transgenderism, Lesbian Desire, & Catalina de Erauso.* Austin: University of Texas Press.

Wyatt, Jean. 1995. On Not Being La Malinche: Border Negotiations of Gender in Sandra Cisneros's 'Never Marry A Mexican' and 'Woman Hollering Creek'. *Tulsa Studies in Women's Literature* 14: 243–271.

Transforming Borders: Resistant Liminality in *Beloved*, *Song of Solomon*, and *Paradise*

Danielle Russell

> 'Gimme the tea.... No geography.' 'No geography? Okay no geography. What about some history in your tea? Or some sociopolitico-No. That's still geography.... I do believe my whole life's geography.... I live in the North now. So the first question come to mind is North of what? Why, north of the South. So North exists because South does.'[1]

The exchange between Guitar Bains and Milkman Dead in Toni Morrison's *Song of Solomon* highlights the fact that geography is never neutral. It carries a history in Morrison's texts. Ideological, cultural, and political concerns inform both our understanding and depictions of space. There is an all-too-human need to classify the spaces we occupy; boundaries can provide a comforting containment. Borders also impose a constricting confinement. Practices of inclusion/exclusion hinge on power dynamics which are rarely democratic. "Borders ... distinguish *us* and *them*," argues Gloria Anzaldua. She cautions, "[A] border is a dividing line, a narrow strip along a steep

[1] Toni Morrison, *Song of Solomon* (New York: Penguin, 1987), 114.

D. Russell (✉)
Glendon, York University, Toronto, ON, Canada

J. Elbert Decker, D. Winchock (eds.), *Borderlands and Liminal Subjects*, https://doi.org/10.1007/978-3-319-67813-9_6

edge."[2] "Steep edge" suggests a firm division—a physical emblem of an imaginative or psychological barrier—between "us" and "them." As Guitar points out, "North exists because South does"; the emphasis on difference which privileges one space/one group over another is crucial to that division. The "us/them" binary has become such a common aspect of Western culture that it is often accepted without question. Binaries, whether physical or conceptual, are artificial constructs. They fulfill prescriptive rather than descriptive functions.

Morrison's writing is an exercise in denaturalizing racial binaries. The historical legacy of slavery and continuing practices of systemic racism have created emotionally fraught and politically charged physical and psychological spaces in America. Literature can be a means of continuing the insistence on borders or an act of resistance by destabilizing binary divisions. In *Playing in the Dark: Whiteness and the Literary Imagination*, Morrison insists that "the contemplation of [a] black presence is central to any understanding of our national literature and should not be permitted to hover at the margins of the literary imagination."[3] She challenges readers to confront the ideological borders created by the reality of racial discrimination in America. One of Morrison's key approaches is to reject the "white as default" mentality of American literature; she writes complex and compelling black characters who take center stage while white characters, if present, are relocated to the periphery. Lives traditionally marginalized or ignored in literature comprise Morrison's fictional worlds. Those worlds, however, are firmly anchored in American geography—with all its historical, legal, and social implications—and this infuses Morrison's novels with a political strategy which can, in turn, be extrapolated as a real-world practice. Morrison insists on the amelioration of the margin.

To be marginalized is to be pushed to the side—discounted, discredited, disempowered; life on the margin is a precarious state Morrison acknowledges in her narratives, but it is also potentially empowering. bell hooks concedes that "locating oneself there is difficult yet it is necessary."[4] On the margin, hook contends, "we are transformed … we make radical creative

[2] Quoted in Gayle Wald, *Crossing the Line: Racial Passing in Twentieth-Century U. S. Literature and Culture* (London: Duke UP, 2000), 1.

[3] Toni Morrison, *Playing in the Dark: Whiteness and the Literary Imagination* (Cambridge, Massachusetts: Harvard UP, 1992), 5–6.

[4] bell hooks, *Yearnings: Race, Gender and Cultural Politics* (London: Turnaround Press, 1989), 206.

space which affirms and sustains our subjectivity...."[5] Morrison creates characters who learn to use the margin—the space between the binaries—as a site and source of resistance. Liminality is a dominant feature in Morrison's fiction. Her body of writing incorporates characters poised on borders; they are situated on the periphery by race, class, gender, culture, and history. The transformative possibility of borders is particularly evocative in *Beloved, Song of Solomon*, and *Paradise*. The titular character Beloved is arguably the most striking of Morrison's characters to challenge borders. Bridging the spirit and physical worlds, the young woman embodies "an apocalyptic demolition of the boundaries," asserts Susan Bowers.[6] Characters on the periphery in *Song of Solomon* and *Paradise* lack the incendiary influence of Beloved's character but are no less engaged in resistant acts of self-definition.

Spatial borders in all three novels function as a means of asserting power. By claiming or reclaiming territory, individuals attempt to impose order on their worlds. Whether externally or self-imposed, boundaries divide space into manageable sections; these areas exist on both a practical and conceptual level—street names, city limits, national borders are territorial markers and ideological categories. Morrison's fiction exposes the artifice of, and power dynamics embedded in, official mappings of space. The collision of official and unofficial naming takes a quasi-comical form in *Song of Solomon*. The Southside residents use "Not Doctor Street" as a resistant landmark:

> Town maps registered the street as Mains Avenue, but the only colored doctor in the city had lived and died on that street, ... his patients took to calling the street, ... Doctor Street. ...when other Negroes moved there, ...envelopes ... began to arrive addressed to people at house numbers on Doctor Street. The post office workers returned these envelopes.... Then in 1918, when colored men were being drafted, a few gave their address at the recruitment office as Doctor Street. In that way, the name acquired a quasi-official status.[7]

The residents redefine the street based upon their perspective of it. They personalize it, not through the doctor's name, but what he represents: as "the only colored doctor," he is a challenge to white society. Their own

[5] Ibid., 209.

[6] Susan Bowers, "*Beloved* and the New Apocalypse," in *Toni Morrison's Fiction: Contemporary Criticism*, ed. David L. Middleton (New York: Garland Publishing, 1997), 211.

[7] Morrison, *Song of Solomon*, 4.

challenge is met with resistance: city legislators "saw to it that 'Doctor Street' was never used in any official capacity."[8] The attempt to establish "Doctor Street" is undermined by the powers-that-be.

Defiance takes a different direction after the official quashing of the name. Residents continue to use it, prompting a more pointed intervention:

> ... since they knew that only Southside residents kept it up, they had notices posted ... in that part of the city saying that the avenue running northerly and southerly from Shore Road fronting the lake to the junction of route 6 and 2 leading to Pennsylvania, and also running parallel to and between Rutherford Avenue and Broadway, ... would always be known as Mains Avenue and not Doctor Street.[9]

The campaign is pointed and precise: it is targeted at the transgressors and very specific in demarcating the territory in question. In point of fact, the official notices fuel more resistance from the disenfranchised populace who are not granted the power to participate in the naming of their environment. They interpret it as a "genuinely clarifying public notice because it gave Southside residents a way to keep their memories alive and please the city legislators .... They called it Not Doctor Street, and were inclined to call the charity hospital at its northern end No Mercy Hospital. ..."[10] The addition of "Not" strikes a comical note of defiance, but the reference to the hospital which only accepts white patients invokes the systemic racism lurking behind what could be construed as a petty squabble over a street name.

The ramifications of definitions are exposed in a tragic way in *Beloved*. Once again, the power to define is the prerogative of white men, and the definitions are imposed on the black population. The male slaves on Sweet Home plantation are men because Mr. Garner determines they are. Paul D recalls Garner's provocative conversations with other farmers

> 'Beg to differ, Garner. Ain't no nigger men.' 'Not if you scared, they ain't.' Garner's smile was wide. 'But if you a man yourself, you'll want your niggers to be men too.' 'I wouldn't have no nigger men round my wife.' It was the reaction Garner loved.... 'Neither would I,' he said ... there was always a pause before the neighbor ... got the meaning.... Garner came home bruised

[8] Ibid.
[9] Ibid.
[10] Ibid.

> and pleased, having demonstrated one more time what a real Kentuckian was: one tough and smart enough to make and call his own niggers men.[11]

In one fell swoop, Garner asserts his masculinity, undercuts that of his auditor, and insults the fidelity of that man's wife. The owner's words grant his property the title of men, but it is a status contingent on location—only on Sweet Home plantation—and designed to reinforce *his* reputation. It is a lesson that will be driven home to the slaves after Garner's death; his brother-in-law will not only reject the label of "men" but undermine their very humanity. Sethe overhears Schoolteacher, "'which one are you doing?' And one of the boys said, 'Sethe.' ... I heard him say, 'No .... put her human characteristics on the left; her animal ones on the right.'"[12] While under the control of the Garners, Sweet Home has been a relatively benign system of slavery. Schoolteacher's arrival exposes what has been masked: slavery defines its victims as non-human. The boundaries are clear and leave no room for self-definition. Resistant acts of definition, possible in *Song of Solomon* because a (comparatively) free black community exists on the margin of mainstream society, are impossible in *Beloved*.

The effects of slavery are directly visited on Sethe's children in *Beloved*, but the consequences of racial barriers are equally apparent in *Song of Solomon* and *Paradise*. Milkman's grandfather was murdered by whites for his property; the legacy of that injustice is passed down damaging multiple generations in *Song of Solomon*. In contrast, the experience of racial injustice seems, oddly, to be empowering in *Paradise*. Borders, in the minds of the "founding fathers" of Ruby, are protective barriers when self-imposed. A policy of isolationism and a strategy of entrenchment are adopted in response to personal and collective experiences of racism:

> Ten generations had known what lay Out There: space, once beckoning and free, became unmonitored and seething; ... a void where random and organized evil erupted.... Out There where your children were sport, your women quarry, and where your very person could be annulled... But lessons had been learned and relearned in the last three generations about how to protect a town.[13]

[11] Toni Morrison, *Beloved* (New York: Penguin, 1998), 10–11.

[12] Ibid., 193.

[13] Morrison, *Paradise* (New York: Penguin, 1999), 16.

The absence of barriers between themselves and their persecutors has driven home the practical need for an impenetrable division. "Out There" requires an "In Here" mentality, the men conclude. The all-black town of Ruby, a town where "outsider" and "enemy" "mean the same thing," is conceived as the perfect antidote to the threats looming "Out There."[14] What begins as a defense established by one generation, however, soon becomes a restrictive practice to the next generation. Bunkering down behind what seems to be self-imposed borders can only be a temporary strategy. The youth of Ruby seek an active political engagement with the larger world rather than the retreat from it enacted by their elders.

Beloved also opens with a black community apparently isolated from the larger world, but it quickly becomes clear that the separation is not as complete as might be inferred. The central location—124 Bluestone Road—is owned by white abolitionists despite Sethe's view of it being her home. It is the site of a terrible event eighteen years prior to the novel's commencement. Discovered by slave catchers, Sethe's maternal instinct takes a violent turn: she attempts to kill her children rather than allow them to be claimed as "property." The decision is meant to send her children "through the veil, out, away, over there where no one could hurt them. … Outside this place, where they would be safe."[15] Sethe is relying on a firm division between the worlds of the living and the dead. Beloved, the murdered child returned as a young woman, is a direct challenge to the notion of rigid boundaries.[16] She is the tenuous bridge between the spiritual and physical worlds. Articulating where she has been is complicated by her childlike perspective—Beloved is seemingly frozen at the toddler stage when she died—and the lack of words to describe a "reality" beyond the known boundaries of reality. Denver, who survived their mother's violent act, asks:

> 'What's it like over there, where you were before?' … 'Dark,' said Beloved. 'I'm small in that place. I'm like this here.' She … lay down on her side and

[14] Ibid., 212.

[15] Morrison, *Beloved*, 163.

[16] Beloved can be read as a damaged woman rather than a ghostly presence made flesh. To do so, however, involves reading against the text; the debate falls outside of my current discussion, but it does surface in the novel. Initially, Sethe believes "Beloved had been locked up by some whiteman for his own purposes …." Denver accepts Beloved as "the true-to-life presence of the baby that had kept her company," and Sethe soon embraces her as her missing child. Ibid., 119.

> curled up. ... 'Nothing to breathe down there and no room to move in.' 'You see anybody?' 'Heaps. A lot of people is down there. Some is dead.'[17]

"Over there" and "that place" demarcate a separate space from the one the girls now occupy. Its characteristics are vague but clearly unpleasant. The specification that only "some are dead" further complicates the depiction as it implies others are not, blurring the boundaries between "there" and "here." The contrast is clear: "here" is the desired space of home with Sethe, while "there" is a place of suffering and disconnection. With the gradual expulsion of Paul D, the home becomes a sanctuary for the three women. It offers asylum from a threatening world. Asylum soon takes on a different meaning as Sethe and Beloved descend into madness—"if the whitepeople ... had allowed Negroes into their lunatic asylum they could have found candidates in 124."[18] Destruction comes from within the home, not the outside world. The collision of Sethe's crippling guilt and Beloved's all-consuming love cannot be contained; what begins as a protective gesture—retreat from a threatening world—devolves into a cannibalistic relationship. Denver watches her mother sit "like a chastised child while Beloved ate up her life ...."[19] The distorted and distorting mother/daughter love transforms the home into a self-defeating space.

Home, as a self-contained space, fails to fulfill its desired purpose in all three novels. Closed borders shift from protecting to imprisoning as the inhabitants cannot see beyond their own boundaries. The resulting stasis is psychologically crippling: holding onto the past prevents them from engaging with the present or anticipating an alternative future. Sethe is too focused on justifying her past actions in *Beloved* to concern herself with the present fates of her daughters. The responsibility shifts to Denver: "to step off the edge of the world and die because if she didn't, they all would."[20] Like her mother, Denver's world has been reduced to a house and its grounds; unlike Sethe, she recognizes the need to move beyond those boundaries in order to survive and, ultimately, thrive. Neither Sethe nor Beloved realizes that they are fighting a losing battle; their past cannot be altered or erased, only endured. Sethe in particular has forgotten the

[17] Ibid., 75.
[18] Ibid., 250.
[19] Ibid.
[20] Ibid., 239.

lesson of her mother-in-law, Baby Suggs: "Freeing yourself was one thing; claiming ownership of that freed self was another."[21] Legally emancipated, Sethe is enslaved by her past and bound to her aggrieved child in a mutually destructive way. In limiting her world to her home, and her worldview to her own history, Sethe is blind to the historical factors that mitigate (if not exonerate) her guilt. The legalized practice of brutality—the institution of slavery—is the central cause of Sethe's own violence. Literally bearing its scars, the mother cannot condemn her children to the same fate—death as deliverance, not punishment. Obsessed with, and seemingly by (in the form of Beloved), the past, Sethe never deals with it in its entirety. The past is a border she cannot cross on her own. Denver's movement out into the community will, however, set in motion events which will force Sethe to cross that psychological boundary.[22]

Psychic trauma as the legacy of racially motivated violence is equally pervasive in *Song of Solomon* and *Paradise*. Haunted by the murder of his father by white landowners, *Song of Solomon*'s Macon Dead II passes the trauma to his son and daughters. He loses sight of his father's legacy of hard work and loving familial bonds. He teaches Milkman to "Own things. And let the things you own own other things. Then you'll own yourself, and other people too."[23] Macon misconstrues wealth with self-worth. Tangible objects, in his philosophy, equal the intrinsic values needed for self-possession; powerlessness over his father's fate leads to the pursuit of compensatory economic power. The approach, while understandable, is misguided and self-destructive. Macon Dead II gains property and money at the price of a loveless marriage, estrangement from his emotionally damaged children, the black community he looks down on, and the sister he once cherished. The borders he attempts to impose on his painful past—containing it so it cannot reoccur—are more porous than he thinks. Macon fails to anticipate that the trauma will trickle down to his own children.

Generational conflict surfaces in *Paradise* as the children of the founders of Ruby actively resist their isolationist approach to life. The two worldviews collide around the town's central symbol, the communal Oven. What begins as "a utility . . . became a shrine . . ." to the older men and a lightning

[21] Ibid., 95.

[22] I will address this process in a subsequent section of this chapter.

[23] Morrison, *Song of Solomon*, 55.

rod to the younger ones.[24] The appearance of a "fist, jet black" on the Oven triggers a confrontation.[25] The black power symbol reflects the youths' desire to engage with the world beyond Ruby's boundaries. The new generation's demand for active resistance hinges upon a movement beyond Ruby's borders. Not surprisingly, the older generation's response is defensive; it shuts down the conversation with a show of power. The symbol of communal strength becomes a source of conflict. It reveals the changing needs of Ruby's inhabitants, but the older men project their fears outward, to the edge of town.

Paradise opens with a provocative line highlighting the importance of racial boundaries to the men: "They shoot the white girl first."[26] Race is foregrounded, yet it is impossible to determine which of the characters is white. It is not a case of reverse passing in that the white girl is not undercover: she is identified but not identifiable. The racial division is invoked, and then not quite revoked since race figures prominently in the novel, but it is destabilized in a haunting way. Gender is the determining factor in the assault: the "prey" are pursued because they are women and the "hunters" attack to reassert their masculinity.[27] The opening section, focalized through the men, reveals their "rationale" for mass murder: "their target ... is ... throwaway people ... the venom is manageable now. Shooting the first woman (the white one) has clarified it like butter: the pure oil of hatred on top, its hardness stabilized below."[28] Race is reduced to parentheses—not irrelevant but seemingly not the central fact in the assault—five women are dehumanized and disposed of—four of whom are black. On second read, however, the quotation implies that race is a motivation for the violence; the fresh "hatred on top" is directed at the women while "its hardness stabilized below" is the result of the continuing wounds of past racial injustice: "that is why they are here.... To make sure.... That nothing inside or out rots the one all-black town worth the pain."[29] The possibility that the (perceived) threat can come from within Ruby is briefly conceded, but the attack on the Convent is to eradicate an external enemy.

[24] Morrison, *Paradise*, 103.
[25] Ibid., 101.
[26] Morrison, *Paradise*, 3.
[27] Ibid., 224.
[28] Ibid., 4.
[29] Ibid., 5.

The women become a scapegoat for the discord in Ruby. Change, the men conclude, is the fault of the outsiders, and "they did not think to fix it by extending a hand in fellowship or love. They mapped defense instead. . . ."[30] The response is to insist on the rigidity of their borders—a defensive insistence on their world map and a refusal to tolerate the existence of those who threaten, even if inadvertently, that vision. Refusing to be introspective, they project their fears on the women who fail to live by their norms. One of the invaders thinks how "there wasn't a slack or sloven woman anywhere in town. . . its people were free and protected. A sleepless woman could . . . walk . . . down the road . . . nothing for ninety miles around thought she was prey. . . ."[31] The fact that he is now stalking a group of women who have been too free—both "slack" and "sloven" by Ruby standards—is perverse to say the least. Their "crime" is that they challenge the values on which the town prides itself: "out here . . . no one to bother or insult them – they managed to call into question the value of almost every woman . . . ."[32] Willfully blind to the fact that he is bringing armed "insult" to the women, he sees only the threat to his concept of a woman. The legitimate fear of "Out There where your children were sport, your women quarry . . ." has been transformed into an "out here" where the Ruby men become the source of violence against the most vulnerable.[33] The men become what they abhor: predators hunting the marginalized because they can. In so doing, they betray themselves and throw into question their self-righteous stance of protectors.

Life on the margins of Ruby—the women and the racial unrest in the rest of the country—encroaches on the town despite the efforts of the men. Borders in *Paradise* are more fluid than many of the townspeople suspect. The concluding section will bring to light what has been hovering on the periphery: an alternate yet co-existing spirit world.[34] The presence of this differing reality is woven into *Beloved* and *Song of Solomon* in a more overt way than in *Paradise*, but all three novels will have timely interventions from this realm. The resurrection of the murdered daughter in *Beloved* is

[30] Ibid., 275.

[31] Ibid., 8–9.

[32] Ibid., 8.

[33] Ibid., 16, 8.

[34] Spirit is used to indicate a state that defies the limitations of "reality," a space where the seemingly impossible is made possible. It may or may not have a spiritual aspect, but this otherworldly territory empowers the marginalized in a way that their real world cannot.

the starkest example, but the community's acceptance of ghosts recognizes that there is more beyond the known world. Sethe's explanation of "rememory" lays the theoretical ground for Beloved's return. As she explains to Denver, "Places ... are still there. If a house burns down, it's gone, but the place ... stays ...."[35] The lesson could be interpreted as a frightened mother's dread of the past and fear for the future. The idea that space leaves a trace is supported by the work of Henri Lefebvre, "no space disappears completely .... 'Something' always survives ...."[36] Boundaries between the past and the present, the abstract and the concrete are not rigid in this context.

Beloved is "rememory" made flesh. She crosses the boundary between the worlds of the living and the dead. Life on the margin, the threshold between the two realms, is an extremely vulnerable position. Beloved's presence in the physical world is tentative at best. The loss of a tooth triggers a recurring fear: "Next would be her arm, her hand, a toe. Pieces of her would drop .... Or on one of those mornings before Denver woke and after Sethe left she would fly apart. It is difficult keeping her head on her neck ... when she is by herself."[37] Beloved's physical vulnerability reflects her precarious escape from the spirit realm. She believes she exists corporeally because Sethe and Denver keep her alive.

Beloved's destructive potential is indisputable. She is a powerful threat to Sethe and all-but alienates her from Denver. There is truth to their neighbor Ella's observation that while "a little communication between the two worlds" is acceptable, "this was an invasion," but the interaction can also be interpreted as an intervention.[38] Sethe and Denver endured an isolated existence prior to the past-made-flesh intervening in their lives. The marginal figure—Beloved—is a catalyst for both her family and the community. Negative actions lead to positive reactions. Denver faces her fear of "out there" and "step[s] off the edge of the world ... to ask somebody for help."[39] Journeying out into a threatening environment is made necessary by the

[35] Morrison, *Beloved*, 36.

[36] Henri Lefebvre, *The Production of Space*, trans. Donald Nicholson-Smith (Oxford: Blackwell Publishers, 1992), 402.

[37] Morrison, *Beloved*, 133.

[38] Ibid., 133.

[39] Ibid., 243.

conditions of her home; it is made possible by a conversation with her dead grandmother:

> Denver stood on the porch ... and couldn't leave it. ... and then Baby Suggs laughed ... 'You mean I never told you nothing about Carolina? ... You don't remember nothing about how come I walk the way I do and about your mother's feet, not to speak of her back? ... Is that why you can't walk down the steps?' But you said there was no defense. 'There ain't.' Then what do I do? 'Know it, and go on out the yard.'[40]

The past, however horrific, is precisely the reason Denver needs to seek out the community. Baby Suggs offers Denver a lesson in resiliency: the past can be endured and the present must be lived. Denver has heard her family's history but does not appreciate its significance until Beloved intercedes. The outcome, for Denver, is quite positive: she is welcomed into the community, finds employment, and gains a suitor.

The community is also healed through their interaction with Beloved. They are granted, and seize, the opportunity they rejected eighteen years ago. Hearing of Sethe's plight, thirty women come to her defense:

> ... it was as though the Clearing had come to her ... the voices of women searched for the right combination ... Building voice upon voice ... a wave of sound wide enough to sound deep water .... It broke over Sethe and she trembled like the baptized in its wash.[41]

Harmony defeats the chaos. A communal voice reminds Sethe of the Clearing, the space in which Baby Suggs preached a sermon about self-love.[42] It is a lesson Sethe is desperately in need of, but still does not internalize. She retreats to her bed awaiting death after the second loss of Beloved. Paul D must remind her "You your best thing, Sethe. You are."[43] Sethe's response is indeterminate—"Me? Me?"—but promising.[44] Survival, the novel makes clear, requires community, a sense of self-worth, and an acknowledgment of the past that does not impede the present. Beloved is ultimately an ameliorating force despite her negative actions.

[40] Ibid., 244.
[41] Ibid., 261.
[42] Ibid., 87–89.
[43] Ibid., 273.
[44] Ibid.

The interaction between the physical and spiritual realms is, initially, ambivalent in *Song of Solomon*. Milkman dismisses Freddie's insistence that "ghosts" are "in the world."[45] Unwilling to concede the existence of the two spheres, he rejects Freddie's insistence on a fluid boundary between them. The dream he has about his mother, however, reveals Milkman's awareness of a more complex reality. In narrating the vision of his mother buried "under a mound of tangled tulips bent low over her body, which was kicking to the last," Milkman omits the fact "that he had really seen it."[46] Guitar's question—"why didn't you go help her?"—is telling: it indicates his own acceptance of the reality of the "dream" and highlights Milkman's utter selfishness.[47] Milkman's "world" is his own life; his needs, his desires create a boundary he does not think to cross until he is guided by his aunt Pilate.

Pilate Dead is not a spirit guide like Beloved, but her body does mark her as otherworldly in the eyes of the community. While Beloved bears her mother's mark—"the little curved shadow of a smile ... under her chin" created by the saw—Pilate lacks the more traditional mark of a navel: "it was the absence of a navel that convinced people that she had not come into this world through normal channels ...."[48] Early in her life, the absence alienates Pilate from several communities. The fear of her origins prompts distinct boundaries; unable to cross them psychologically, the others expel her physically. In time, Pilate transforms this liminal status into a positive: "she threw away every assumption she had learned and began at zero."[49] The self-born baby becomes a self-made woman with no concern for social conventions, but she develops "a deep concern for and about human relationships."[50] A positive presence "who never bothered anybody, was helpful to everybody," Pilate is also "believed to have the power to step out of her skin, set a bush afire from fifty yards, and turn a man into a ripe rutabaga – all on account of the fact that she had no navel."[51] Pilate's power comes from within, not a magical source, but she is shaped by interaction

[45] Morrison, *Song of Solomon*, 109.
[46] Ibid., 105 and 104.
[47] Ibid., 105.
[48] Morrison, *Beloved*, 239 and *Song of Solomon*, 27–8.
[49] Morrison, *Song of Solomon*, 149.
[50] Ibid.
[51] Ibid., 94.

with the spirit realm. She pays "close attention to her mentor – the father who appeared before her … and told her things."[52] The dead father's message is rather cryptic: "'Sing. Sing,' …. 'You just can't fly on off and leave a body.'"[53] Pilate's response is literal—she sings and collects what she thinks are the bones of the "man she and Macon had murdered"—misconstruing their actual reference to her mother and the story of Solomon and Ryna.[54] The task of translation will fall to Milkman as he internalizes Pilate's lesson of love and concern for humanity. The journey "home" to Shalimar will strip Milkman of his material goods, his social status, and his self-absorption. As a result, he will discover a new community and, significantly, a spiritual connection to the land: "walking it like he belonged on it …."[55] The choice of "belonged" is telling: Milkman does not seek ownership like his father, but belonging like his grandfather.

Pilate and his grandfather are catalysts for growth in Milkman. He deciphers the family riddle and aids Pilate in burying her father on Solomon's Leap. What is briefly a peaceful moment of reconciliation, however, is interrupted by violence as Guitar shoots Pilate. Pilate's final words—"I wish I'd a knowed more people. I would of loved 'em all"—and the symbolic release of the impromptu grave marker—her earring is scooped up by a bird—suggest that she has, in some way, transcended her violent death.[56] Her earlier conversation with Milkman's mother (potentially) softens Pilate's death; she believes "people die when they want to and if they want to."[57] Interactions between Pilate and her father further throw into question the finality of death. The psychological barrier—the inability to accept an alternative reality—seemingly is more rigid than any physical barrier.

Song of Solomon and *Beloved* incorporate peripheral figures who serve as sources of inspiration for characters who are themselves marginalized figures. Milkman, Sethe, and Denver, to varying degrees, open themselves to the life-altering lessons provided by Pilate and Beloved. The pattern in *Paradise* is more complicated. The men of Ruby devalue life on the periphery to the point of exterminating it. Rather than accepting any connection

[52] Ibid., 150.
[53] Ibid., 147.
[54] Ibid.
[55] Ibid., 281.
[56] Ibid., 336 and 335.
[57] Ibid., 140.

to the marginalized, they see themselves as the center—the source of authority and arbiters of justice: "God at their side, the men take aim. For Ruby."[58] One of the "crimes" they ascribe to the women is godlessness; there is a suspicion of the kind of influence that the women have been exerting. The mistrust is a convenient mask for the origins of unrest in the town, but it is also an indication that they have forgotten their own history. Proud of their roots, the men neglect the fact that a spirit guide leads them to the location of Haven. Lost in the wilderness, the "walking man" delivers them to "freedom without borders and without deep menacing woods where enemies could hide."[59] The descendants of Haven's founders become the imposers of borders and the menacing enemy, not because of the women, but because of the illusory nature of Ruby. The division they insist on cannot be absolute. Ruby is in danger of stultifying and, thus, in desperate need of a catalyst.

Despite being denigrated by the men, the Convent functions as a sanctuary for the wounded—the women who live there and the townspeople who shelter there in times of need—but it is Consolata who exercises healing powers. The discovery that she can "step in" another person and prolong life initially strikes Consolata as "devilment," but Lone chastises her, "God don't make mistakes. Despising His gift, now that it is a mistake."[60] Contextualizing it as God's gift soothes Consolata's fears; it also throws into question the men's assumption that God is "at their side."[61] Consolata's teaching does what the men fail to do for their people: "unlike some people in Ruby, the Convent women were no longer haunted."[62] The peripheral figure is clearly a catalyst in the lives of the marginalized and damaged women; her influence on the people of Ruby is less clear.

The absence of bodies leaves space for the various sides to spin their own narratives about the events at the Convent. Lone is convinced: "God had given Ruby a second chance. ... He had actually swept up and received His servants ... ."[63] For her, the lesson is obvious: Ruby must mend its ways; the process, however, requires a degree of soul-searching few in Ruby will face.

[58] Morrison, *Paradise*, 18.
[59] Ibid., 97 and 99.
[60] Ibid., 247 and 246.
[61] Ibid., 18.
[62] Ibid., 266.
[63] Ibid., 297–8.

The individual affected the most is Deacon Morgan; his newfound introspection leads him to the recognition that he has "become what the Old Fathers cursed: the kind of man who set himself up to judge, rout and even destroy the needy, the defenseless, the different."[64] Although he concedes, "I got a long way to go," Deacon's self-awareness holds out the possibility of positive change.[65]

The epilogue to the novel also has the potential to be positive. The missing bodies appear as corporeal beings and seemingly experience moments of "closure"—contact with key people. There is a fitting element of transcendence in the women's fates; while undergoing the healing process, "they had to be reminded of the moving bodies they wore, so seductive were the alive ones below."[66] The distinction between moving bodies and alive ones complicates the concept of reality. The threshold between the physical and the spiritual is more dynamic than a mind/body split would suggest. Morrison transforms a seemingly finite space—death—into an infinite space through the intersection of the physical and spirit worlds. The reaction in Ruby is to the missing bodies; the text, however, implies that the focus on the body is misleading. The women exist outside the borders of Ruby. They enter a new kind of peripheral state. One of the lingering questions is where they might be moving on to, but for Billie Delia, the question is "When will they reappear, with blazing eyes, war paint and huge hands to rip up and stomp down this prison calling itself a town?"[67] She is hoping for an apocalyptic intervention. Morrison withholds certainty about the fates of the women. The fate of the town is equally ambiguous, but the fissures in its boundaries suggest the status quo of the past is unlikely to hold.

Song of Solomon and *Beloved* also end with an element of suspense. The final moments of the former leave Milkman suspended in mid-air as he leaps toward Guitar. The phrase "it did not matter which one of them would give up his ghost in the killing arms of his brother" does not bode well for either man, but the negative act never happens in the text.[68] Milkman's conviction that "if you surrendered to the air, you could ride it" holds out a more

[64] Ibid., 302.
[65] Ibid., 303.
[66] Ibid., 265.
[67] Ibid., 308.
[68] Morrison, *Song of Solomon*, 337.

hopeful outcome, but it too is unrealized.[69] Morrison does not pick a side of the "border" between defeat and triumph. Without the narrative boundary of a closed ending, as was the case with *Paradise*, the final pages remain a space of multiple possibilities. This point is also true of *Beloved*; uncertainty lingers as to Beloved's fate: that she is absent is clear, what has happened to her is not. In the last two pages, there is an insistence that it is "not a story to pass on."[70] It is a haunting story, and despite the seeming disclaimers, it is a story which must be passed on—as in handed down. "Passed on" can also be read as rejected or neglected, passed without recognition. Morrison, in all three novels, actively engages with the tendency in American literature to do just that: to pass by the marginalized.

Territorialization, imposing borders, is a way of asserting power. It is an attempt to impose order in the physical world and on the conceptual world. Morrison uses peripheral characters who defy this approach; Beloved, Pilate, and the women of the Convent offer a counter way of making sense of the world. They recognize the blurred boundaries and their potential. The connection to an alternative space highlights the transformative power of the border; malleable, not rigid, the line between physical and spirit realms is empowering for those with the vision to see it. Visiting the deserted Convent, Richard Misner, and Anna Flood, "saw it. Or sensed it, rather, for there was nothing to see. A door, she said .... 'No, a window,' he said laughing .... focusing on the sign rather than the event .... to avoid ... saying out loud .... what would happen if you entered? What would be on the other side?"[71] The means of entrance is domesticated, but the movement into the unknown is still threatening. Neither Richard nor Anna can cross the threshold imaginatively; the sudden revelation is too abrupt. They lack a guide to help them access the unfamiliar space. Richard will reflect on the encounter during a funeral "when he bowed his head and gazed at the coffin lid he saw the window in the garden, felt it beckon toward another place – neither life nor death – but there, just yonder, shaping thoughts he did not know he had."[72] Richard's awareness of co-existing spaces and their interconnection highlights the fluidity of the border and its transformative potential.

[69] Ibid.

[70] Morrison, *Beloved*, 274–5.

[71] Morrison, *Paradise*, 305.

[72] Ibid., 307.

Morrison's use of magic realism—itself a blurring of the literary "boundaries" of realism and fantasy—pushes the reader to reconsider divisions between physical and spirit worlds, past and present. Arguably, the first border contested in a Morrison novel is the one between text and reader. She issues a challenge: "My writing ... demands, participatory reading .... My language has to have holes ... so the reader can come into it."[73] Part of that participation is a willingness to engage with a variety of ideological boundaries—to reconsider our tendency to rely on binaries to shape our reality. Morrison invites the reader to occupy the margin: "the ability of [readers] to imagine what is not the self, to familiarize the strange and mystify the familiar, is the test of their power."[74] The quotation is actually addressed to writers, but the test is applicable to readers; their willingness to imaginatively embrace resistant liminality is a crucial factor in Morrison's efforts to transform the border.

Bibliography

Bowers, Susan. 1997. Beloved and the New Apocalypse. In *Toni Morrison's Fiction: Contemporary Criticism*, ed. David L. Middleton, 209–230. New York: Garland Publishing.

hooks, bell. 1989. *Yearnings: Race, Gender and Cultural Politics.* London: Turnaround Press.

Jenkins, Candice M. 2006. Pure Black: Class, Color, and Intraracial Politics in Toni Morrison's *Paradise*. *Modern Fiction Studies* 52 (2): 270–298.

Lefebvre, Henri. 1992. *The Production of Space.* Trans. Donald Nicholson-Smith. Oxford: Blackwell Publishers.

Morrison, Toni. 1983. Interview. In *Black Women Writers at Work*, ed. Claudia Tate, 124–125. New York: Continuum Company.

———. 1987. *Song of Solomon.* New York: Penguin.

———. 1992. *Playing in the Dark: Whiteness and the Literary Imagination.* Cambridge, MA: Harvard UP.

———. 1996. *Paradise.* New York: Penguin.

———. 1998. *Beloved.* New York: Penguin.

Wald, Gayle. 2000. *Crossing the Line: Racial Passing in Twentieth-Century U. S. Literature and Culture.* London: Duke UP.

[73] Toni Morrison, "Interview," in *Black Women Writers at Work*, ed. Claudia Tate (New York: Continuum Company, 1983), 124–5.

[74] Morrison, *Playing in the Dark*, 15.

“Gone Over on the Other Side”: Passing in Chesnutt’s *The House Behind the Cedars*

Irina Negrea

“You are black, my lad, and you are not free.”[1] Addressed to John Walden in Charles Chesnutt’s *The House Behind the Cedars*, these words are uttered by a white judge. They are followed by a list that sums up the odds stacked against John in his attempt to become socially and racially mobile: the inability to travel without “papers,” to vote, to testify in a court of law, to be out after the curfew, to obtain accommodations at an inn, to return the blow if a white man strikes him. The same odds were stacked against any person who was defined as “black,” legally or otherwise, especially right after the Civil War, when antiblack sentiment was at its peak,[2] and when Chesnutt’s novel is set.

John has to fight a binary racial system that is designed to lock people into rigid categories, with no room in between for people of mixed blood, like him and his sister, Rena. Classified as black, John is contemplating a lifetime of servitude and discrimination, added to the social stigma of his

[1] Chesnutt, Charles W. *The House Behind the Cedars* (Ridgewood: The Gregg Press, 1968), 169.

[2] Fredrickson, George M. *Racism: A Short History* (Princeton: Princeton University Press, 2002), 81.

I. Negrea (✉)
Shaw University, Raleigh, NC, USA

J. Elbert Decker, D. Winchock (eds.), *Borderlands and Liminal Subjects*, https://doi.org/10.1007/978-3-319-67813-9_7

illegitimacy. Therefore, he needs to choose his weapons carefully if he wants to fight the system. Despite his protests that he, in fact, is not black but white (because he looks white), the judge introduces John to another concept that is designed to maintain the system: the one-drop rule: "One drop of black blood makes the whole man black."[3] It is a rule that makes John legally black and bars him from the rights and privileges of the whites. The only way he can gain access to them is by passing.

Racial passing is a much-discussed phenomenon that appeared as a consequence of the rigid binary racial system in America. The categories black/white are meant to contain and control, leaving no room for the people with mixed racial ancestry. One of the topics of discussion about passing centers around its possibilities to subvert the binary system. At first glance, it is hard to say how someone who crosses the color line from one rigid category to another would actually subvert the system in any way. However, applying several theoretical models of analysis to the phenomenon will show these possibilities. One important concept is Anzaldúa's "consciousness of the Borderlands," or *mestiza* consciousness, which deals specifically with identities that are not containable by the rigid limits set by a culture.[4] Performative passers are Borderland dwellers because they live between cultures. Their liminality is threatening to the binary system, hence the subversive possibilities that are inherent in such a position, even though sometimes the passer is completely unaware.

Drawing on Althusser, Chela Sandoval's concept of "mobility of identity"[5] is also very helpful in analyzing passing. Sandoval discusses how "the citizen-subject can learn to identify, develop, and control the means of ideology, that is, marshal the knowledge necessary to 'break with ideology' while at the same time also speaking in, and from within, ideology."[6] What else is passing than "speaking from within the ideology," breaking the rules, and showing mobility of identity? Both John and Rena do so in Chesnutt's novel.

[3] Chesnutt, *The House Behind the Cedars*, 170.

[4] Anzaldúa, Gloria. *Borderlands/La Frontera: The New Mestiza* (San Francisco; Aunt Lute Books, 1987), 89.

[5] Sandoval, Chela. *Methodology of the Oppressed* (Minneapolis: University of Minnesota Press, 2000), 43.

[6] Ibid., 44.

The House Behind the Cedars makes claims about two specific types of passing that it portrays: identificatory and performative. Identificatory passing involves a social and psychological identification with whiteness. In the case of identificatory passing, the passer embraces the identity of a white man/woman, along with its accompanying ideology—the way John Walden does in the novel. The identificatory passer crosses the color line with a clear intention not to come back to the black side, to his/her family and community. Identificatory passing is usually permanent and has mainly economic and social reasons, but to really identify with whiteness, the passer has to have a "white" intellectual background. Sandoval's concept is especially useful in discussing this type of passing: John is a "citizen-subject" who develops that mobility of identity needed to become socially mobile as well.

The other type of passing the novel depicts is performative. It is based on the view of race as performance—a matter of props, makeup, and/or behavior. The passer crosses the color line and "acts" white. Performative passing can be temporary (usually for economic reasons or for obtaining one's freedom), but it can also be permanent. In this case, the passer tries to find a means of reclaiming his/her double identity as both black and white, and he/she keeps ties with both communities, but is defined by neither on its own. This type of passing seems to present more opportunities to mine the system from within: the passer's liminality, his/her existence in two cultures (or on the Borderlands) renders visible the tenuousness of the binary system. Rena Walden illustrates this type of passing in Chesnutt's novel. The author's ambivalent views on the act itself and his critical attitude toward a system that makes passing necessary are also present in the depiction of these two types of passing.

Telling a passing story is in itself an act that challenges the racial status quo in America, an act that reveals a Borderland space which critiques the binary. In order to be effective, passing has to be surrounded by secrecy at all times. However, when a passer is "outed," the act produces anxiety in whites. A passing novel proves to a white contemporary reader how unstable racial identity really is, and how the Other can turn into the Same. *The House Behind the Cedars* was published in 1900; judging by the status of race relations at that time, it is neither difficult nor inaccurate to assume that reading about people crossing the color line caused many (white) readers to feel anxious about how tenable the race system was in America. For those used to thinking in racial binaries, it is unsettling to see how those binaries fail to account for the Borderland space between "black" and "white," the space that both John and Rena occupy at certain moments in the novel. Therefore, it is safe to say that perhaps the most subversive act of all is Chesnutt writing a passing story because he shows how easy it is for biracial individuals to cross the color line at will. Moreover, even though Rena is contained by the end of the novel, John's disappearing act makes him a threat to the system once more, since he presumably continues his personal war against the system.

In the novel, John is an identificatory passer because he initially models himself after his father—intellectually by reading his books, and racially, by convincing himself that he is white, despite the beatings he receives from the white boys in town. John's reasoning is built on his lack of physical "visible" marks of blackness: "His playmates may call him black; the mirror proved that God, the father of all, had made him white; and God, he had been taught, made no mistakes – having made him white, He must have meant him to be white."[7] John uses this mixture of religious devotion and empirical evidence to build the conviction that he is white. However, an identificatory passer does not merely pretend to be white, just as John does not merely perform whiteness. Since childhood, he has identified with "white" values and ideologies, from his father's books, from Molly's unwavering adoration of her white lover and admiration for all things white, and from witnessing race relations in his hometown. The narrator discusses John's rationale for passing:

> Once persuaded that he had certain rights, or ought to have them, by virtue of the laws of nature, in defiance of the customs of mankind, he has promptly sought to enjoy them with no troublesome qualms of conscience whatever.[8]

The narrator himself explains the difference between an identificatory and a performative passer. It lies in the distinction he makes between how John and Rena conceive of, and react to, passing. Both are aware of how unfair the system is, and both know they should have the same rights as all humans. Even so, Rena experiences those "troublesome qualms of conscience" (or what Anzaldúa calls "psychic restlessness"[9]), while John's self-conviction has helped him evade any remorse. His emotional self-defense

[7] Chesnutt, *The House Behind the Cedars*, 161.

[8] Ibid., 78.

[9] Anzaldúa, *Borderlands*, 100.

works to protect him from the trauma that is usually associated with a passer who decides to break away from family and community.

When analyzing John's return to his native Patesville after an absence of ten years, de Certeau's notions of "space" versus "place" are also useful in bringing to light the implications of Chesnutt's writing. John's walk through town gives Chesnutt the opportunity to run through a list of acts of injustice, exploitation, and discrimination, committed by whites against blacks. The town serves as a reminder of the hell John decided to leave, or his first battlefield. According to de Certeau, *place* represents a location that is controlled by the dominant culture, with rules that have to be respected by all the users. In contrast, *space* is wild, uncivilized, savage. Rules do not apply. It is temporary, and created within *places* by members of subordinate cultures, in order to cope with the rules set by the dominant culture. The connection with Sandoval's concept is clear: creating a *space* is a *tactic* of survival, which is done from within the dominant ideology. De Certeau argues: "The space of a tactic is the space of the other. Thus it must play on and with a terrain imposed on it and organized by the law of a foreign power. It is a maneuver 'within the enemy's field of vision' ... and within enemy territory."[10] Consequently, Patesville is enemy territory for John, and a *place* that is racially organized. He is able to see this organization because he is part of "the other," of those who were punished for transgressing the laws of the dominant system. *Place* and *strategy* go hand in hand, imposed by the dominant culture, while *tactics* and *spaces* are temporarily developed by the powerless in order to survive and cope with the system. It is a way of fighting the system from within. Thus, by displaying mobility of identity, a passer has the power to turn a *place* into a *space*, merely by being present where blacks are not allowed. The clue is within the reader's grasp all along: Patesville represents the *place* in which John has developed his *tactics* of beating the system. Because his racial identity is known in Patesville, John cannot transform this *place* into a *space*—not even for a short time, so he does that elsewhere. By placing a passer in a clearly racialized *place* that is established by, and belongs to, the dominant culture, Chesnutt is making the reader aware of the difficulties, as well as the subversive possibilities inherent in passing.

[10] Certeau, Michel de. *The Practice of Everyday Life* (Berkeley: University of California Press, 1984), 37.

Even though John experiences the town by remembering injustice, racism, and murder, by the end of the chapter, the reader is still kept in the dark about his racial makeup: Chesnutt seems reluctant to clarify it. William Andrews sees this as a strategy devised in order to win the reader's sympathy before John and Rena's racial identity is disclosed.[11] The racial ambiguity cultivated by Chesnutt in his characters is indeed destined to win the reader's sympathy, but also to make the reader question the validity of the one-drop rule and the black-white binary, although this will come into play only when Rena's racial identity is beyond any doubt. The very first clue in this respect is their mother's speech. Molly Walden speaks like the other African American characters in the novel, a fact that is discussed by the narrator with irony: "The corruption of the white people's speech was one element – only one – of the negro's unconscious revenge for his own debasement."[12] Thus, Molly's speech, along with the information that she is John's mother, should clue the reader in as to John's race. Even so, Chesnutt does not state it explicitly, so the ambiguity still exists, increased by references to a shameful secret in their past, which could be either their illegitimacy or their race. It is only in Chapter XVIII that Chesnutt tells the story of the affair between Molly Walden—"a free colored woman"—and a wealthy white man, which represents yet another border crossing and a bridge across the two sides.[13] So the reader learns that apart from illegitimacy, the secret that both brother and sister try to keep has to do with the fact that—according to the one-drop rule—they are legally black, and as such, subject to prejudice and discrimination.

The chapter "Under the Old Regime" contains the solution to the puzzle that Chesnutt has so carefully constructed for his reader in the previous chapters. It also discusses John's intellectual background, limited to the books that his father brought to the house behind the cedars: Fielding, Walter Scott, and many other European writers have built John's intellectual makeup and his outlook on the world. Had his father not been white, his learning would have been limited to what the black school taught him—something he quickly outgrows. With this background, John seems to be convinced that he is white, when—in a scene reminiscent of DuBois'

[11] Andrews, William. *The Literary Career of Charles W Chesnutt* (Baton Rouge: Louisiana State University Press, 1980), 159.

[12] Chesnutt, *The House Behind the Cedars*, 9.

[13] Chesnutt, *The House Behind the Cedars*, 155.

"fall into race"—he is told by white boys in the street that he is black. What is more, John is beaten into race: "When he had been beaten five or six times, he ceased to argue the point, though to himself he never admitted the change."[14] His own conviction that he is white is unwavering, not only because of his intellectual background, but also because his mother tries to erase any sign of blackness in her children (including "the wave" in Rena's hair).

The mental step that young John has to take after his discussion with Judge Straight, from acknowledging the one-drop rule to stating his intention to pass, is rendered by Chesnutt through the dialogue between the two characters. John's reply, "It is not right," referring to the one-drop rule, is followed by "I had thought . . . that I might pass for white. There are white people darker than me."[15] The narrator shares no personal comments about this exchange, although this is the defining moment of John's life. He recognizes the injustice and lack of logic of an arbitrary rule that boxes him into a rigid, limiting category, out of which there is no escape; he rebels against it; and finally he makes a decision to use his lack of "visible" markers of blackness as a tactic to become racially (and socially) mobile. It is in this very moment that he becomes a threat to the racial status quo because he questions its rules, and ultimately defies them, declaring war on a system that wants to break him.

There are two moments in John's story when he can be considered the most subversive, and this is one of them. His awareness of the possibility of moving between fixed identities, to be *in passing*, along with his decision to claim a space that—according to the laws of his state—is not his, make him threatening. Sandoval would call him a "citizen-subject" who learned to break the rules working from within the dominant ideology.[16] For a few moments, John is hovering between two identities, and his liminality renders the whole racial classification system inoperable—at least for him. Had he stayed in this space in between (or in the Borderlands), he would have been a bigger threat to the system than he is when passing. However, he chooses another fixed identity—albeit one that he assumes illegally—and here we can discuss another level of subversiveness. John turns into a spy in the enemy territory, and he uses the knowledge he gleans about white

[14] Ibid., 160.

[15] Chesnutt, *The House Behind the Cedars*, 170.

[16] Sandoval, *Methodology of the Oppressed*, 43.

society in order to infiltrate himself deeper in their midst. His initial tactic is unconventional: his discovery that he could pass, since he is not racially marked. Ultimately, the most important outcome of the meeting between John and Judge Straight is that John gets help and advice on how to bypass the law—develops the tactics he needs to beat the system from within. The fact that he "need not be black" in South Carolina—as opposed to North Carolina, where he was born—bespeaks the unexpected unevenness of the racial system that tries to cover the unstable nature of "pure" whiteness.

The tenuous nature of the racial system is part of American history. From the seventeenth century on, the American judicial system has made strenuous attempts to define and construct race in order to keep boundaries in place and to make biracial individuals visible as black. Teresa Zackodnik discusses some of these attempts, arguing that one of the reasons why the definitions and conceptions of race were so different and varied especially in the South was that biracial people posed a "corporeal challenge" to the system of racial classification, a challenge that a system based on a binary had enormous difficulties containing.[17] What is clear from all the constructs and definitions of race is that the main intention of the judicial system was to "police and enforce the limits of whiteness."[18] Luckily for John Walden, South Carolina laws seem to be more flexible when it comes to the one-drop rule, and he is not considered black there. But, as the judge tells him, it would be impossible for him to pass in Patesville, not only because he would break the law, but because he is known as Molly Walden's son. Finally, John turns eighteen and decides to leave Patesville and his former life behind, crossing two borders: the state border to South Carolina and the color line. Asked about him, his mother would only say that "he's gone over on the other side," which is an indication that she knows he is passing.[19]

The events of John's life in the ten years after he leaves Patesville are gleaned by the reader from what he tells his mother and Rena on the first night of his visit: during the Civil War, he worked as a manager of an estate where he ended up marrying the owner's daughter and inheriting all his wealth. He has also become a lawyer, so it seems that John Warwick has

[17] Zackodnik, Teresa. "Fixing the Color Line: The Mulatto, Southern Courts, and Racial Identity." *American Quarterly* 53.3 (2001): 422.

[18] Ibid., 423.

[19] Chesnutt, *The House Behind the Cedars*, 174.

achieved everything that John Walden dreamed of in the house behind the cedars. His infiltration into the white camp is now complete.

John Walden is a fascinating figure, partly because even Chesnutt seems to be ambivalent about him, and that is what makes the character very sophisticated, unlike any other passing figure portrayed before. To begin with, John may be read as a "traitor" to his race, because he models himself after his white father; he is also brought up by Molly, who thinks whites are superior; finally, he actually owns slaves for a short time after he inherits his father-in-law's fortune. Equally damning is the fact that, at first glance, John seems to accept racial classifications as long as the system defines him as white. It is true that he has moments when he rebels against the system: when he is beaten into race by the white boys and when he is angry that he has to hide in order to come visit his mother. The very fact that he returns to Patesville speaks in his favor. While Andrews argues that the reason for his return is to get Rena as a free governess for his son,[20] the narrator is clear on the reason for John's return: "an overmastering impulse had compelled him to seek the mother who had given him birth and the old town."[21] No matter how white-identified he might be, John is still thinking about the past and about the ones he left behind. With these arguments in his favor, Chesnutt still weighs facts against him: his identification with whiteness to the point where he owns slaves; the fact that he cut all ties with his mother and sister for ten years; and his thoughts that all the sacrifices he had made to obtain his status and wealth had been worth making.

Chesnutt describes John as a product of a system as cold and calculating as he appears to be. Without these character traits, the writer implies, he would not have succeeded. Chesnutt blames the system for creating John, since he has no choice but to pass in order to become a lawyer and fulfill his childhood dream. His position is one to be envied and coveted by others, and herein lies John's power and also his vulnerability. He is aware that keeping the secret of his origin is paramount, in order to keep his status, but at the same time, he feels lonely because of his situation, so Rena's presence in his life is welcome. He stands to lose everything that he has achieved so far if he is exposed as a passer, and there are two such moments in his life: first, when Rena wants to tell Tryon that she is passing (but John convinces her

[20] Andrews, *The Literary Career of Charles W. Chesnutt*, 150.

[21] Chesnutt, *The House Behind the Cedars*, 28.

not to), and second, when Tryon discovers Rena's true identity and her racial makeup and writes him a letter.

Given John Walden's character traits and the narrator's ambivalence toward him, the question remains: In what way(s) does he question and challenge the racial system? From the very beginning of the novel, the reader realizes that John is sharply aware of the gap the color line imposes between whites and African Americans. The reader sees him angry enough at the system to realize that John has been questioning it since his youth. The incident with the white boys who beat him up is also revealing. John is made aware of the existence of rigid racial categories and of the necessity to stay on "his" side of the color line. The fact that he decides—despite what he is told—to actually use his racial ambiguity and to become racially mobile makes him a threat to a system whose very existence depends on keeping African Americans "in their place." The moment he decides to pass for white is probably his most subversive act, because it finds him in the borderland between racial classifications. John's racial invisibility is the best weapon that he uses against the system. It renders him racially mobile, and the efforts to contain him are useless, since he can't be *seen* as a black man. Unlike his social mobility—which can be visualized as a vertical axis—his racial mobility represents a movement from one side to another on a horizontal continuum. This movement is not allowed by the racial system, but John is determined to infiltrate himself into the other camp, and his tactic is passing. He cannot be contained by the racial category "black."

Even though once he is passing for white, John seems to accept the racial system as long as he is on the white side of the color line, there is one more act that he performs which truly makes him subversive: his disappearance. After Tryon breaks his engagement to Rena because he finds out she is passing, John tries to convince her one more time to move away and start life under another (white) identity. Tryon's discovery does not deter John from making plans. He sees the opportunity to go away to another place where he can carve a space for himself and, possibly, his sister—a space where he can once more make himself invisible to the dominant culture. The advantage of a tactic, as de Certeau suggests, is that it is "determined by the absence of a proper locus."[22] As a citizen-subject, John is free to pick a safe location and develop his tactic in order to actualize a space for himself. It is another moment when he is mobile and between identities, on the

[22] De Certeau, 37.

Borderland. According to Charles Duncan, John's disappearing act may very well be his (and Chesnutt's) most subversive move in the novel:

> John's disappearance becomes an act of double passing, both textual and social. He fades out of the scope of the novel's plot while, more subversively, he disappears into (*not* out of) the culture at large.[23]

One of the last references to John in the novel is made by Molly—"My son's gone"—and his disappearance is bound to be unsettling, since John is no longer visible to the white reader.[24] John is meant to create questions and doubts in the minds of Chesnutt's readers because there could be others who are passing, thus further eroding the myth of pure whiteness.

As for the narrator's attitude toward passing, it is clarified in the chapter entitled "A Loyal Friend." He discusses critically how, in post-war America, "the taint of black blood was the unpardonable sin," dangerous especially when kept secret.[25] As much as he identifies with the dominant culture, John does not see his "black blood" as a sin. The opening lines of the novel attest to that, since the description of Patesville through John's eyes tells the reader that privately, John acknowledges his blackness. Aware that some of his readers might see passing as deceiving and as lying, Chesnutt challenges those readers and finds moral and political grounds for his characters' actions. By birth, they are Americans, so they should have the same rights as all Americans, but they are barred from those rights—and from fully developing to the best of their abilities—by being born on the "wrong" side of the color line. Chesnutt does not disapprove of passing because he sees it as a tactic to obtain their rights. He also sees it as an effect of how the racial system functions, as he notes in his journal:

> it was only natural for colored people to pass if they could as long as it had advantages for them. The only way to stop it was to give colored workmen and artists a chance to succeed without having to pass.[26]

[23] Duncan, Charles. *The Absent Man: The Narrative Craft of Charles W. Chesnutt*. (Athens: Ohio University Press, 1998), 15.

[24] Chesnutt, *The House Behind the Cedars*, 187.

[25] Chesnutt, *The House Behind the Cedars*, 127.

[26] Qtd in Gartner, Carol B. "Charles W. Chesnutt: Novelist of a Cause." in *Critical Essays on Charles W. Chesnutt*, ed. Joseph R McElrath, Jr. (New York: G. K. Hall & Co., 1999), 163–4.

Passing is not lying or betraying, Chesnutt argues. On the contrary, "to undertake what they tried to do required great courage."[27] He implies that by discriminating against African Americans, the system itself has brought about a phenomenon like passing, and that the passers are nothing short of courageous to take such risks.

If John has enough resources to move away and recreate himself, the situation is different for Rena Walden. The reader sees Rena for the first time through John's (incestuous) gaze. He sees Rena in town and does not recognize her, and is attracted by her beauty. Believing that she is white, he follows her through the town. He realizes who she is when she unknowingly leads him to the house behind the cedars.

At first sight, Rena's attitude toward racial classification is—to a certain extent—similar to John's. She perceives the injustice of being boxed into a binary system: "As Rena listened, the narrow walls that hemmed her in seemed to draw closer and closer, as though they must crush her."[28] She feels—almost physically—the pressure of having to fit in a category that cannot account for her identity. Unlike John, who is portrayed as active, Rena appears more passive in the first half of the novel. One possible reason why Chesnutt portrays Rena as passive is that he wants to prove how innocent people are caught in, and crushed by, a relentless and inadequate binary system. She dies in the end not necessarily because she has to atone for the sins of her father, but because she is the tool that Chesnutt uses to criticize and condemn the system.

Unlike John, Rena becomes a performative passer. Performative passing is based on the view of race as performance—a matter of props, makeup, and/or behavior. Rena approaches passing in a different way than John because she does not have the same intellectual background and convictions as her brother. Molly tells John that Rena does not "take to books" the way he did, probably because—as a woman of those times—Rena was never expected to be an intellectual.[29] While John convinced himself that he was white, Rena does not seem to think so. She intends to keep her ties with her community even after she leaves with her brother: "'You don't think, Frank,' asked Rena severely, 'that I would leave my mother and my home

[27] Chesnutt, *The House Behind the Cedars*, 128.

[28] Chesnutt, *The House Behind the Cedars*, 23.

[29] Ibid., 18.

and all my friends, and *never* come back again?'"[30] Even though Rena intends to keep contact with her mother and her friends, she realizes as well that she has to do so covertly. Her departure itself was unannounced, and she stays hidden during the trip to her brother's estate.

Rena's journey represents much more than a physical move from Patesville to Clarence, South Carolina. It is a journey that takes her up on the social scale and over the color line, from one side of the racial continuum to the other. The time she spends locked in her cabin is the time she spends between racial classifications, when her racial mobility is asserted. Ironically, this is the time she dwells on the Borderlands, when her liminality gives her freedom from any and all classifications. The cabin on the ship, then, is a place, and as such, it is subject to the rules and strategies imposed by the dominant culture. Rena's presence, however, re-actualizes the cabin as a space, where the rules of the dominant system and her relation to them are temporarily suspended, and her tactics of resistance and infiltration are developed. It is interesting to note that even at home, in her space, Rena feels constricted, so she feels the same in the one she creates in the cabin. The fact that Rena does not seem to feel completely at home in any of her spaces seems to foreshadow the tragic ending of the novel.

The psychology of being in-between is brilliantly explained by Anzaldúa in her mention of the "fear of going home" and of what people on the Borderlands do in order to avoid rejection: "conform to the values of the culture, push the unacceptable parts into the shadows."[31] It is what Rena does during her trip to John's estate at a great emotional cost to her. She undergoes an "inner war,"[32] as she tries to cope with her separation from her mother and her community and she prepares to take up a role she has never played before—that of a white woman. Unlike John—who does not seem to care for regrets and emotional farewells—Rena feels uprooted. The maid on the ship sees that she has been crying: "'Po'chile,' murmured the sympathetic colored woman. 'I reckon some er her folk is dead ...'"[33] Indeed, for all intents and purposes, Rena's folk are dead, and she suffers from homesickness already.

[30] Chesnutt, *The House Behind the Cedars*, 39.

[31] Anzaldúa, *Borderlands*, 42.

[32] Ibid., 100.

[33] Chesnutt, *The House Behind the Cedars*, 41.

Thus, while Rena Walden enters the ship's cabin in Patesville, Rowena Warwick emerges from it at Wilmington, and is sent to a boarding school where she will learn all the skills she needs to be a "lady." The difference between John and his sister is clear by now: his whiteness is a matter of self-conviction and identification with Euro-American culture, while Rena has to be taught everything. She has to perform whiteness, since she still identifies with everything she left behind in Patesville. Her weapon against the system is the same as her brother's, however: the lack of racial markings which makes her invisible to whites. Rena needs to learn how to "act white," since being "white" is only an act for her. The year spent in the finishing school readies her to play Rowena Warwick, the sister of rich (and white) John Warwick. On her first public appearance, she catches the eye of George Tryon, which makes her brother comment: "Well, Rena, you have arrived. ... You are winning the first fruits of your opportunity."[34] John's choice of words is interesting: he refers to Rena's goals in spatial terms. To be a white woman, then, is to "arrive" at a certain locus that would grant her everything she wanted. Literally, Rena receives recognition as a rich white woman in a very public place (the reenactment of a medieval tournament, and the parallels with Walter Scott's *Ivanhoe* are obvious), which is definitely functioning under rules imposed by the dominant culture. However, John's words indicate to her that there is the possibility of strategically creating one's own space that does not follow the rules of the larger place.

As a performative passer, Rena has managed to play her role so well that not only is she taken for a white woman, but she is proclaimed the ideal white woman—the Queen of Love and Beauty—by white and wealthy George Tryon, who goes as far as to propose to her. However, even though Rena has fallen in love with George, she does not feel free enough to set a wedding date because she feels like she is lying to George by not disclosing to him her racial makeup.

Even though she eventually decides to marry Tryon, Rena remains a performative passer. The narrator dwells on the oppressiveness of her secret, compounded with her homesickness. Unlike John, Rena actually keeps in touch with her mother and she retains her old beliefs, and this makes her a Borderland dweller. That is why she trusts the dreams she has about her mother dying, later proven to be true. Ferguson argues that because of her "superstitious ignorance," Rena cannot keep her status. She is portrayed as a

[34] Ibid., 57–8.

"postbellum naïf," and her fault is that she tries to stay "psychologically black" while she passes.[35] It is true that Rena stays "psychologically black" while she passes, if that means keeping in touch with her mother, and through her, with the community she had left. That is the main characteristic that makes her a performative passer, after all, as opposed to John. However, Chesnutt does not find this a fault with Rena (as Ferguson implies), nor does he dismiss these dreams as ignorant superstitions. In both *The House Behind the Cedars* and *The Conjure Woman*, Chesnutt considers premonitions and dreams as intrinsic parts of African American culture. Thus, Rena is maintaining the ties that keep her close to her African American roots and her liminality.

As a performative passer, Rena has a certain subversive power, but also a tremendous vulnerability. In fact, her power is contingent on her vulnerability, for while Rena's power consists in her looks, in her ability to unsettle whites and create racial anxiety, it is—paradoxically—manifested primarily when Tryon finds out she is passing. Chesnutt carefully describes Tryon's emotional turmoil and his wavering between anger, disgust, and horror at the realization that he had been about to commit "the unpardonable sin against his race of marrying her"[36] (143). Fueling his anxiety about blacks seems to work for Tryon, as he tries to convince himself that a marriage with Rena would never have been a viable option. At the center of this anxiety is, of course, Rena—living proof that the color line has been crossed before, and "an example of how permeable the boundary between races [is]."[37] Through her visibility, Rena has unknowingly threatened the very existence of the color line, since she has the possibility to dwell on either side of it.

After the shock of her broken engagement wears off, Rena's decision to teach at a black school brings her to Tryon's neighborhood, although neither of them is aware of that initially. According to Andrews, Rena's fate from this point of the novel is similar to that of other heroines of passing novels and conforms to the conventions of the tragic mulatta fiction.[38] However, it is important to discuss the way Rena makes white people

[35] Ferguson, SallyAnn. "Rena Walden: Chesnutt's Failed 'Future American.'" In McElrath, *Critical Essays*, 201.

[36] Chesnutt, *The House Behind the Cedars*, 143.

[37] Cathy Boeckmann – *A Question of Character: Scientific Racism and the Genres of American Fiction, 1892–1912.* (Tuscaloosa: The University of Alabama Press, 2000), 32.

[38] Andrews, *The Literary Career*, 167.

uncomfortable, albeit unintentionally. On her way to her school, she has to explain to several inquiring whites that she is black. As soon as she offers the explanation, nobody questions it—as Chesnutt bitterly comments—since "no white person of sound mind would ever claim to be a Negro."[39] Rena is constantly subjected to scrutiny from whites because her appearance represents a source of concern and insecurity. She is repeatedly asked to "declare" her racial identity, even by Tryon's mother, who pays her a visit to the schoolhouse because she is "interested in the colored people."[40] As the ones who uphold the binary system, whites feel uneasy about ambiguity because any blurring of the border between races would question their (imagined and self-asserted) superiority, which is to be manifested in the racial binary. It is interesting to note that, had she been passing, Rena would not have caused any anxiety in whites because her "blackness" would have been invisible; it is her refusal to do so in this instance that causes unease.

Discussing Rena's vulnerability as a young African American woman, Boeckmann argues that the scene where she is pursued by Tryon and Wain

> is a metaphor for the twin vulnerabilities of her position. When she rejects both her suitors and sets into the uncharted swamp, she succumbs both to the powerlessness of her gender position and the liminality of her racial identity.[41]

To this I add M. Giulia Fabi's very apt comment, "the once-Queen of Love and Beauty will turn into a fugitive slave pursued by obtrusive suitors turned slave catchers."[42] At this point in her life, Rena has managed to heal her wounds and to become an independent professional woman. She does not want Wain, a wife abuser who is looking for another mother for his children and a free servant. Neither does she want Tryon, who has finally realized that he loves her in spite of her race, because she realizes that a life with Tryon would submit her to constant scrutiny, if not from him, then from others around him, and she does not want to pass again. Rena's acceptance of either man means also accepting one or another rigid racial classification—white if she accepts Tryon and black if she accepts Wain. It is quite possible that

[39] Chesnutt, *The House Behind the Cedars*, 229.

[40] Chesnutt, *The House Behind the Cedars*, 239.

[41] Boeckmann, *A Question of Character*, 166.

[42] Fabi, Giulia M. *Passing and the Rise of the African American Novel* (Urbana: University of Illinois Press, 2001), 79.

Rena feels the need of being in between, of having both her black and her white blood accounted for, which would not have been possible with either man. Her escape into the unknown territory of the swamp (which in itself is an ambiguous space, both water and land) is an expression of her attempts to cope with her complex identity, which is still an unknown territory to her, a space beyond the places of the white and black parts of the town. Thus, her tragic end begs the question: Why do Rena's "in-between" moments end up by being so fatally confining? Rena's death is Chesnutt's critique of the binary racial system: it makes it impossible for biracial individuals to exist on the Borderlands. They either have to be classified as "black" or have to pass for white. Since for Rena passing was a traumatic experience, she tries to stay outside classifications, but she cannot survive there. Chesnutt is highly critical of the racist system in America, to the extent of showing how innocent people fall victim to it because of its relentless attempts to contain and control. There is no end in sight—Chesnutt seems to contend—unless segregation and racial prejudice are abolished.

The author tries to educate his white readers against the dangers of believing that passing is an endeavor that is always doomed to failure, and that all biracial people fit the stereotype of the tragic mulatto. These positions, meant to reassure the whites, were prevalent in the works of his contemporary Southern white writers Thomas Dixon and Thomas Nelson Page. He is also trying to show them what happens when innocents are trapped in a binary system. In Chesnutt's own words,

> The object of my writings would be not so much the elevation of the colored people as the elevation of the whites ... a moral revolution which must be brought about in a different manner. The subtle almost indefinable feeling of repulsion toward the Negro, which is common to most Americans – cannot be stormed and taken by assault; the garrison will not capitulate, so their position must be mined, and we will find ourselves in their midst before they think it.[43]

Chesnutt uses a war vocabulary—"storm," "assault," "garrison," "revolution"—to describe the walls that white supremacy has built in order to protect whites, and the actions needed to tear them down. He recommends stealth and secrecy—and what better way to infiltrate an enemy camp than telling the story of passing, of people who have secretly

[43] Qtd in Ames, Russell. "Social Realism in Charles W. Chesnutt," in McElrath, *Critical Essays*, 149.

crossed the color line, "mined" the positions of the whites, and lived among them, undetected? If his own characters are subversive—each in their own way—telling the story of passing must be the most subversive act of all because not only does he achieve his goal of educating his readers, but he also manages to render them uneasy. By portraying John and Rena as intelligent, articulate, and capable of holding their own in the wealthy white world, Chesnutt contradicts all the tenets of scientific racism that he discusses in the novel, and renders his white readers uncomfortable. Moreover, in creating a character like John, so different from the typical tragic mulatto, Chesnutt thwarts the expectations of his white readership, while "the novel's final silence concerning John's whereabouts sends an inflammatory message to that very audience."[44]

While himself of mixed ancestry, Chesnutt focuses his attention on characters that challenge the American racial system and question its functionality and validity. White Southern writers who focused on biracial characters (Page, Dixon) have typically represented them as "a dangerous element among the freedmen, [as a] despoiler of white womanhood, the corruptor of white gentlemen, and the usurper of political power," according to Penelope Bullock.[45] Chesnutt changes this image by portraying dignified and intelligent characters who can use their lack of "visible" marks of blackness as a tactic to escape white scrutiny. They actualize spaces where they can use their silent tactics and create a better life for themselves. But perhaps more than his characters' invisibility, racial mobility, and infiltration into the "enemy camp," Chesnutt's telling of their story is unsettling to white readers, to the extent of making them question the validity of "pure" whiteness and of a binary racial system that is unforgiving and bent on containing African Americans and people of mixed ancestry into one narrow racial category. *The House Behind the Cedars* does its share in "elevating" whites, educating them about the identity struggles of biracial individuals, because even if John seems at home in the white world, Rena cannot seem to find her place on either side of the color line. Telling the story of passing forces the reader to ask anxious and uncomfortable questions about "real" cases of passing, about the binary's ability to contain the passers, about its validity in general. If Chesnutt's readers asked themselves these questions, then the novel has fulfilled one of

[44] Duncan, Charles. *The Absent Man: The Narrative Craft of Charles W. Chesnutt.* (Athens: Ohio University Press, 1998), 15–16.

[45] Bullock, Penelope. "The Mulatto in American Fiction," in McElrath, *Critical Essays*, 142.

its author's aims: to "mine" the positions of the whites that seemed so stable and so unapproachable before, or, in Chesnutt's words, "I hope the book may raise some commotion."[46]

Bibliography

Ames, Russell. 1999. Social Realism in Charles W. Chesnutt. In *Critical Essays on Charles W. Chesnutt*, ed. Joseph R. McElrath Jr., 147–155. New York: G. K. Hall & Co.

Andrews, William. 1980. *The Literary Career of Charles W. Chesnutt*. Baton Rouge: Louisiana State University Press.

Anzaldúa, Gloria. 1987. *Borderlands/La Frontera: The New Mestiza*. San Francisco: Aunt Lute Books.

Boeckmann, Cathy. 2000. *A Question of Character: Scientific Racism and the Genres of American Fiction, 1892–1912*. Tuscaloosa: The University of Alabama Press.

Bullock, Penelope. 1999. The Mulatto in American Fiction. In *Critical Essays on Charles W. Chesnutt*, ed. Joseph R. McElrath Jr., 142–147. New York: G. K. Hall & Co.

Chesnutt, Charles W. 1968. *The House Behind the Cedars*. Ridgewood: The Gregg Press.

de Certeau, Michel. 1984. *The Practice of Everyday Life*. Berkeley: University of California Press.

Duncan, Charles. 1998. *The Absent Man: The Narrative Craft of Charles W. Chesnutt*. Athens: Ohio University Press.

Fabi, Giulia M. 2001. *Passing and the Rise of the African American Novel*. Urbana: University of Illinois Press.

Ferguson, SallyAnn. 1999. Rena Walden: Chesnutt's Failed 'Future American'. In *Critical Essays on Charles W. Chesnutt*, ed. Joseph R. McElrath Jr., 198–205. New York: G. K. Hall & Co.

Fredrickson, George M. 2002. *Racism: A Short History*. Princeton: Princeton University Press.

Gartner, Carol B. 1999. Charles W. Chesnutt: Novelist of a Cause. In *Critical Essays on Charles W. Chesnutt*, ed. Joseph R. McElrath Jr., 155–170. New York: G. K. Hall & Co.

Sandoval, Chela. 2000. *Methodology of the Oppressed*. Minneapolis: University of Minnesota Press.

Zackodnik, Teresa. 2001. Fixing the Color Line: The Mulatto, Southern Courts, and Racial Identity. *American Quarterly* 53 (3): 420–451.

[46] Qtd. in Gartner, "Charles W. Chesnutt," 164.

PART III

Borderlands of Sexuality and Gender

Queering and Gendering Aztlán: Anzaldúa's Feminist Reshaping of the Chicana/o Nation in the US–Mexico Borderlands

Tereza Jiroutová Kynčlová

The Chicana/o Movement's neglect of gender-related issues and its tacit imperative of heteronormativity earned the political platform a well-articulated criticism from Chicana feminists.[1] Besides the myopic political agenda of androcentrism, Chicanas targeted *El Movimiento's* exclusionary nationalism as well as the biased symbolic representation of the emergent nation as engendered by Aztlán—the originary, patriarchal fatherland. A counterhegemonic, non-nationalist example of a feminist reconceptualization of the mythical homeland is Gloria Anzaldúa's subversive portrayal of her relationship to the region that stretches from the Valley in South Texas to the shores of the Pacific Ocean. It is an area that is both integral to the mythical *patria* and, concurrently, spans the entire length of the US–Mexico border. She combines the narratives of "grand histories" with the seeming ordinariness of stories of her family's daily agricultural routines, thereby undermining the authority of Western versions of (masculinist) history. Moreover, the traditional, patriarchal familial sphere—a miniature analogy to nation—is toppled by the author's

[1] Cf. Alma García, ed., *Chicana Feminist Thought: The Basic Historical Writings* (London and New York: Routledge, 1997).

T. Jiroutová Kynčlová (✉)
Charles University, Prague, Czech Republic

J. Elbert Decker, D. Winchock (eds.), *Borderlands and Liminal Subjects*, https://doi.org/10.1007/978-3-319-67813-9_8

broadening of the concept of the family as an inclusive, non-heteronormative, and relational alliance.

Fencing at San Diego/Tijuana Divide

Anzaldúa's Aztlán is introduced in the first chapter *of Borderlanads/La Frontera—The New Mestiza* in a complex manner that in fact concerns the critical concepts she devises so as to navigate and explicate her Chicana feminist identity politics communicated throughout her writing career. The argumentation unfolds with a preludial poem in which Anzaldúa sees herself standing by the rusty fence she later claims her home, upon which the salty waters of the Pacific wash, break, and gnaw it away. The iron structure in San Diego's Border Field Park literally lacerates the urban agglomeration of the Californian metropolis and Mexican Tijuana, or more graphically, it embodies the border where "the Third World grates against the first and bleeds."[2] To the writer, the border represents the following:

> 1,950 mile-long open wound
> dividing a *pueblo*, a culture,
> running down the length of my body,
> staking fence rods in my flesh,
> splits me splits me
> *me raja* *me raja*
> This is my home
> this thin edge of
> barbwire [...]
> This land was Mexican once,
> was Indian always
> and is.
> And will be again.[3]

The colonial mixture of the "brown blood" Anzaldúa evokes earlier in the poem that oozes from the "1.950 mile-long open wound" that "divid[es] a pueblo, a culture, running down the length of [the writer's] body, staking fence rods in [her] flesh" brings together—despite the agony conveyed—two

[2] Gloria Anzaldúa, *Borderlands/La Frontera: The New Mestiza* (San Francisco: Aunt Lute, 1999), 25.

[3] Ibid., 24–25.

worlds and forms "a third country – a border culture."[4] This single poem thus outlines the principal concepts of Anzaldúan thought such as the constructedness of the border, borderlands, border culture, *mestizaje*, hybridity, gendered embodiment, location, and their potential transpositions.

If for Homi Bhabha everything starts at the border as he implies invoking Heidegger in the very opening lines of *The Location of Culture*,[5] it certainly does so for Anzaldúa. Most of the aforementioned concepts are engaged in the following excerpt from the poem partially quoted above. It actually commences on the first page of the introductory chapter of *Borderlands/La Frontera*—the opening page being both symbolically and formally a border in its own right.

> I walk through the hole in the fence
> to the other side.
> Under my fingers I feel the gritty wire
> rusted by 139 years[6]
> of the salty breath of the sea.
> Beneath the iron sky
> Mexican children kick their soccer ball across,
> run after it, entering the U.S.[7]

The poem's subject matter provides a blueprint for interpreting Anzaldúa's transformation of "the abject identity into which she has been interpellated into a resistant identity, intent on exposing and dismantling the history of oppression to which both her identity and the border stand as citations."[8] The space left out immediately before and after "I walk" in the first line of the passage itself represents the activity Anzaldúa describes she is doing; it marks the distance traveled *to* the border fence from somewhere within the USA—presumably her home state of Texas, and *through* the

[4] Ibid.

[5] Homi, Bhabha, *The Location of Culture* (London and New York: Routledge, 1994), 1.

[6] At the time of the writing of *Borderlands/La Frontera – The New Mestiza*, 139 years had elapsed since the Treaty of Guadalupe-Hidalgo that established the US–Mexico border in its current form.

[7] Anzaldúa, *Borderlands/La Frontera*, 24.

[8] Robert McRuer, *The Queer Renaissance: Contemporary American Literature and the Reinvention of Lesbian and Gay Identities* (New York: University of New York Press, 1997), 128.

border fence into Mexico, without leaving Aztlán. Thus, the author can claim the border to be her home as mentioned earlier. At the same time, the space between the words points to the hole in the fence as well as to the slit, the open wound incurred by the artificial presence of the man-made iron structure. Further, the exact counting of years since the delimitation of the border alerts us to Anzaldúa's awareness of the grand history of what in Aztlán is perceived as a double colonial conquest executed through Spanish/European *conquista* and later US imperial and capitalist imposition. The poem ruptures the grandness of this history, which is often attributed to global significance, by the everyday triviality of children's accidental kicking of the soccer ball across the border to, officially, a foreign country. Anzaldúa's analogy between her walking to Mexico and the soccer ball entering the USA thoroughly demonstrates her disrespect both for the artificial and arbitrary border and for the historical master narratives that relegate Chicanas'/os' multiple otherness beyond the realm of accepted and respected existence.

The painful, bleeding wound caused by the fence rods, which metaphorically represent the ongoing historical oppression and that invade the writer's body, her *pueblo* (people) and her culture, also stands at the roots of resistance. Consequently, Anzaldúa's oppositional articulation of Chicana counterhegemonic thought dismisses the arbitrary division of "us" versus "them" that the "steel curtain [...] crowned with rolled barbed wire, rippling from the sea where Tijuana touches San Diego" both metaphorically and materially represents.[9] The binarism performed by the chain-link fence also points to its inherent failure; any attempt at unequivocal division always produces groups of people who do not fit into either category. Or as the poem aptly reminds us, "the skin of the earth is seamless, the sea cannot be fenced, *el mar* does not stop at borders."[10]

Here, the sea, of course, stands for the Pacific Ocean, or the human race in general, but more specifically it may also symbolize the peoples of the Americas, i.e. the waves of immigrants making the United States the vastly diverse society it conceives of itself to be. Moreover, in yet another interpretative twist the sea may represent Emma Lazarus' "tired, [...] poor, [and] huddled masses yearning to breathe free" greeted by the Statue of

[9] Anzaldúa, *Borderlands/La Frontera*, 24.
[10] Ibid., 25.

Liberty upon arrival to Ellis Island.[11] But, on the opposite, western shore, the looming "Tortilla Curtain,"—Anzaldúa's apparent reference to the Iron Curtain once fracturing Europe—discourages migration across the US Southern border. The Pacific here, unlike the Atlantic, is not a sea of promise, but a sea of limits. It embodies the final frontier beyond which there is no farther/further expansion. The Pacific hems the Anglo myth of Manifest Destiny, but what tacitly matters in the migrant influx evoked by Anzaldúa's poem are the incomers' countries of origin and their racial backgrounds.

The celebrated and acknowledged historical European inflow establishing the United States as a Western power on the one hand, conflicts with the contemporary Mexican and Latin-American immigration that is government-, military-, and vigilantes-targeted on the US–Mexico border on the other hand. This oblique cultural and racist/racial double standard is, however, undercut by the fact that the events in Border Field Park are taking place on Easter Sunday, which brings about the "resurrection of the brown blood in [the writer's] veins."[12] The poem, in other words, gradually evokes a sort of redemption, or at least recognition, brought about by the strategic re-vision of the abject, i.e. migrant, mestiza/o identity. By association with the Christian concept of Jesus' resurrection where salvation applies to all individuals, regardless of socially constructed categories, the poem conveys a subtle hope for the settlement of historical inequalities. The claim to land that "was Mexican once [and] Indian always [...] and will be again" supports the need for historical, cultural, and social re-evaluation of the presence of postcolonial, native, and/or indigenous subjects in US society and culture.[13]

Anzaldúa's walking with ease across the San Diego/Tijuana divide corresponds with her free-flowing switching between English and Spanish. To Anzaldúa, transgressing and crossing borders are fundamental steps which must be taken so that a new epistemology reflective of her specific position can be arrived at. Both the contents and the form of the poem in terms of its layout as well as language alternation buttress her message. Anzaldúa consistently tries to diminish the significance of the border by exposing its

[11] Emma Lazarus, "*The New Colossus,*" *National Park Service*, Accessed December 18, 2016, https://www.nps.gov/stli/learn/historyculture/colossus.htm

[12] Anzaldúa, *Borderlands/La Frontera*, 24.

[13] Anzaldúa, *Borderlands/La Frontera*, 25.

triviality and arbitrariness, but she is well aware that no effortless and easy stepping across is actually possible. She illustrates this by stories of (racial) misrecognition. The issue is voiced in a grotesque and rather tragic story of Anzaldúa's relative Pedro, a fifth-generation American, whom *la migra* thinks to be an illegal Mexican immigrant. While working on the fields near the border, Pedro fails to show the Immigration and Naturalization Service officers his documents proving his US citizenship for he never carries them to work. His primary language being Spanish together with his being unable to find proper English words to explain his situation, the youth is deported by plane to Guadalajara, Mexico, although the "deepest [he'd] ever been to Mexico was Reynosa, a small border town opposite Hidalgo, Texas, not far from McAllen."[14] Anzaldúa's deliberate deconstruction of the border then springs from the concept's intended purpose and signification, i.e. its supposed capacity to provide lucid, clear-cut separations and categorizations. As Pedro's case shows, however, rather than producing two distinct entities, the demarcation line paradoxically contributes to beclouding of the immanent differences on either side of the border.

Robert McRuer correctly reads Anzaldúa's rendering of her and Pedro's mestiza/o identity not as an attempt to show that this identity *automatically* works toward disruption of institutions invested in maintaining the border status quo, such as the Immigration and Naturalization Service, even though its hybrid character challenges cultural and racial purity. To him, Anzaldúan thought is a representation of a process whereby the mestiza grasps and navigates all her multiple identities "as results of unsuccessful attempts to divide people and transposes the meaning of those identities, turning them against ongoing attempts to maintain hierarchical divisions."[15] The border is thus a marker of Chicanas'/os' otherness that claims them in their very native region.

In the US—Mexico borderlands, mestiza/o racial identity severely complicates Chicanas'/os' everyday life and equally impedes their relationship to their nation, homeland, and home. Encounters such as the one resembling Pedro's that consistently reiterate misrecognition and denial of belonging from the majority US society constitute a part of Chicana/o existence. This has caused many Chicanas/os to internalize—as McRuer[16]

[14] Ibid., 26.

[15] McRuer, *The Queer Renaissance*, 131.

[16] Ibid., 128.

and Aldama[17] go to great lengths to word it in Julia Kristeva's psychoanalytical terms—the abject racial identity. Anzaldúa describes the self-loathing as "the agony of inadequacy" and elaborates: "we Chicanos blame ourselves, hate ourselves, terrorize ourselves. Most of this goes on unconsciously; we only know that we are hurting, we suspect that there is something 'wrong' with us, something fundamentally wrong."[18]

Reproduction of External Oppression on the Inside and Queer Resistance

Although the complexes Chicanas/os grapple with are attributable to the colonial and capitalist history or multiple external oppressions, Anzaldúa also denounces the internal hierarchies existing within her own folk. As McRuer notes, Anzaldúa initially shows how "subjects are cast into abject positions as a result of binary thinking and how identities emerge as casualties of oppression," but she does not yet quite hint at whether such "locations might be transformed into sites of resistance."[19] The internal investigation of Chicana/o interior otherings is the subject matter of "*Movimientos de rebeldí a y las culturas que traicionan* (Movements of rebellion and cultures of betrayal)." As the chapter title suggests, Anzaldúa accentuates the depreciation and ostracism that takes place inside the Chicana/o society and exposes it with the same thrust as she exposes the external, mostly race- and culture-related pressures. While the failed racial profiling performed by the Immigration and Naturalization Service officers from outside the writer's community primarily targets Pedro for his brown-skinned appearance, Anzaldúa ethnicity is just one of the categories that needs to be negotiated by Chicanas/os:

> I abhor some of my culture's ways, how it cripples its women, *como burras*, our strengths used against us, lowly *burras* bearing humility with dignity. The ability to serve, claim the males, is our highest virtue. I abhor how my culture makes macho caricatures of its men. No, I don't buy all the myths of the tribe into which I was born. I will not glorify those aspects of my culture which have injured me and which have injured me in the name of protecting me.[20]

[17] Arturo J. Aldama, "Millennial Anxieties: Borders, Violence and the Struggle for Chicana/o Subjectivity," *Arizona Journal of Hispanic Cultural Studies* 2 (1998): 52.

[18] Anzaldúa, *Borderlands/La Frontera*, 26.

[19] McRuer, *The Queer Renaissance*, 139.

[20] Anzaldúa, *Borderlands/La Frontera*, 43–44.

It is apparent that gender-related norms are central to the author's critique. Remaining faithful to the chapter's title, Anzaldúa explains how (specifically women's) sexuality is turned into a locus of Chicana/o culture's betrayal and reprimand of its females while also providing a potential for resistance to such a treatment via queerness and non-hierarchical collectivity. Thus, Anzaldúa's defying of heteronormativity, androcentric tenets of social organization, and Chicana/o patriarchal familial structures suggests a challenge to established conceptualizations of commonality and nation based on gender difference.[21]

The writer's queer identity—declared a willed choice—is a parallel to what she coins in the concluding chapter of *Borderlands/La Frontera* as mestiza consciousness. The concept crowns the transformation of hybrid identity in terms of recognition and embrace of all sorts of conflicting affiliations and contradictions on a collective, communal level.[22] Similarly, Anzaldúa's employment of queerness is at the outset individual as she deals with the sphere of her family, and only then is the personal aspect replaced with the collective and alliance-building quality of queer identity. The author thus proceeds from the singular to the plural, but she constantly ascertains that her argument is contextualized and soundly situated so that generalizations are avoided. To put it differently, queerness and mestiza consciousness are indivisible from one another; in Anzaldúan thought they both share transformative functions and come together in similar disruptive and liminal ways.[23]

The breach of the compulsory heterosexuality imperative comprises the greatest jeopardy to *El Movimiento*'s nationalist agenda in particular and the Chicana/o people's cultural integrity in general. Anzaldúa is well aware of the threat that an undermining, non-compliant sexuality in women (as cultural transmitters and reproducers) poses for the nationalist as well as familial discourses. She therefore wields it as yet another tool with which to question hierarchies and internal discrimination within her community. To put it differently, queer identity exposes the duality and limits of the Chicana/o family ideology which—should all its logical outcomes and

[21] Cf. Anne McClintock, "Family Feuds: Gender, Nationalism and the Family," *Feminist Review* 44 (1993): 61–80. Nira Yuval-Davis, *Gender & Nation* (London, Thousand Oaks: SAGE Publications, 2005).

[22] Anzaldúa, *Borderlands/La Frontera*, 109.

[23] McRuer, *The Queer Renaissance*, 142, 143, 153.

consequences be taken into account—render love and respect no longer unconditional (contrarily to the beliefs regarding parental and/or romantic love one is socialized to adhere to and identify with, as Ulrich Beck and Elisabeth Beck-Gernsheim minutely demonstrate in their study *The Normal Chaos of Love*), but dependent on one's becoming a subject of and to patriarchy and heteronormativity. By no means is this a unique observation; the history of feminism engenders a tradition of revealing the highly political and public aspects of the seemingly private, domestic sphere. Having been "raised Catholic and indoctrinated as straight, [Anzaldúa] made the choice to be queer" claiming queerness as both an effective means of relating to the world and other people and as a political means, whereby she reaches an epistemological vantage point not dissimilar to the positionality of hybrid, border subjects occupying the ambiguous US–Mexican borderlands.[24] Or as McRuer summarizes it, "Anzaldúa's work puts into play a new and transgressive identity but at the same time resists mere transgression for transgression's sake."[25]

A key aspect of Anzaldúa's identity arises: being able to make a choice concerning her queerness, the author exposes her identity as strategically constructed, politically charged, and contextually negotiated. Simultaneously, Anzaldúa points out, she imbues it consciously with "the coming together of opposite qualities within," a stance perfectly aligned with the aforementioned notion of mestiza consciousness.[26] She acknowledges that "[f]or a lesbian of color, the ultimate rebellion she can make against her native culture is through her sexual behavior. She goes against two moral prohibitions: sexuality and homosexuality."[27] Queer self-identification enables her to attack the tacit normativity of gender and sexual duality that causes trauma in queer persons and their families (and the nation, by extension), which as a consequence may undermine the politics of recognition within Chicana/o familial structures of kinship and their love for family members. By so doing, Anzaldúa criticizes the social dictates that pressure us to choose loyalties restrictively only within the Western binary system as she states: "What we are suffering from is an absolute despot duality that

[24] Anzaldúa, *Borderlands/La Frontera*, 41.

[25] McRuer, *The Queer Renaissance*, 128.

[26] Anzaldúa, *Borderlands/La Frontera*, 41.

[27] Ibid.

says we are able to be only one or the other. It claims that human nature is limited and cannot evolve into something better."[28]

Anzaldúa's queer mestiza defiance of hindering categories of social organization and normative institutional power actually unmasks this "despot duality" or repression—thoroughly in line with Foucault's dispersion of power and resistance described in *The History of Sexuality*—as productive or as one "giving rise to new forms of behaviour rather than simply closing down or censoring certain forms of behaviour."[29] In this regard, the writer performing her queer identity may be interpreted as a productive effect of her navigating the constant negotiation of power and resistance as universally suggested by Foucault. Likewise, Judith Butler's perspective of social norms inherently containing a potential for their own disruption and dilution is informative here. Since Anzaldúa's sexually transgressive and racially and culturally hybrid Chicana identity inevitably challenges the mentioned duality of Western thought, such an identity partakes in upending the established norms by exposing their fragility that stems from their dependence on their binary opposites. As Butler phrases it: "[the] resignification of norms is thus a function of their *inefficacy*, and so the question of subversion, of *working the weakness in the norm*, becomes a matter of inhabiting the practices of its rearticulation."[30] It would be a mistake, however, to idealize Anzaldúa's queerness and identity constructions in any sort of romanticized notions of unlimited, unrestrained, free, and independent choices. Rather, I concur with McRuer's suggestion that Anzaldúa's mestiza queer agency is not "simplistically voluntaristic" and reveals the intricacies of the question of one's agency.[31] The writer's agency is discursively delimited and her subject position is that of conflicting intersections which are being resisted and rearticulated, but which are also resistant and in their effect bearing on Anzaldúa's possibilities of articulating mestiza subjectivity. Or as Judith Butler has it, the subject "is always the nexus, the non-space of cultural collision, in which the demand to resignify or repeat the very terms which constitute the 'we' cannot be summarily

[28] Ibid.

[29] Sara Mills, *Michel Foucault* (London and New York: Routledge, 2003), 33.

[30] Judith Butler, *Bodies That Matter: On the Discursive Limits of "Sex"* (London and New York: Routledge. 1993), 257; emphasis hers.

[31] McRuer, *The Queer Renaissance*, 150.

refused, but neither can they be followed in strict obedience."[32] In fact, Butler's argumentation in *Bodies That Matter* employs Anzaldúa's notion of the "crossroads" for the subject as a "juncture of discursive demands" to disclose how "cultural and political discursive forces" render the subject "chiasmic" and non-existent prior to its constructions, and neither determined by those constructions.[33] To use Anzaldúa's phrase, "[that] focal point or fulcrum, that juncture where the mestiza stands, is where phenomena tend to collide."[34] This crossroads of cultures and competing discursive practices gives rise to mestiza subjectivity and a new (mestiza) consciousness which—although being "[sources] of intense pain," as the author admits—simultaneously represent a "continual creative motion that keeps breaking down the unitary aspect of each new paradigm."[35] In this regard, the queer mestiza is produced by the US–Mexico border and, to the same degree, by the boundaries of dual Western categories, but is also never fully contained by them.

Thus, Anzaldúa's hybrid and queer position facilitates the rearticulation of the nationalist notions of Chicana/o identity in general and the homeland of Aztlán in particular, both of which she seeks to reinvent as ideally inclusive, non-discriminatory, and welcoming alliances. Only such approach corresponds with the non-binary, multilayered, and complex character of Chicana/o existence. In other words, in Anzaldúa's perspective, all othering practices conducted internally *within* and *by* the Chicana/o community as declared in *El Movimiento's* nationalist, androcentric, and heteronormative rhetoric represent a form of violence the people performs on its own bodies and minds and may be perceived as the nation's misinterpretation and misconception of its own multiple origins. Thus, to feel at home in her culture in an attempt to make it "evolve into something better," Anzaldúa launches her critical attacks against the nation's "intimate terrorism" aimed both at women and the queer.[36]

[32] Butler, *Bodies That Matter*, 124.

[33] Butler, *Bodies That Matter*, 124.

[34] Anzaldúa, *Borderlands/La Frontera*, 101.

[35] Ibid., 102.

[36] Ibid., 41, 42.

Complicating Home and Nation: Tribal Alliances

The author aptly relates the difficulties her queerness constitutes for the institutions of Chicana/o family and nation. The androcentric and heteronormative dictates of nationalism complicate the acceptance of the community's "others" into the national body: a university student of Anzaldúa's once totally misread the term homophobia as a fear of going home and not being taken in after a long time spent away.[37] The student's error concerns both the etymology and the meaning of the word homophobia; most significantly, however, it utterly obfuscates the sexual connotations and heterosexism conveyed by the miscomprehended term and lets Anzaldúa shift her readers' attention away from the identity that causes heterosexual angst and direct it to the concept of home in terms of kinship as well as—in the broader sense—culture, community, or homeland. In fact, later on in her notes, Anzaldúa defines home as "comfort zones, both personal and cultural."[38] In this manner, the writer targets the rigidity of Chicana/o social organization in order to expand the content of what being a Chicana/o means not because she wants to shatter Chicana/o cultural significance and devitalize her people's political struggle, but because she feels a genuine love for her origins and home that "permeates every sinew and cartilage in [her] body"[39] and because—in correspondence with her belief in betterment achieved through accepting ambiguity—she has a vision of a hybrid, inclusive Aztlán as "a community of those previously excluded."[40]

In this regard, the valorization of mestiza/o identity and queerness serves to disrupt the patriarchal, masculine-coded nationalist rhetoric and offers a more democratic alternative—a liminal or interstitial space of Aztlán *sin fronteras* (without borders). What matters in Anzaldúa's conception of the homeland is not the mere overcoming or disposing of borders; rather it is the emphasis put on liminality and interstitiality, or more specifically, it is the recognition of the ambivalences that are brought about by the (present or historical) existence of borders that leave an imprint not only on the

[37] Anzaldúa, *Borderlands/La Frontera*, 42.

[38] Gloria Anzaldúa, *Light in the Dark/Luz en lo Oscuro: Rewriting Identity, Spirituality, Reality*. Ed. AnaLouise Keating (Durham and London: Duke University Press, 2015), 67.

[39] Anzaldúa, *Borderlands/La Frontera*, 43.

[40] Elizabeth Jacobs, *Mexican American Literature: The Politics of Identity* (London and New York: Routledge, 2006), 146.

landscape, but also the mind. Anzaldúa's Aztlán implies a consciousness that acknowledges collectivity and community, but not necessarily in geographically, linguistically, and racially conditioned nationalist terms. To paraphrase McRuer, Anzaldúa avoids fixing a new Chicana/o nation and/or nationalism by rigorously querying both the concepts.

In fact, shortly after the publication of *Borderlands/La Frontera*, precisely in 1991, Anzaldúa started formulating the notion of "new tribalism," an innovative alternative to nationalism. While she explores the concept in a number of essays and notes, it never truly constitutes the major topic of these writings; rather new tribalism seeps through her work and theorizing continually. As related in *Light in the Dark/Luz en lo oscuro*, new tribalism means "being part of but never subsumed by a group, never losing individuality to the group nor losing the group to the individual. [It] is about working together to create new 'stories' of identity and culture, to envision diverse futures."[41] The latest and perhaps the most pertinent and sophisticated delineation of the theory is contained in an archival Word document Anzaldúa sketched out six weeks before her untimely death in 2004. It reads: "The new tribalism disrupts categorical and ethnocentric forms of nationalism. By problematizing the concepts of who's us and who's other, [...] the new tribalism seeks to revise the notion of 'otherness' and the story of identity. The new tribalism rewrites cultural inscriptions, facilitating our ability to forge alliances with other groups."[42]

The refusal of Anzaldúa's new tribalism to establish national(ist) kinship solely on race and/or on shared genetic pools resists customary nationalisms' conformity with essentialism. By contrast, both Anzaldúa's expansion of social categories and the simultaneous critique of their insufficiency point to the author's conception of a collective/coalition/alliance/community or a nation—with a modified sense of the last word—in constructivist, inclusive terms. Her theory of home/land and mestiza/o existence in *Borderlands/La Frontera* moves from the national, physical homeland of Aztlán to a new, hybrid and flexible awareness that executes a capacity for doing away with the duality-burdened category of nation.[43] Unlike other competing interpretations of Chicana/o Aztlán, such as Rudolfo Anaya's "homeland

[41] Anzaldúa, *Light in the Dark*, 85.

[42] Anzaldúa, *Light in the Dark*, xxv.

[43] McRuer, *The Queer Renaissance*, 145.

without boundaries"[44] or Bill Ashcroft's "transnation" that could both be read as partially gender-blind conceptualizations of the Chicana/o nation or as a Western, markedly affirmative projection of borderland subjects' ingenuity in terms of their inventing flexible notions of a body politic,[45] Anzaldúa deserts the nation(alist) sentiments. For one thing, it is because she is concerned about the material conditions of the mentioned community; for another, she cautions against the dangers nationalist categories themselves pose within the androcentric and capitalist world.

The author's non-nationalist approach to Aztlán and Chicana/o community can also be extrapolated to her views of women-of-color feminism and women's movement as these vastly inform her agenda. An accent is always put on commonly shared, critical, and reflective cooperation and alliance building since this activist and political aspect, as Anzaldúa perceives it, leads to social change and helps detect and counter oppressive relations of power. In an essay whose title "Bridge, Drawbridge, Sandbar or Island" is akin to *Borderlands/La Frontera* for it elicits imagery of geographical locations associated with division, isolation, and connection and shifting, she marks the importance of collective action: "*coalition work attempts to balance power relations and undermine and subvert the system of domination-subordination* that affects even our most unconscious thoughts."[46] At the same time she concedes the difficulties inherent to identity politics; joint cooperation entails complex negotiation of internal differences, i.e. a critical recognition of the inner heterogeneity of any given collective. Cognizant of the vital role played by intersectionality in this regard, she critiques white lesbians for their "unconsciously rank[ing] racism a lesser oppression than sexism," or feels empathy with men of color and their struggle against racist emasculation by white masculinity only to be "saddened that they [need] to be educated about women-only space." No less significant is her appeal to her family to scrutinize their antifeminism or a call to the whole

[44] Rudolfo Anaya, "Aztlán: A Homeland without Boundaries" in *Aztlán: Essays on the Chicano Homeland,* eds. Rudolfo Anaya and Francisco Lomelí (Albuquerque: University of New Mexico Press, 1989), 241.

[45] Bill Ashcroft, "Chicano Transnation" in *Imagined Transnationalism: U.S. Latino/a Literature, Culture, and Identity,* eds. Kevin Concannon, Francisco Lomelí, and Marc Priewe (New York: Palgrave Macmillan, 2009), 14, 19, 27.

[46] Gloria Anzaldúa, "Bridge, Drawbridge, Sandbar or Island. Lesbians-of-Color Hacienda Alianzas," in *Bridges of Power: Women's Multicultural Alliances,* eds. Lisa Albrecht and Rose M. Brewer (Philadelphia: New Society Publishers, 1990), 224–225; emphasis hers.

Chicana/o nation to sift through its "heterosexist bullshit" and exclusionary rhetoric.[47] By such a *cri de coeur* Anzaldúa once again points out the fact that Chicana/o nationalism *internally* replicates and perpetuates exactly those kinds of ostracism, discrimination, and othering of its own members who "go through the confines of the 'normal'" which all Chicanas/os are subjected to *externally* by the US majority society.[48]

The exposure of this internal conflict helps Anzaldúa reclaim Chicana/o nation and Aztlán not only as inclusive and fluid, but as a community with an alliance-forging potential; as Peréz-Torres remarks, Chicanas/os now "come to be seen as transfiguring themselves – moving between the worlds of indigenous and European, of American and Mexican, of self and other."[49] Being both an activist and a writer, Anzaldúa theorizes the issue of conflicts and friction in the course of the communal transfiguration both *within* and *beyond* alliances, communities, or tribes by adopting rich, figurative, symbolic language, which—redolent of the multilayered use of border and borderlands in *Borderlands/La Frontera*—again exposes the fundamental interconnectedness of a geographical location, its historical and cultural specificity, and one's epistemology reflective of one's positionality. While certainly the concepts of border, borderlands, and the aforementioned crossroads highlighted by Butler are the climax in Anzaldúa's conjoining literary imagery and political and activist thought, the metaphors of bridge, drawbridge, sandbar, and island from the eponymous essay also speak volumes about the author's drive to fashion a space for communication, acting, and interacting *within* a nation or alliance and *with* an outreach beyond Aztlán to other communities, especially white US society.

Although out of the four concepts—bridge, drawbridge, sandbar, island—Anzaldúa does not incorporate the latter three in her writing beyond the mentioned essay on alliance forging and replaces them with other culturally more relevant terms, such as the indigenous nepantla—an expression for liminal, hybrid position on the threshold that comprises cultural multiplicities and spiritual and psychic dimensions as yet another mode of epistemological perspective—the geographical concepts are

[47] Ibid., 218, 219.

[48] Anzaldúa, *Borderlands/La Frontera*, 25.

[49] Rafael Peréz-Torres, *Movements in Chicano Poetry: Against Myths, Against Margins* (Cambridge, MA: Cambridge University Press, 1995), 96.

informative of the contextual rootedness combined with flexibility and contradictoriness of Chicana/o experience as conveyed by Anzaldúa throughout her literary and political work. The poem "To live in the Borderlands means you" is no exception.

On Being a Crossroads

The piece reflects Anzaldúa's theorizing of the mestiza, Chicana subjectivity and, by extension, provides a map for a broader conception of Aztlán as a borderland. She no longer sees Aztlán as a static, historical location in which the mythical homeland is set, but as a dynamic, interstitial border region, where events take place and contradictions are interrogated; Aztlán is viewed as a borderland or a non-discriminatory cultural crossroads—a point of permanent movement and constant flow—where difference is embraced. Thus, Anzaldúa's conception of an inclusive, encompassing Aztlán functions as a manifestation of the collective and the communal and is therefore empowering for it permits the assumption of various subject positions, especially those formerly proscribed by the discourse of Chicana/o nationalism. Or as Peréz-Torres eloquently sums up the aims of the author's conception of Aztlán and her attempt to bring the individual and collective together, "[the] refusal to be delimited, while simultaneously claiming numerous heritages and influences, allows for a rearticulation of the relationship between self and society, self and history, self and land."[50] The theoretician's focus on diversity fully corresponds with Anzaldúa's push for inclusiveness; her approach inherently discerns that the social and cultural inhomogeneity needs to be explicitly addressed. Moreover, according to Peréz-Torres, "the transformation of 'Aztlán' from homeland to borderland signifies an opening within [Chicana/o] cultural discourse. It marks a significant transformation away from the dream of origin toward an engagement with the construction of cultural identity."[51] Anzaldúa's reconceptualization of Aztlán embodies Chicana/o culture's radical departure from essentialism and nostalgic insistence on common roots and the concurrent paradigmatic move toward constructivism.

While in the opening poem of *Borderlands/La Frontera* Anzaldúa embraces the US–Mexico border as an "open wound," calls the

[50] Peréz-Torres, *Movements in Chicano Poetry*, 96.

[51] Peréz-Torres, *Movements in Chicano Poetry*, 96.

demarcation line her "home," and addresses the internalized pain of othering practices symbolized by the steel "Tortilla Curtain,"[52] the poem "To live in the Borderlands means you" illustrates coping strategies or modes of survival in navigating borderland characteristics. In brief, the titleless Border Field Park poem dissected earlier may be read as a lead-in, a description of the nuances faced by borderland subjects straddling the artificial divide or as a confession of the hurt the divide elicits. By contrast, "To live in the Borderlands means you" suggests, upon listing the series of contradictory and (seemingly) irreconcilable positions, a method of handling dualities, or offers advice, if not a direct solution. The formal properties of the poem make shifts in syntactical meaning possible as Peréz-Torres observes.[53] The title serves simultaneously as the first line of the poem which heralds transgression of both the physical border and social boundaries, i.e. motifs the piece intimately explores. Most importantly, however, the "you" in the title may represent an addressee of the poem, but at the same time the addressee gets conflated with the Borderlands it refers to. The merging of separate, individual aspects in the title and the poem itself is representative of the hybridity inherent to the borderlands, which is, actually, the fact the poem aims to communicate. The text performs exactly what it tries to convey; the form complements the content.

In terms of content, Anzaldúa throughout the whole poem aptly diagnoses the antagonistic pulls a borderland subject faces in regard to his/her gender, race, culture, and situatedness:

> To live in the Borderlands means you
> are neither *hispana india negra española*
> *ni gabacha, eres mestiza, mulata*, half-breed
> caught in the crossfire between camps
> while carrying all five races on your back
> not knowing which side to turn to, run from;
>
> To live in the Borderlands means knowing […]
> that denying the Anglo inside you
> is as bad as having denied the Indian or Black;

[52] Anzaldúa, *Borderlands/La Frontera*, 24.

[53] Peréz-Torres, *Movements in Chicano Poetry*, 94.

Cuando vives en la frontera
people walk through you, the wind steals your voice,
you're a *burra, buey*, scapegoat,
forerunner of a new race,
half and half – both woman and man, neither –
a new gender [. . .][54]

The liminal condition of multiracial identity that confirms colonial desires, but rubs against the (unattainable and racist) ideal of racial purity, places the mestiza at a center of warfare over belonging that, at this point in the poem, seems to lack a solution. Rather, identity emerges from the multiple mixtures of various forms of affiliation, such as racial, linguistic, cultural belonging, etc., that are antithetical. Although it poses a genuine challenge to her identity which may seem to coerce the mestiza to turn against herself and incite self-hatred, acknowledging the significance of the background that she shares with her oppressor, the Anglo, as related in the second stanza, is a key factor in Anzaldúa's identity politics. Not only does she expand the concept of a woman-of-color by recognizing the mestiza's partial whiteness, she also subverts race as a concept of social construction per se. Concurrently, identifying the colonial and racial oppressor within empowers the mestiza against what Pierre Bourdieu termed symbolic violence.[55] The acknowledgment resists the epistemological denial and incapacitation by uneven power relations that Bourdieu's concept describes. Further, the poem introduces gender as fluid; femininity and masculinity are not presented as extremities, but may shift along the gender continuum. This perspective inevitably opens a wider space for experiencing (rather than defining, therefore fixing) one's sexuality, a strategy obviously aimed at validating dissenting sexual relationships and desires of those who do not adapt to compulsory heterosexuality, such as Anzaldúa's queer mestiza. A subject's agency is vastly conditioned by language, discourse, and the capacity to speak and be heard.[56] Therefore, the wind that steals one's voice in the third stanza can be read as a factor impeding such an agency. Since non-conforming identities are frequently silenced by

[54] Anzaldúa, *Borderlands/La Frontera*, 216.

[55] Pierre Bourdieu, *Masculine Domination* (Stanford: Stanford University Press, 2001), 35.

[56] Cf. Sneja Gunew and Gayatri Chakravorty Spivak, "Questions of Multi-Culturalism," *Hecate* 12.1–2 (1986): 136–142.

dominant discourses,[57] the borderland subject needs to acquire a voice and carve a discourse that sustains and nurtures the hybrid and liminal existence that embodies "the battleground / where enemies are kin to each other," where "you are at home [and] a stranger."[58] In order to voice the complexities of what being a borderland subject entails, the poem actually forges a discourse of interstitiality. It "speaks" both English and Spanish in terms of form as the excerpt above confirms, and at the same time, in terms of content, it explicitly shows that language choices (as well as culturally conditioned cuisine preferences) are contextually and socially informed:

> To live in the Borderlands means to
>   put *chile* in the borscht
>   eat whole wheat *tortillas*,
>   speak Tex-Mex with a Brooklyn accent [...].[59]

According to Peréz-Torres, "[the] poem's interlingual expression and evocation of interstitial spaces represents the power of transgression."[60] I conceive of the discourse of interstitiality in a parallel manner: it embraces ambiguity and provides a platform for articulating borderland subjectivity. However, as Foucault reminds us and as Anzaldúa is well aware, discourses may fail to deliver, which, in effect, testifies to the constant negotiation of power relations.[61] An example of such a failure is contained in Pedro's story of deportation and misrecognition of his citizenship by Immigration and Naturalization Service officers as I relate above.

In Pedro's case, the discourse of interstitiality by means of which he can make sense of his borderland subjectivity is overridden by a discourse that allows for practicing of racist prejudice by the immigration officers. In a similar manner, the discourse of interstitiality is undermined by the fact (arising from discourses of national security and anti-immigrant sentiments) that living in the borderlands means being repeatedly "stopped by *la migra* at

[57] Gayatri Chakravorty Spivak, "Can the Subaltern Speak?" in *Marxism and the Interpretation of Culture,* eds. Cary Nelson and Lawrence Grossberg (Urbana: University of Illinois Press, 1988).

[58] Anzaldúa, *Borderlands/La Frontera*, 216.

[59] Anzaldúa, *Borderlands/La Frontera*, 216.

[60] Peréz-Torres, *Movements in Chicano Poetry*, 95.

[61] Michel Foucault, *The History of Sexuality. Volume I. An Introduction* (New York, Pantheon Books, 1978), 100.

the border checkpoints." This is a reality of a global scale which starkly clashes with Anzaldúa's views of seamless earth and sea and migrant people(s) who can neither be contained by a fence nor stopped by a border, an image drawn by the initial Border Field Park poem. Once again, the writer demonstrates her knowledge that subjectivity is constantly in the making, has to be permanently negotiated, and that success and failure are effects of shifting power relations. Yet, having recounted in seven stanzas the various intricacies of living in the borderlands, such as the ones discussed, Anzaldúa then turns to a swift conclusion and provides a succinct climax to the borderland conundrum:

> To survive the Borderlands
> You must live *sin fronteras*
> be a crossroads.[62]

The image of the crossroads, an evident interstitial space, deconstructs the duality produced by the US–Mexico border and is accepting of the incompatibility of the multiple phenomena that are inherent to borderland subjectivity. In this regard, the conclusion of the poem seems to suggest a solution to and summation of the hybrid, borderland ambiguity in the very concept of the crossroads; in addition, the concept is also indicative of the extrication from the border's othering and discriminatory effects. An aspect of the poem that also deserves attention lies in Anzaldúa's conscious avoidance of painting unrealistic vistas of an ultimate riddance concerning internalized historical traumas on the one hand, and of a simple acquiring of skills for living without borders, on the other. The development is gradual and possible only with an honest introspection and self-reflexivity that invites (self-)doubt. Although such moderation and continence could be viewed as insufficiently revolutionary and radical, I view it as an asset to Anzaldúa's theorizing. It demonstrates her ability to link theory, art, and dailiness of the lived experience; in short, it testifies to her activist concern for both the material and social reality of the borderland subjects and their imprint in artistic forms of representations.

To conclude, Chicana feminists target Aztlán's nationalist representations for not truly conveying a homeland without boundaries as Anaya and Ashcroft mentioned above suggest. Contrariwise, Chicanas expose the enduring

[62] Anzaldúa, *Borderlands/La Frontera*, 217.

boundaries that arise from gender bias and from malestreaming masculinity as the default representation of humanity. Thus, Aztlán is in Chicana feminism and most notably in Anzaldúa's reinvention posited in terms of one's relationship to and location in a (border)land, i.e. a hybrid physical and geographical place. Concurrently, Anzaldúa's Aztlán and by extension the Chicana/o nation call for a reformulation of the notions of a home and belonging beyond the restrictive nationalistic, androcentric, and heterosexist terms. As a result, this rearticulated Aztlán emerges as a more inclusive, collective, and inherently fluid nation. Or in Anzaldúa's vision, it is a nation as an alliance; an alliance of resistance against any one kind of a discriminatory, hierarchical practice.

Bibliography

Aldama, Arturo J. 1998. Millennial Anxieties: Borders, Violence and the Struggle for Chicana/o Subjectivity. *Arizona Journal of Hispanic Cultural Studies* 2: 41–62.

Anaya, Rudolfo. 1989. Aztlán: A Homeland without Boundaries. In *Aztlán: Essays on the Chicano Homeland*, ed. Rudolfo Anaya and Francisco Lomelí. Albuquerque: University of New Mexico Press.

Anzaldúa, Gloria. 1990. Bridge, Drawbridge, Sandbar or Island. Lesbians-of-Color Hacienda Alianzas. In *Bridges of Power: Women's Multicultural Alliances*, ed. Lisa Albrecht and Rose M. Brewer. Philadelphia: New Society Publishers.

———. 1999. *Borderlands/La Frontera: The New Mestiza*. San Francisco: Aunt Lute.

———. 2015. In *Light in the Dark/Luz en lo Oscuro: Rewriting Identity, Spirituality, Reality*, ed. AnaLouise Keating. Durham/London: Duke University Press.

Ashcroft, Bill. 2009. Chicano transnation. In *Imagined Transnationalism: U.S. Latino/a Literature, Culture, and Identity*, ed. Kevin Concannon, Francisco Lomelí, and Marc Priewe. New York: Palgrave Macmillan.

Beck, Ulrich, and Elisabeth Beck-Gernsheim. 1995. *The Normal Chaos of Love*. Cambridge: Polity Press.

Bhabha, Homi. 1994. *The Location of Culture*. London/New York: Routledge.

Bourdieu, Pierre. 2001. *Masculine Domination*. Stanford: Stanford University Press.

Butler, Judith. 1993. *Bodies That Matter: On the Discursive Limits of "Sex"*. London/New York: Routledge.

Foucault, Michel. 1978. *The History of Sexuality, An Introduction*. Vol. I. New York: Pantheon Books.

García, Alma, ed. 1997. *Chicana Feminist Thought: The Basic Historical Writings*. London/New York: Routledge.

Gunew, Sneja, and Gayatri Chakravorty Spivak. 1986. Questions of Multi-Culturalism. *Hecate* 12 (1–2): 136–142.

Jacobs, Elizabeth. 2006. *Mexican American Literature: The Politics of Identity.* London/New York: Routledge.
Lazarus, Emma. 1883. *The New Colossus.* National Park Service. https://www.nps.gov/stli/learn/historyculture/colossus.htm. Accessed 18 Dec 2016.
McClintock, Anne. 1993. Family Feuds: Gender, Nationalism and the Family. *Feminist Review* 44: 61–80.
McRuer, Robert. 1997. *The Queer Renaissance: Contemporary American Literature and the Reinvention of Lesbian and Gay Identities.* New York: University of New York Press.
Mills, Sara. 2003. *Michel Foucault.* London/New York: Routledge.
Peréz-Torres, Rafael. 1995. *Movements in Chicano Poetry: Against Myths, Against Margins.* Cambridge, MA: Cambridge University Press.
Spivak, Gayatri Chakravorty. 1988. Can the Subaltern Speak? In *Marxism and the Interpretation of Culture*, ed. Cary Nelson and Lawrence Grossberg. Urbana: University of Illinois Press.
Yuval-Davis, Nira. 2005. *Gender & Nation.* London/Thousand Oaks: SAGE.

Achilles and the (Sexual) History of Being

William Koch

The first word of Western literature is “rage”, *menin*.[1] Western thought begins from the rage of Achilles. Despite the political gambits of Agamemnon, which seem to trigger this rage, it is pathological in the deepest sense. It is a *pathe*, a passion, with a *logos* or logic of its own that it lays upon all the events which unfold in the *Iliad*. It may just be a *pathe* that drives Western history from the space beyond the limits of this history’s constitutive fantasies. This is a space occupied by the Outside in all its many guises, that which rejects the central pillars of a culture’s frameworks of meaning.

Achilles’ rage cannot be disentangled from the specter of death that he holds constantly before himself:

> [A] man’s life cannot come back again, it cannot be lifted
> nor captured again by force, once it has crossed the teeth’s barrier . . .
> I carry two sorts of destiny toward the day of my death. Either,
> if I stay here and fight beside the city of the Trojans,
> my return home is gone, but my glory shall be everlasting;
> but if I return home to the beloved land of my fathers,

[1] Homer *Iliad*.

W. Koch (✉)
New York City College of Technology, Brooklyn, NY, USA

J. Elbert Decker, D. Winchock (eds.), *Borderlands and Liminal Subjects*, https://doi.org/10.1007/978-3-319-67813-9_9

> the excellence of my glory is gone, but there will be a long life
> left for me, and my end in death will not come to me quickly.[2]

Faced with the choice between a death that births immortality or a life destined to end without immortal offspring, Achilles chooses life. Achilles chooses the present over future immortality. This choice is not made in cool deliberation, in the spirit of pragmatism, but rather arises from the logic of his rage, a rage that is turned against the entire social edifice of the heroic ethic and the justification of the Trojan War:

> Yet why must the Argives fight with the Trojans?
> And why was it the son of Atreus assembled and led here
> these people?[3]

Achilles insists, "For not worth the value of my life are all the possessions they fable were won for Ilion ..."[4] Yes, Achilles *insists* in life rather than *desisting* in death pacified by the fantasy of an immortality born from his desistence. This is the heart of Achilles' rage; it is an insistent persistence giving rise to:

> devastation, which put pains thousandfold upon the Achaians,
> hurled in their multitudes to the house of Hades strong souls
> of heroes, but gave their bodies to be the delicate feasting
> of dogs, of all birds ...[5]

The *Iliad* is haunted with the terrible force of this rage, a destructive force that threatens even the stability of Olympus and the divine order itself as the gods repeatedly come to blows over the fate of Troy. Within the figure of this rage at the well-spring of Western history we find humanity's confrontation with time, death, and the fantasy of immortality. This confrontation threatens from the very beginning the entire social world.

When seeking the first words of Western thought Heidegger didn't go as far as we have; instead, he delved into the lone short extant fragment of

[2] Homer *Iliad* Richard Lattimore trans. Book Nine, 408–416.

[3] Ibid., 337–338.

[4] Ibid., 400–402.

[5] Ibid. Book One, 2–5.

Anaximander. There, Heidegger suggests, Being is thought entirely in terms of time and the ongoing flow of coming-to-be and passing-away. This passing of time can, however, either be *Fug* or *un-Fug*. These German words are translated generally as "order" and "disorder", but the German contains the sense of things either fitting with each other, joining together, or suffering from a lack of jointure. What, however, places the temporal world of passing out-of-joint? Heidegger suggests that an entity:

> may insist upon its while solely to remain more present, in the sense of perduring. That which lingers persists in its presencing. In this way it extricates itself from its transitory while. It strikes the willful pose of persistence, no longer concerning itself with whatever else is present. It stiffens – as if this were the only way to linger – and aims solely for continuance and subsistence.[6]

Disorder arises, then, from an insisting on present persistence over passing. The parallels to Achilles should be obvious. It is precisely this persistence that Zizek thinks opens up the space for a theory of the Freudian and Lacanian drive in Heidegger's philosophy. Is not this persistence precisely the insistence of the drive beyond the satisfaction of the pleasure principle or the instincts that gives rise to the reality principle? It is Zizek's proposal that we ground Heidegger's conception of temporality, whiling, and order in an underlying insistent drive that both breaks and gives rise to temporal order.

These preliminary considerations have made things far too easy for ourselves, for Achilles does achieve his immortality. Doesn't he choose it? The answer is that he does not. Achilles' slaying of Hector is as pathological as his rejection of the war with Troy, born not from a futural commitment to glory and immortality but rather from a rage at the slaying of his "most beloved companion"[7] Patrocles. Achilles does not choose to die, but he chooses to kill, and we will suggest that his rage over Patrocles is the same rage we have seen throughout the entire story. It is another aspect of his *insistence*, his figuring of the drive. Let us stress, for a moment, some of the aspects of the sketch we have offered so far. Achilles' rage is a rejection of a fantasy, the fantasy that immorality can be achieved in and through our sacrifice to a social whole. It is fundamentally a rejection of futurity in favor of the present, a rejection that undermines the structure of all political order

[6] Heidegger "The Anaximander Fragment" as quoted in Zizek *Less Than Nothing* p. 883.
[7] "*polu philtatos . . . hetairos*" *Iliad* Book 17 line 411.

to the extent that politics is always committed to achieving or preserving some future. When read as such, the first word of Western literature is a challenge to the futurity Heidegger proposes as the basic constitution of Dasein's temporality in *Being and Time*; it is a rejection of being-toward-death. There Heidegger claims that humanity, or Dasein, is always engaged in projecting itself into the future through its commitments and choices and that the most basic aspect of this futurity is the recognition of an end to all these choices in their fundamental limited, or finite, nature. A resolute facing up to this inevitable finitude is our being-toward-death, and the attempt to forget or deny this inescapable finitude is understood by Heidegger to be an inauthentic form of human life. Could it be that Western Thought began in inauthenticity, through Achilles' own rejection of the future? Or, rather, might it have begun by "traversing the fantasy" in the Lacanian sense, by realizing the pathological foundation of the future-oriented being-toward-death in the sexual drive? Here we see the way in which the futurity Heidegger understood to be a basic aspect of human existence can be understood as a psychological illusion by Lacan. It is this possibility that drives me to suggest that we should rethink Heidegger's History of Being by means of a Sexual History of Being, one beginning with Achilles as the embodiment of the drive, the synthomosexual.

My thesis is that, in Achilles, we witness Western Culture's first engagement with what has been conceptualized as the drive in psychoanalysis. We assume that Heidegger is right that the only way to free ourselves from the destructive distortions of the metaphysical tradition is to think our way beneath that tradition by finding the moments of its origins and what was concealed within those origins. We repeat this path in returning to Achilles, but in hopes of uncovering something Heidegger failed to see. This "something" is a sexual aspect of Being that brings with it distinct political implications precisely in grounding the nature of politics on the sexual nature of Being.

But what is the drive? It has been conceptualized in several ways, and it is our hope that the investigation of Achilles will help us navigate between these modes of conceptualization. Freud, in "Beyond the Pleasure Principle", articulates the drive in terms of the compulsion to repeat found in cases of both trauma and the basic play of children. Freud considers the compulsion to repeat to be a basic characteristic of all biological life; it is "... an urge inherent in organic life to restore an earlier state of things".[8] Lacan,

[8] Freud *The Essentials of Psycho-Analysis* p. 244.

though claiming to remain true to Freud, dramatically changes this formulation by making the drive an effect of the symbolic structure of language and social practice. At the very end of his 1954 seminar, *The Ego in Freud's Theory and in the Technique of Psychoanalysis*, he specifically identifies the drive with the Symbolic itself:

> This is the point where we open out into the symbolic order ... It tends beyond the pleasure principle, beyond the limits of life, and that is why Freud identifies it with the death instinct . . . the death instinct is only the mask of the symbolic order ... The symbolic order is simultaneously non-being and insisting to be, that is what Freud has in mind when he talks about the death instinct as being what is most fundamental – a symbolic order in travail, in the process of coming, insisting on being realized.[9]

This, in turn, will be characterized by Zizek as the manner in which "desires lose their mooring in biology"[10] with the advent of language in human life. The drive is an effect of the "transposition from the immediate biological reality of the body to the symbolic space of language"[11] which is experienced as the most primordial trauma from which the original compulsion to repeat arises. This drive is the insistent repetition of language itself, a repetition however that cannot be simply grounded in language or justified through it. Objecting to Heidegger's focus on language as the house of Being, Zizek insists that Lacan's theory presents the satisfaction of the drive, called *jouissance*, as something which "... resists symbolization, remains a foreign kernel within it, appearing as a rupture, cut, gap, inconsistency, or impossibility ...".[12] This lines up with Lacan's formulation of the drive as the nature of the Symbolic as both non-being and insistence. It is the form in which language, as always failed and incomplete, nonetheless repeats its way insistently into Being. In this sense we can see how the entire Symbolic, and language itself, is pathological. It is the *logos* of the *pathe* that is drive.

[9] Lacan *The Ego in Freud's Theory and in the Technique of Psychoanalysis* p. 326.

[10] Zizek *Less Than Nothing* p. 873.

[11] Ibid.

[12] Ibid., 874.

We note, by way of foreshadowing, that there is a connection to be made here with the pulsations of Heidegger's History of Being understood as the events of disclosure and concealment of Being which constitute epochs through the *epoche* or "bracketing" of Being. The history of Being consists, then, in the ways in which Being appears in terms of varying aspects, aspects that themselves conceal more than they reveal. We might, then, suggest that Being shares the aspects Lacan grants the Symbolic; it is a non-being which nonetheless insists, and this insistence and failure to fully *be* constitutes the compulsive repetition we call history. In relation to Heidegger Freud's reflections on the a-temporal nature of the unconscious become particularly suggestive. In the heart of "Beyond the Pleasure Principle", Freud offers a single paragraph that "hints", as he says, at a topic too large for him to fully discuss at the time:

> [W]e are to-day in a position to embark on a discussion of the Kantian theorem that time and space are 'necessary forms of thought'. We have learnt that unconscious mental processes are in themselves 'timeless'. This means in the first place that they are not ordered temporally, that time does not change them in any way and that the idea of time cannot be applied to them.[13]

Freud's insistence that the drive is the deepest level of unconscious mental processes and is a-temporal might suggest the possibility of grounding the temporality Heidegger makes central in *Being and Time* in a deeper reality. Of course, to do so, the drive must be something other than an "unconscious mental processes" or basic characteristic of biological life. It must be ontological, perhaps another term for the groundless insistence of the Heideggerian event of disclosure, the *Ereignis*, which originates a history.

Despite these brief ontological speculations, the drive has pressing political implications. To uncover these, however, we will have to consider the difference between the *jouissance* of the drive and the pleasure of achieved desire through the mediating factor of fantasy. The drive can never be fully satisfied; there is no object toward which it aims, but its repeated insistence produces its own type of satisfaction. This is *jouissance*. The drive and its *jouissance* give rise, however, to the full collection of desires that structure the more obvious characteristics of our mental and social lives. The manner in which we move from the objectless drive to the object-directed desire is

[13] Freud *The Essentials of Psycho-Analysis* p. 237.

by means of fantasy. Fantasy channels the circular pulse of the drive toward specific objects by presenting the myth that something specific can, at last, satisfy the insistence of the drive. The most basic structure of fantasy has a temporal characteristic; specifically it is future directed. Fantasy tells us that something specific, to be achieved or worked toward, will provide the fulfillment the drive constantly lacks. Thus, desire for this object is born from the drive. Fantasy is fundamentally the belief that the future will satisfy the drive, but the drive knows only insistence and the present. As Lee Edelman makes clear in *No Future: Queer Theory and the Death Drive*, this future-oriented characteristic of fantasy takes as its easiest object the image of the Child. According to fantasy, the drive of the parent or society in general will achieve satisfaction in the child. This child-focused future orientation, Edelman points out, is the shared collective fantasy of all political projects. Despite their differences, all politics insist that we must think about the children and strive for the world of the future that they deserve. It is also this future-oriented nature of fantasy that grounds the demand for sacrifice within the human psyche. The drive itself is satisfied, as far as it can be, in its very insistence, but fantasy and the satisfaction of the desire it creates demand postponement and self-denial for the sake of the future. This, in turn, grounds all politics in an assault upon those people who are not willing to sacrifice the present for the future or who are, at the very least, seen as doing this. From homosexuals who, it is claimed, can't contribute to the creation of the child but rather insist on non-future-oriented pleasures to childlike savages in need of civilizing to the inner-city "irresponsible" poor—politics is populated with phantasmal enemies threatening society as a whole through their rejection of the collective futural fantasy. Politics is grounded in this endless war against its margin where stand those who are seen as unwilling to become living sacrifices to the future.

The drive, then, can manifest in society in one of two general ways. Either it is sublimated by fantasy and becomes the desire embodied in the perennial image of the Child or it is to some extent unsublimated and shows up in non-future-oriented terms. As we saw, the drive in Freud is the force that gives rise to the repetition compulsion seen most clearly in the response to trauma but present to some degree in all psychic phenomenon. As mentioned, Lacan transforms this view by identifying the drive with the entirety of our social symbolic practices. This, in turn, gives rise to a clarification of the repetition compulsion Freud is engaged with. Once we recognize the drive in, and as, language we see repetition arises in terms of the insistence and, indeed, autonomy of language itself. We enter language from the start already part of an ongoing symbolic process as marked by our names. Before we can even speak, people speak of us, for us, and to us. We enter a world of conversations already, as it were, under way. This fairly basic observation, however, gives rise to a deep insight concerning the nature of language itself. Language speaks on its own and we are the product of this speech. Lacan refers to this as the *automaton*, or automatic characteristic of signifying chains that lead, according to their own logic, from one formulation to another. Language does not require thought as much as it, as a thoughtless playing out of a mechanical structure driven by repetition of rote formulations and references, provides the thoughtless background that enables thought to show up in the breaks and inconsistencies of this mechanical process.

The Symbolic as a whole, the automatic signifying mechanism, speaks us but is not itself internally consistent. For this reason it fixates upon various points of failure which alone hold the entire structure together. It is these key points, which ground both the possibility of any signification at all and make clear the impossibility of a complete system of signifier-signified matching, that make clear the sense in which the Symbolic is a nothing or non-being that nonetheless insists. The Symbolic speaks but, ultimately, fails at key points to actually say anything. It is at these points of failure/fixation that we find such Lacanian key ideas as the Master Signifier or the Big Other. The Master Signifier is supposed to signify that which provides for the completeness and consistency of the entire system. God, for whom all things are meaningful and have an appropriate name, is one example but so too is Science, as that system in which eventually all things will find their place and full explanation, or History, as that story within which all events will eventually be meaningful.

When we move to the personal level and the play of individual desires, the formulation that this understanding of the Symbolic takes on is that of the *objet a*, the symptom,[14] and *sinthome*. The *objet a* is that object which one believes will satisfy the insistence of the drive. It may change its identity, moving, for example, from the achievement of successfully wooing

[14] For two brilliant investigations of the concept of the "symptom" in the Ancient Greek context, see Emanuela Bianchi's *The Feminine Symptom: Aleatory Matter in the Aristotelian Cosmos* and Brooke Holmes' *The Symptom and the Subject: The Emergence of the Physical Body in Ancient Greece.* The importance of each of these books for the investigation I have undertaken cannot be understated, but length considerations do not allow me to explore these implications here.

a certain lover to the winning of a given job, but it consistently seems to offer the missing thing that the drive is experienced as calling out for. The *objet a* is that which we feel will fulfill the lack in the subject around which it seems the drive insists. In what are traditionally considered "healthy" social-psychological subjects, this object is located in various future-oriented figures such as the Child, the Career, Posterity, and so on. When the *objet a* is located in non-future-oriented objects, however, it gives rise to the fetish and various obsessive symptoms. In the example of someone with a shoe fetish, the dream of fulfillment is located not in some goal toward which one can lead a meaningful life but rather in an immediately present object which, once obtained, threatens to become an obsession since the failure of this object to fully satisfy leads toward endless fascination and accumulation. The fetish provides no ground for future ambition, but rather only presents indulgence and accumulation, and so shows up as anti-social. The *objet a*, then, becomes symptomatic to the extent that it loses its support in future-oriented fantasy and instead collapses into simple immediate insistence and repetition.

Sinthome is an old spelling of the word symptom and is used by Lacan to designate the deep structure of the drive's insistence in individuals which underlies the logic of the *objet a* and can either give rise to symptoms or sublimating fantasies. When speaking of the *Sinthome* we mean the very specific form that points of impossibility and insistence take on in individual subjects. After all, even in "healthy" fantasy, the desire is never just for "the Child" as a general concept. Instead one desires the strapping-football-playing-son, the physicist-daughter, and so on. Our desires are overly specific. These specific characteristics of the fantasy/desire mark the arbitrary point of the fixation of the drive. Something has to become the focus of the drive, something always does, but the details of this something are both arbitrary and the central motif of our entire social-psychic life. While everyone may not have "symptoms", everyone has *sinthomes.*

This brings us to the point where we can begin discussing the second manifestation of the drive in society in general. As mentioned it can show up in the figure of the Child and those who obediently sacrifice all for the future in the figure of the Child or it can manifest in what Edelman has termed the *sinthomosexual.* The *Sinthomosexual* is one who either hasn't developed the full prop of fantasy to sublimate her or his drive into future-oriented desires or one who has lost the prop of fantasy for various reasons. For this reason the *Sinthomosexual* is unmoved by the sacrificial demands of the future, the Child, and all the various synonyms for responsibility that arise around these concepts. Where others manifest desire, the *Sinthomosexual* manifests the drive through a present-oriented indulgence in the always incomplete satisfaction of the drive that can't help but appear as purposeless and without a goal to society in general. From the standpoint of society, the *Sinthomosexual* is engaged in a dramatic rejection of, and even assault upon, the blessed object of the Child and the future. As Edelman's clever analysis of literary and cinematic figures, such as the figure of Scrooge in Dicken's *The Christmas Carol,* shows, the *Sinthomosexual* almost always shows up as the villain engaged in selfish and inherently dangerous meaningless forms of indulgence that ultimately result in the destruction of the Child.

From the previous reflections it should be clear the role an understanding of the drive may play in understanding the political forces of racism, sexism, homophobia, and indeed the full spectrum of Othering which figures in the execution of social power as well as the form taken by class conflict. But in Heidegger we have the opportunity to understand the role the drive plays in structuring the nature of history itself, but to do this we need to engage with his History of Being. Heidegger's History of Being first prominently comes to appearance in his 1936–1938 thought as captured in his *Contributions to Philosophy (of the Event)* and his Nietzsche lectures given from 1936 to 1940. However, it is arguably contiguous with his earliest thinking on history and his attempt to arrive at an appropriate phenomenological method for engagement with history, developed especially in his 1920 lecture course *Phenomenology of Intuition and Expression.*[15] It can, further, be understood as a development of the project planned to constitute part two of *Being and Time*, "basic features of a phenomenological destruction of the history of ontology, with the problematic of Temporality as our clue".[16] Roughly speaking, then, the project of the History of Being can be understood as the attempt to arrive at an understanding of the meaning of Being through an analysis of the history of ontology focused on the temporal characteristics of the various phases of ontological thought. This investigation will allow us to escape from the frameworks of understanding

[15] For a more extensive presentation of the continuity between Heidegger's phenomenological approach to history from his earliest to latest work, see William Koch "Phenomenology as Social Critique" in *The Horizons of Authenticity: Essays in Honor of Charles Guignon's Work on Phenomenology, Existentialism, and Moral Psychology,* Hans Pederson, Megan Altman ed., (Springer, 2015).

[16] *Being and Time* p. 63.

established by tradition which has been unthinkingly adopted as long as the idiosyncratic turns of that tradition's history have gone unnoticed. In short, when we understand where our understandings have come from we also understand their contingency and are so opened up both to develop possibilities left in that history which have been unpursued and to experience radically new ways to understand the world that sedimented understandings have kept from appearing.

Our rough presentation of the History of Being above brings to appearance the central paradox of Heidegger's project. To endeavor an exploration of history guided by the issue of conceptions or manifestations of temporality leaves unaddressed the basic fact that history itself is understood on the basis of an understanding of temporality. According to Heidegger, history as understood by the science of historiology will view history as a series of fully constituted past events or facts accessible to us through reports, investigations such as archeology, and inference. Time, from this view, is a sequence of moments following upon one another and history is the collection of the moments that have already occurred. Consistently throughout his career Heidegger offered critiques of both this conception of temporality and its conception of history.[17]

In laying out in greater detail Heidegger's conception of the History of Being from the late 1930s and early 1940s, we will be able to clarify the conception of temporality at work within it. Heidegger presents the History of Being as an attempt to think our way back through the history of Western Thought to its First Beginning in the experience of Being present primarily in Pre-Socratic Ancient Greek thought. The First Beginning consists of an experience of Being as the temporal coming to appearance of beings as a total meaningful world. This formulation captures the understanding of truth as the *alethea*, or unconcealing, of beings within the clearing of a world from out of a primordial *lethe* or hiddenness. Swiftly however, in the development from Pre-Socratic to Platonic philosophy, the thinking of

[17] Interestingly, his critique of this concept of history pre-dates any fully developed critique of the serial conception of temporality and appears very clearly in 1920 as part of a critique of the concept of the a priori in philosophy, a fact which should discourage any overly transcendental readings of Heidegger's investigations of temporality in *Being and Time*. See *Phenomenology of Intuition and Expression* Part One: "On the destruction of the problem of the a priori" especially Section 6: "The six meanings of history and first bringing-out of the pre-delineations in them" and Section 10 part b: "The phenomenological dijudication of the genuine enactments of the meaning-complexes in question".

Being as an event of presencing gets forgotten and the Guiding Question of philosophy becomes "what are beings?" rather than "what is it that allows for the appearance of beings within a meaningful totality or world?". The development of the first question, and the forgottenness of the temporal coming-to-be and passing-away of *alethea* in favor of presence over presencing, leads to various attempts from Plato, through Aristotle and Medieval thought, until Descartes and finally contemporary scientific and transcendental understandings of Being to ground change in some unchanging foundation which would be universal and not itself subject to change. In short, the forgottenness of the temporal understanding of Being leads to investigations into the a-temporal and ahistorical until even history is understood in an ahistorical sense to the extent that it is taken to consist of stable unchanging facts about events which have been.

The First Beginning of Western thought consists, then, in a forgetting of temporality that leads to a focus upon the Guiding Question "What are beings?". Heidegger hopes, however, that we will be able to think our way out of this history and leap into a new history constituted by the Grounding Question of philosophy that is "What is Being?". This would be the leap into the Other Beginning of Western Thought, the beginning that was possible but never fully actualized. This Grounding Question is tentatively answered by Heidegger with the word *Ereignis*, or Event. Being is the Event that gives a meaningful context, world, or clearing in which beings can appear. This move can alternatively be conceptualized as a move from a thinking of the being of truth, that is, the fact of what it is to be for a being, to the thinking of the truth of being, that is, what it means for being itself to appear as a temporal Event of disclosure/concealment.[18]

Although the ground we have covered above is far from simple, the most difficult element of understanding what has already been said is to grasp that neither the history being investigated nor the Event (*Ereignis*) which that history attempts to bring to appearance consist of factual moments, events as specific presencings, which have passed. Rather, the history in question can best be understood in terms similar to the way that Gadamer discusses "effective history". This is an understanding of history as living and not past. In other words, in contrast to the First Beginning's privileging of presence

[18] A third formulation of the First and Other Beginnings consists in the move from asking about the essence of truth, or what allows anything to appear as what it is, to asking about the truth of essence, or what allows for the clearing in which alone things can appear or essence in a verbal sense.

over coming-to-be and passing-away, living effective history is understood in terms of the way that we carry the past forward through our future-oriented projects. Living time, such as the temporality of Dasein presented in *Being and Time*, is never present but rather always exists as a past projecting itself into the future. We are always behind and ahead of ourselves. In the same way, the only understanding of history possible is one that takes its origin from the meanings and practices through which we reach into a future and by which we have been given an understanding of the past as heritage and an inheritance. This means, as Heidegger stresses, that the investigation into the past that the History of Being seems to involve is always also an attempt to step forward into a future opened up for us. In this sense, the Event of *Ereignis* is always both lost before Western History and beaconing as an event yet to come; it precisely lives in this having-been-as-pursued-into-the-future. As Charles Guignon puts it:

> [I]nsofar as the meaning of any happening is determined by what is fulfilled or realized through it, history understood in the Heideggerian sense is not about something that is past. Instead, 'the happenings of history are primordially and always the future, that which ... comes towards us ... The future is the beginning of all happening' (GA 45: 36). So 'genuine history' is not a sequence of events, but consists of 'the goals of creative activity, their rank and their extent,' and this forms the subject matter for historical reflection (GA 45: 36).[19]

The key here is that the History of Being has a primordial and necessary futural aspect; it relies on the projective future-oriented characteristic of temporality that Heidegger had made central to his analysis in *Being and Time*. To understand history according to the Grounding Question "What is Being?" is to understand it as a living temporally extended event lagging behind us through our future-oriented pursuit of it. It is within the context of this larger History of Being that the engagement with Anaximander that we have already discussed takes place and which leads to Heidegger's discussion of the possibility of a thing's refusal to succumb to the temporal imperative to change in carrying its past into the future. It is within this context, then, that Zizek raises the question of whether Heidegger has not momentarily touched upon the concept of the drive and whether a full

[19] Charles Guignon "The History of Being" in *A Companion to Heidegger* Dreyfus and Wrathall ed. p. 393.

embrace of this concept might not entirely change the conception of history Heidegger embraces.

It is our contention that Heidegger could have extended his analysis beyond the Pre-Socratics to Homer, something he utterly fails to do in his unproductive engagement with Homer in his discussion of the Anaximander fragment but which he hints at as possible in the "Bremen Lectures".[20] Had he done so he might have struck upon the drive as manifest in Achilles. It is our challenge to clarify how this experience of the drive might deepen Heidegger's own analyses and challenge Zizek's conception of the drive.

In our discussion of the *sinthomosexual* we have already made clear the extent to which the drive is a force opposed to futurity. Indeed, from the standpoint of the drive, the future-oriented nature of meaning itself only arises by means of the prop of fantasy. The drive itself knows only insistence, without goal or past, and the full scope of temporality arises as a secondary misdirection of the drive onto impossible futures that will satisfy it. The manifestation of the drive, in breaking with future-oriented fantasy, threatens meaning as a whole. It appears as the abyss at the foundation of the Symbolic. This is because of the distinct temporal nature of meaning. Meaning is grounded on a life-world of projects constituted out of fantasy. It is precisely the characteristic of Achilles' rage as meaningless and abyssal that mystifies both his comrades who would talk him into being more reasonable and later scholars who would seek to understand his speech within the Homeric context. Adam Parry, son of the great Classicist Milman Parry who renovated forever Homeric studies and an important scholar of ancient philosophy in his own right, states that Achilles:

> is the one Homeric hero who does not accept the common language … [He] has no language with which to express his disillusionment. Yet he expresses it, and in a remarkable way. He does it by misusing the language he disposes of. He asks questions that cannot be answered and makes demands that cannot be met.[21]

It is in this sense that we have discussed Achilles' rage as pathological. Despite his rage appearing first in the story due to a slight to his honor he has suffered at the hands of Agamemnon, it swiftly becomes clear to the

[20] Heidegger *Bremen and Freiburg Lectures* Andrew J. Mitchell trans.

[21] A. Parry, "The Language of Achilles", *Transactions and Proceedings of the American Philosophical Association 87* (1956).

perplexity of his friends that his anger is not actually about the slight. Despite more than adequate compensation for the slight being offered, Achilles makes it clear that his rage is not to be understood based on any scale the heroic ethic can provide. It is honor itself, and the ideal of the hero, which Achilles' rage drives him to reject. But this, as Parry points out, is to reject the only language Achilles has access to as well as the entire social world it supports. This is why his demands cannot be met.

This rage is pathological in a very precise sense; it is the *pathe,* passion, or drive out of which the *logos*, speech, and reason of Achilles rise. In this regard we can see even Achilles' pathetic dream of returning to his homeland to have a peaceful life as a non-hero is not so much the positing of a new goal as the rejection of goals in general and the entire game of pursuing futures. We see this just as clearly in the second manifestation of Achilles' rage, his return to battle to kill Hector. He knows this will be his death, that once he kills Hector his own death will soon follow, but what he displays is anything but being-toward-death. Despite his meditations on finitude and death, he has not embraced this fact but rather rages against it even in his pursuit of Hector. There is no pause in his rage from which he can achieve resolute action. Much like Agamemnon's slight, even Patrocles' death is an event illuminated in light of rage and not a cause.

Achilles' rage seems, then, to embody an insistence that defies the futurity of only apparently coherent social fantasy. As such, it would seem to nicely fit a particular's refusal to succumb to time on the model presented by Heidegger in his discussion of Anaximander. It is clear within the context of Heidegger's own thought that this injustice can be read as a proto-enframing, a prefiguring of the technological reduction of all beings to mere force to be translated and used, which Heidegger understands as the nihilism at the end of the history of metaphysics. This enframing arises out of the triumph of subjectivism, the process whereby humanity's own drive for mastery becomes a universal measure for what is real and constant such that becoming as the flux of force is absolutized. As Heidegger asserts of Nietzsche's thought, Being is identified with Becoming but in a way that reduces real change or temporality to a gray base of forces to be manipulated. Ultimately, however, the end of this absolutism of subjectivity is the dissolution of subjectivity into the forces themselves such that there is no longer any subject or object, no material to be used, or humanity to use it.

The unjust refusal of the particular to pass becomes, then, this chain of subjective willful self-assertion eventually dissolved into a universal understanding of Being as timeless force. When we recognize this we realize first that, far from marking an intimation in Heidegger never fully developed as Zizek implies, the discussion of the individual's insistent rebellion against time is a major theme Heidegger has extensively developed throughout his project. Second we realize that an understanding of the drive based on this model will leave us caught within the end of metaphysics with Nietzsche but not outside of it in an Other Beginning that Heidegger hopes to prefigure. To accept Zizek's proposal we must give up the entire project of the History of Being and surrender to the nihilism Heidegger finds at the end of that history. This brief evaluation will seem more convincing when we recognize that we have, as yet, only partially analyzed the rage of Achilles. A fuller analysis makes clear a break with Zizek's proposal that illuminates, rather than overturns, Heidegger's History of Being.

What we know of as the *Iliad* is just one part of the story cycle that would have constituted the full Homeric story of the Trojan War, its pre-history, and its effects. Specifically it deals with the story of Achilles' rage. But by considering what we know of the full scope of the war's story, we can reasonably assert that Achilles' rage is at the very center of the entire event's structure. Despite common attempts to moralize the Trojan War, Homer and Ancient Greek myth make clear it is a story that forcefully resists any reading in terms of moralistic cause and effect. The stealing of Helen by Paris was no human crime; for example, it wasn't a breach of the famous Greek guest code or at least any reading of it as such is inadequately partial. Helen was given to Paris by Aphrodite. It was a match made in Heaven, or rather in Olympus. But Achilles is himself at the center of this very event and is, from the very beginning, the manifestation of a force that threatens Olympus to its very core.

The story of Achilles' birth is the story of the fall of Olympus barely averted. Achilles' mother, Thetis, is herself a goddess and was desired by both Zeus and Poseidon before she married Achilles' mortal father Peleus. Already his birth, then, is prefigured in strife between two mighty gods. Prometheus, however, was aware of a terrible secret that Zeus somehow finds out. Specifically, Thetis' son is destined to be greater than his father. To Zeus, who had overthrown his own father who in turn overthrew his father, this is clearly the grimmest threat imaginable. It is a threat he himself had dodged by devouring his first partner Metis who, similarly, was destined to give birth to a son greater than his father. By devouring her and taking onto himself the power of birth, he transforms the son who would overthrow him into the daughter, Athena, who most supports his rule. Thetis, however, threatens this delicate balance. For this reason Zeus marries Thetis off to a mortal, transferring the force that would destroy Olympus down into the mortal realm.

Though alleviated, the doom represented by Thetis' child-to-be cannot be fully silenced. At her wedding we see the first manifestation of the destructive force Zeus sought to redirect. What follows is the famous story of Eris, goddess of strife who was not invited to the party, and her golden apple. In revenge for being snubbed, Eris rolls a golden apple engraved with the word *kallisti* or "for the most beautiful one", into the wedding. This leads Athena, Hera, and Aphrodite to argue over which of them the apple is intended for. This, in turn, leads to their selecting Paris to judge between them. In exchange for giving her the apple, Aphrodite promises Paris the most beautiful woman in the world, Helen. The Trojan War, then, arises out of the marriage of Achilles' parents.[22]

It is clear from what has been said that the gods are as much pawns to the force in play here as are the mortals. We see this even more clearly when we realize that Troy is the one city most beloved by Zeus. He would save it, if he could, but its destiny is determined by an indistinct Fate that not even the king of the gods can alter. Throughout the *Iliad* the Trojan War is as much about the gods joining the battle, both for and against Troy, as it is about mortals. At times the gods themselves come to blows, and it is clear that Olympus itself is shaken by the terrible power that dooms Troy. The rage of Achilles plays a role in the larger drama and is used both to punish the Greeks for daring to destroy a city even Zeus would save if he could and to ultimately bring about the same city's destruction through the death of its military leader Hector. More than this, we can recognize the rage of Achilles as the very force that led to Thetis' wedding, the force that drove the successive generations and revolutions of the gods leading eventually to Zeus' reign. This rage echoes in the very halls of Olympus as the gods bicker over Troy's fate, and we see that even though the doom meant for Olympus and Zeus has been offset to Troy and Priam, it constantly threatens to overflow into universal destruction. The entire history of the Greek gods, with Troy as a footnote, is driven by the rage we find exemplified in Achilles. As rage is the first word of Western history, so too is it its first conception of force, fate, and doom. We might go so far as to say it is its first conception of temporality as well.

[22] For beautiful retellings of the above myths, see, for example, Jean Pierre Vernant's *Ancient Greek Myths*.

The pathological rage, the drive, is here no insistence of a thing beyond its time. No self-asserting particular is represented here as in Anaximander. And no longer does this drive's rejection of futural temporality seem as clear. What is clear is that Zeus, in eating Metis and marrying off Thetis, is facing the basic problem of time, but it is now the rule of succession and, indeed, the female power of generation that order must arise in defiance of. In Ancient Greek myth we find the mother and child prefigured not as the prop of fantasy and hopeful futurity, but rather as the force working perpetually against order, meaning, and coherence. Achilles is the child that destroys rather than fulfilling fantasy, offering us a new image of the *sinthomosexual* as child. Could we not even say that the rage of Achilles is, on a cosmic scale, itself futural?

The drive as figured by Achilles is far from a particular insisting in existence beyond its time. Rather it is a cosmic force, and Achilles happens to be a privileged instantiation of this force. This fits with Lacan's identification of the drive as a pre-subjective force to be identified with the Symbolic order itself in its failure or inconsistent non-being. This point stresses the pathological nature of Achilles' rage. If we consider the term in a Kantian sense we recognize the pathological as the heteronomous and thus as that which isn't free. Pathological actions are determined by the world's influence upon our psychology and physiology, rather than from the transcendental dictates of reason. Thus, far from an independent force of individuation embodied by a particular's rebellion against the rule of time as we might find in Heidegger's reading of Anaximander or Zizek's embrace of this reading, the drive is the point of connection between the world and the self. The drive, in this sense, is the space of a type of Heideggerian *fug* or order, an order or *logos* in opposition to which the human and divine world is built.

Holding in view the vision of the drive as the universal force of change, time, and fate against which Zeus struggles to establish a lasting order—a force identified particularly with the fertile power of the mother and embodied in the destructive advent of the child—allows us to bring together two different versions of the rejected margin. We have, namely, the historical war against both the female gender and the homosexual. Achilles as the *sinthomosexual* is both the destructive force of the mother and the specter of the future denying, social responsibility rejecting, homosexual. In this Achilles is not resisting change and death; rather it is the presumed control over time and change dreamed of through collective social fantasy he rejects and, indeed, violently destroys through both his inaction and action.

Achilles offers us a vision of the pulsion of the drive, the insistence-to-change rather than the insistence-to-be, which far from Freud's atemporality is instead the original pulsion of time itself.

We should recall that Heidegger's History of Being recognizes in history a plurality of clearings and concealings as the world opens up to us and takes on meaning in different ways from the time of the Pre-Socratics through to the final dominance of nihilistic technological enframing. We might suggest that the rule of Zeus, like the rule of the heroic ethic of Agamemnon and Troy alike, is itself a limited clearing or disclosure. These different worlds open and close not just due to their own internal characteristics but also, and arguably ultimately, due to what rests outside of them beyond the limit of their circle of meaning. What they hide, what they reject, what they ignore is the source of their fate. It is the logic which rests beyond the borders of a given Symbolic system or meaningful world which drives that world to its inevitable change, and this is the logic figured forth in Achilles' *pathe*, in his rage. Achilles projects no future; his rage allows him to pursue no desire or coherent course of action, and yet around him and because of him, the entire world that comes to stand-forth in Homer's *Iliad* takes the form and path that it does. Here, far more than in the Promethean creator-artist-thinker of Heidegger's fantasies in the early 1930s who begins a new history by projecting new paths into the future, we find an image of the *Ereignis* that opens up a world. Achilles teaches us to see *Ereignis* as drive, *Ereignis* as *sinthomosexual*, *Ereignis* as the force transgressing and rejection the limit along with its sustaining desires. It is the insistence on change decoupled from fantasy.

Bibliography

Bianchi, Emanuela. 2014. *The Feminine Symptom: Aleatory Matter in the Aristotelian Cosmos.* New York: Fordham University Press.

Dreyfus, Hubert L., and Mark A. Wrathall, eds. 2007. *A Companion to Heidegger.* Hoboken: Wiley-Blackwell.

Edelman, Lee. 2004. *No Future: Queer Theory and the Death Drive.* Durham: Duke University Press Books.

Freud, Sigmund. 2008. *The Essentials of Psycho-analysis.* London: Random House.

Heidegger, Martin. 2010a. *Being and Time.* Trans. Joan Stambaugh. Albany: State University of New York Press.

———. 2010b. *Phenomenology of Intuition and Expression: Theory of Philosophical Concept Formation.* Trans. Tracy Colony. New York: Continuum.

———. 2012. *Bremen and Freiburg Lectures.* Trans. Andrew J. Mitchell. Bloomington: Indiana University Press.

Holmes, Brooke. 2010. *The Symptom and the Subject: The Emergence of the Physical Body in Ancient Greece.* Princeton: Princeton University Press.

Homer. 1951. *Iliad.* Trans. Richard Lattimore. Chicago: University of Chicago Press.

Koch, William. 2015. Phenomenology as Social Critique. In *Horizons of Authenticity in Phenomenology, Existentialism, and Moral Psychology: Essays in Honor of Charles Guignon*, ed. Hans Pedersen and Megan Altman. New York: Springer.

Lacan, Jacques. 1991. In *The Ego in Freud's Theory and in the Technique of Psychoanalysis*, ed. Jacques-Alain Miller. New York: W.W. Norton & Company.

Parry, A. 1956. The Language of Achilles. *Transactions and Proceedings of the American Philosophical Association 87*: 1–7.

Zizek, Slavoj. 2012. *Less Than Nothing: Hegel and the Shadow of Dialectical Materialism.* New York: Verso.

Borderland Spaces of the Third Kind: Erotic Agency in Plato and Octavia Butler

Jessica Elbert Decker

Sexual difference is the foundational lynchpin of patriarchal metaphysics and its corresponding symbolic structures. While feminist readings of Plato's texts often emphasize the dualism of his thought, this dualism is perhaps amplified as Plato is read through the Cartesian and Enlightenment models of rationality that followed. Understood in the context of the mythological and poetic texts of the thinkers that preceded him, Plato's dialogues reveal latent possibilities for unraveling the canonical, dualistic understanding of his thought and for undermining deeply hierarchical and patriarchal systems that rely on binary models for their justification. Adopting Irigaray's method of "jamming the theoretical machinery," I attempt here not a reparative reading of Plato, but a differently focused reading that calls his dualism into question and tarries with the strange interloper in his binary model, the third kind.[1] Using the work of Octavia Butler, I will demonstrate how this third kind disrupts the binary understanding of sexual difference, especially with regard to erotic agency.

[1] Luce Irigaray, *This Sex Which Is Not One* (Ithaca: Cornell University Press, 1985), 78. "The issue is not one of elaborating a new theory of which woman would be the *subject* or the *object*, but of jamming the theoretical machinery itself, of suspending its pretension to a truth and of a meaning that are excessively univocal."

J. Elbert Decker (✉)
California State University San Marcos, San Marcos, CA, USA

J. Elbert Decker, D. Winchock (eds.), *Borderlands and Liminal Subjects*, https://doi.org/10.1007/978-3-319-67813-9_10

In the *Timaeus*, Plato introduces the third kind, which he first names as "receptacle (*hypodoche*), and as it were the nurse, of all Becoming" and posits it as intermediary between the intelligible and the sensible worlds.[2] Timaeus, the speaker for much of the dialogue, tells us that without the necessary mediation of this third kind, no transmission or passage between the sensible and intelligible would be possible.[3] Plato's *Timaeus* will be the focus of this analysis, as this dialogue most directly contests his seemingly binary metaphysics, though the tri-part structure developed in *Timaeus* is not an anomaly, but integral to Plato's thought. As Hampton has pointed out in studying Plato's *Philebus*, "throughout the Platonic corpus there is ample evidence, both implicit and explicit, of his striving to find intermediaries to bridge the gap between the one and the many, the Forms and the sensibles, soul and body."[4] In many of Plato's dialogues, the role of intermediary is played by *eros*, a crucial aspect of Plato's project, as Jill Gordon has persuasively demonstrated in *Plato's Erotic World*.[5]

The cosmology of *Timaeus* uses the model of sexual reproduction as a schematic for the production of the cosmos: Timaeus likens Being (the active "from which") to the Father, the third kind to the Mother (the

[2] Plato, *Timaeus*, trans. R.G. Bury (Boston: Harvard University Press, 1929), 49a. Bianchi has pointed out the suggestive maternal connotations of *hypodoche*: "the verbal form *hypodechomai* more strongly indicates the hospitality of entertaining or welcoming under one's roof, and, said of a woman, also means to conceive or become pregnant." Emanuela Bianchi, *The Feminine Symptom: Aleatory Matter in the Aristotelian Cosmos* (New York: Fordham University Press, 2014), 97. Plato uses several different names for the third kind throughout *Timaeus*, including mother, nurse of all Becoming, and space (*khora*).

[3] At *Timaeus* 31c, "but it's not possible for two things alone to be beautifully combined apart from some third: some bond must get in the middle and bring them both together"; and at *Timaeus* 49a: "Two kinds were sufficient for what was said before: one set down as the form of a model—intelligible and always in the self-same condition—and the second, an imitation of a model, having birth and visible. A third kind we didn't distinguish at that time, since we deemed that the two would be sufficient; but now the account seems to make it necessary that we try to bring to light in speeches a form difficult and obscure."

[4] Cynthia Hampton, "Overcoming Dualism: The Importance of the Intermediate in Plato's *Philebus*" in *Feminist Interpretations of Plato* ed. Nancy Tuana (University Park: Pennsylvania State University Press, 1994): 223.

[5] Jill Gordon, *Plato's Erotic World: From Cosmic Origins to Human Death* (Cambridge: Cambridge University Press, 2012).

passive "receiver"), and Becoming to the offspring they generate.[6] The third kind unsettles the binary model while simultaneously allowing the distinction in the first place, creating an ambiguous borderland space that both joins and separates the sensible and the intelligible. The third kind is a space of motion, described by Plato as shaking and discordant, and most significantly, as a generative space: it is the origin of all sensible forms. However, Plato strategically presents *khora* as feminine and without agency or autonomy, a passive molding-stuff (*ekmageion*) that receives all things but *is* none of the shapes it takes on.[7] In contrast to the passivity of *khora*, the divine male demiurge of *Timaeus*' origin myth creates the cosmos through intelligent mastery. But if we follow Plato's logic, when he tells us that *khora* is neither of the binaries it grounds, then *khora* cannot be passive or active, or male or female; these categories would continually shift because *khora* has no static identity—a problem Plato recognizes in using multiple names for it.

Octavia Butler's work frequently interrogates binary, hierarchical models and their corresponding power structures; her narratives can be read as imaginative meditations on radical alterity: how to approach that which is radically other, without doing violence, without obliterating the other? Given the framework of the *Timaeus*, I will be focusing on Octavia Butler's representations of sexual difference and reproduction, which present us with an alternative reading of a third kind that disrupts binary models of opposition and their metaphysical underpinnings. In her *Xenogenesis* trilogy, Octavia Butler imagines an alien race called the Oankali, and their methods of sexual reproduction involve a third kind, similar to the model presented in Plato's *Timaeus*. The Oankali are nomadic creatures; their ships are living, and they require what they call genetic "trading" in order to survive. The Oankali include male and female individuals, but there is also a third kind, the ooloi, which are neither male nor female but radically other. The ooloi are experts at manipulating genetic material and mixing selected new genes from the species they encounter into the current genetic structures of the Oankali. They, like Plato's *khora*, are the space in which reproduction happens; though, unlike *khora*, they are corporeal and they have agency.

[6] At *Timaeus* 50b Plato describes the three kinds as follows: "that *in which* it comes to be, and that *from which* it comes to be. . .and what's more, it's fitting to liken the receiver to a mother, the from which to a father, and the nature between these two to an offspring."

[7] Plato calls *khora* '*ekmageion*' at *Timaeus* 50c, the full passage is cited later in this article.

This ambiguous wavering between passivity and activity, modeled in the paradoxical concept of *khora*, is one way to imagine this third borderland space that is neither this nor that, but somehow partakes of both. In Plato's *Timaeus* and in Octavia Butler's imaginary worlds, a particular erotic borderland continually erupts: that ambiguous space between force (*bia*) and persuasion (*peitho*). In these origin stories, creation is only possible through a harmony that is also discordant, love that is also war, seduction that is also compulsion. The question of agency is crucial to a feminist reading of Plato's *Timaeus*, since Plato makes *khora*, which takes the place of mother or matrix, a non-agent, a passive medium impressed upon by intelligent (male) mastery like that of the demiurge. As Bianchi has argued, this move "crucially involves a relegation of the feminine to a position of barely knowable, shifting, errant function in the production of a metaphysical system and world in which only men are able to function as agentic, reasoning beings."[8] Binary models of activity versus passivity assume static categories and identities, and, as Judith Butler has suggested, Plato's family structure in the *Timaeus* grounds a "heterosexual matrix" in which the male is always the agent (penetrator) and the female always passive (penetrated).[9] The work of Octavia Butler will present imaginative possibilities for understanding the third kind in a way that disrupts this binary, heterosexual, and patriarchal conception of erotic agency.

The Discordant Motion of Plato's Third Kind

Plato was well aware of the philosophical problem raised by his binary division between the bodily and the intelligible worlds: how can this borderland possibly be crossed? The introduction of the third kind in *Timaeus* is perhaps Plato's most explicit solution to this problem, but, as Jill Gordon has shown in *Plato's Erotic World*, the role of *eros* as intermediary between mortal and divine is a vital and consistent theme in Plato's thought. Of particular interest for reading Plato alongside Octavia Butler's work, a strange pattern emerges in his dialogues: the appearances of the third kind as mediator consistently invoke themes of sexuality and generation: whether it is the figure of *khora*, the mediation of *eros* in human life, or the

[8] Emanuela Bianchi, "Receptacle/Chora: Figuring the Errant Feminine in Plato's Timaeus." *Hypatia* 21, no. 4 (2006): 125.

[9] Judith Butler, *Bodies that Matter* (New York: Routledge, 1993): 23.

demiurge's method of constructing the cosmos in *Timaeus*. As I will demonstrate, in discussing each of these three cases in turn, erotic language or explicit mention of sexual reproduction frames the discussion. This reading emphasizes a consistent strategy of undermining binary opposition in Plato, particularly binary models of sexual difference; the picture that emerges is not one of intractable, separate categories of opposition, but an image of movement, multiplicity, repetition, and difference.

A triangular structure repeats and multiples in the *Timaeus*, a phenomenon fitting to a cosmology, as Pythagorean models indicate that nothing can be built without the triangle. When Socrates begins the discussion in *Timaeus*, he identifies the matter at hand with a subtlety very familiar in Platonic dialogues; he greets Timaeus thus, "one, two, three...but now where's our fourth...?"[10] Socrates then offers a strategically abridged version of the *Republic* (a discussion that reportedly occurred the day before): he mentions only that each man be given the task appropriate to him (his example is the warrior class), that the souls of the guardians need to have a balanced nature, that guardians would be trained in gymnastics and music, and that mating would be done by a rigged lottery and the offspring raised in common.[11] Plato here suggests that the question of sexual reproduction is essential to the production of the cosmos, as both origin and generation are at stake in this narrative, and he introduces the crucial theme of harmony between opposites. The mention of the warrior class also invokes conflict and struggle, a prominent motif in the *Timaeus* dialogue as it is occurring during the feast of Athena.[12]

[10] Plato, *Timaeus*, 17a.

[11] The lottery is rigged because the guardian class would match good with good and bad with bad, though the people would believe it was decided by chance, "in order that they might become, to the best of our power, as good as possible in their natures right from the start, don't we remember how we said that the rulers, male and female, had to contrive some sort of lottery by secret ballots for marital coupling so that the separate classes of bad and good men will respectively be mated by lot with women who are like them; and that no hatred would arise among them on this score since they'd believe that the cause of the allotment was chance." Ibid., 18c.

[12] At *Timaeus* 21a, Critias says that the speakers will "praise the goddess on her feast-day by singing, as it were, in a manner both just and true." As Kalkavadge explains in a footnote, "the feast to which Critias refers is probably the Greater Panathenaea, the celebration of Athena's birthday," 51. The prominence of Athena's presence in this dialogue is reflected in the war stories told by Critias, and underscores Socrates' desire to see the animals engaging in some struggle or conflict.

Socrates tests his listeners by asking them whether or not this summary of *Republic* is sufficient, "or are we still yearning (*pothos*) for something further in what was said, my dear Timaeus, something that's being left out?"[13] Socrates deliberately uses the language of desire, invoking *pothos*, a desire for something missing or lacking. As Kalkavadge remarks on this passage, "by giving us a philosophically deficient summary of the *Republic* here at the beginning of the *Timaeus*, and by following it up with Timaeus' willingness to be satisfied with such an account, Plato indirectly signals the importance of philosophic *eros* for the dialogue."[14] Eros is associated with lack, as Diotima's speech in Plato's *Symposium* makes clear—we desire only that which we do not possess; philosophic eros is what motivates us to seek out the limits and edges of what we know. As a catalyst, eros is essential to a living and moving cosmos, just as it is essential to the animals (human or otherwise) that hope to transcend mortality through sexual reproduction and the production of offspring. But Socrates' next remark is crucial—he identifies the thing missing from the truncated summary of the *Republic* as *motion*, indicating both his desire for what is missing and his inability to possess it. Before Critias and Timaeus begin their speeches, Socrates wishes to see the imaginary city of the *Republic* in motion: "it's as if someone who gazed on beautiful animals somewhere, either produced by the art of painting or truly living and keeping their peace, were to get a desire to gaze upon them moving or contending in some struggle that seemed appropriate to their bodies."[15] Socrates' remark links eros with motion, and indicates the importance of this theme in approaching the cosmology of *Timaeus.*

Socrates tells Timaeus that the class of poets is deficient in giving a true account because they can only imitate what they know and they remain in their place of upbringing, while the class of sophists is deficient because they "wander from city to city" and "would stray from the mark in describing how men at once philosophers and statesman might act and speak."[16] In other words, one stays firmly in place while the other wanders and strays—a familiar Platonic characterization of the realms of Being and Becoming, respectively. Socrates tells Timaeus, "what's been left is the class in your

[13] Ibid., 19a.

[14] Kalkavadge, *Plato's Timaeus: Translation, Glossary, Appendices and Introductory Essay* (Newburyport: Focus Publishing, 2001), 9.

[15] Plato, *Timaeus*, 19c.

[16] Plato, *Timaeus*, 19e.

condition, the class that by nature and upbringing partakes of both at once"—note that this class in which Timaeus is being included is the third, and partakes of both without being limited to either—in other words, the mark of the third kind.[17] Plato reveals the structure and model of this dialogue in this seemingly innocent opening discussion, identifying Timaeus as a properly embodied speaker for the third kind.

The third kind is introduced when Timaeus tells us that the two forms, Model (the intelligible) and Copy (the sensible), respectively, are not sufficient to explain the structure of the cosmos. This third kind is described in detail at *Timaeus* 50c:

> One must always call it by the same name, since it never at all abandons its own power. It both always receives all things, and nowhere in any way has it ever taken on any shape similar to the ones that come into it; for its laid down by nature as a molding-stuff (*ekmageion*) for everything, being both moved and thoroughly configured by whatever things come into it; and because of these, it appears different at different times; and the figures that come into it and go out of it are always imitations of the things that *are*, having been imprinted from them in some manner hard to tell of and wondrous.

Although Plato tells us that *khora* must always be called by the same name, he perplexingly identifies *khora* by multiple names, including mother, nurse of all becoming, receptacle (*hypodoche*), and space (*khora*). As Derrida remarks, "at times the *khora* appears to be neither this nor that, at times both this and that, but this alternation between the logic of exclusion and that of participation...stems perhaps only from a provisional appearance and from the constraints of rhetoric, even from some incapacity for naming."[18] This problem of naming is not new to Plato, but appears as a frequent philosophical problem in Presocratic texts, especially in the fragments of Heraclitus.[19]

[17] Ibid., 19e–20a.

[18] Jacques Derrida, *On the Name*, trans. David Wood, John P. Leavey, Jr., and Ian McLeod (Palo Alto: Stanford University Press, 1995), 89.

[19] Plato is well aware of this reading of Heraclitus, as he refers to Heraclitus repeatedly in the *Cratylus*, where Socrates and his interlocuters interrogate the problem of names and naming. As Jill Gordon notes, "Heraclitus is referred to no fewer than eight times: 401d; 402a–b; 410a; 411b–c; 420a; 439b–c; 440c; 440e. One concern Socrates has is how meaning can emerge if there are two names that refer to the same thing. The first examples Socrates uses is the name of the river, called Xanthus by the gods but Scamander by men; one might argue that this pointed example of a river...may itself be an oblique reference to Heraclitus," *Plato's Erotic World*, 56.

The nature of *khora*, then, must not be a simple identity; its nature must be of a different kind, in fact, of a self-differing kind: an idea prefigured in Heraclitus. His fragment DK 51 reads: "they do not comprehend how a thing agrees at variance with itself; it is a backwards-stretched harmony, like that of the bow and the lyre."[20] Heraclitus' notion of identity, as this fragment illustrates, is of dynamic identity—literally, a self-differing thing. Derrida cites this fragment in his essay "Differance," where he interrogates the metaphysics of presence, as he names it, in its relation to language.[21] If identity is a dynamic flux, as Heraclitus suggests, then any metaphysics or language that relies on static identities has the abyss open up beneath it: multiplicity and ceaseless change. Derrida's description of *khora* echoes this indeterminacy of identity, "with *khora* herself/itself...[it] must not have any proper determination, sensible or intelligible, material or formal, and therefore must not have any identity of its/her own, must not be identical with herself/itself."[22] The indeterminacy and ambiguity of *khora*'s identity in Plato, when understood in this way, is not a concept unique to Plato, but an adaptation of Heraclitean flux.

The problem of naming, especially in Heraclitus, erupts because of *motion*—how can our static names possibly describe self-differing things that are constantly in flux? As his repeated references to Heraclitus attest, Plato was well aware of this problem—especially because of the trouble it spells for his Forms as divine and unchanging truth. Thus Plato's vacillation in naming *khora* reveals a sleight of hand: Plato attempts to *use* this ambiguous "place" as a ground for his distinction between the sensible and intelligible, while at the same time avowing the permanence of these categories. In other words, Plato uses *khora* to quarantine Heraclitean flux and the radical ambiguity of opposites. But the borders of *khora* are permeable and call his categories into question; as Lynn Huffer has noted, "the introduction of the *chora* in fact undermines the mimetic system of identity on which its very articulation is founded, since the *chora* becomes that gap. In other words, by positing the *chora*, the *Timaeus* points to the fissure that

[20] Heraclitus, DK 51. All fragments of Heraclitus use the standard Diels-Kranz numbering, and translations are Charles H. Kahns' unless otherwise specified, from *The Art and Thought of Heraclitus: An Edition of the Fragments with Translation and Commentary* (Cambridge: Cambridge University Press, 1979).

[21] Jacques Derrida, "Differance," In *Margins of Philosophy,* trans. Alan Bass (Chicago: University of Chicago Press, 1982).

[22] Derrida, *On the Name*, 99.

breaks open the entire Platonic system of naming and knowing."[23] The manner in which *khora* disrupts the dualistic, patriarchal system is best imagined as a kind of shaking, swaying motion and discordant music, chaotic and *aleatory*, to use Emanuela Bianchi's appropriate word.[24] This swaying motion is repeatedly described in Heraclitus' fragments as the motion generated by opposites, and *khora* introduces this kind of motion into Plato's cosmos, a dynamic tension and oscillation between poles, a space without static identity. This is especially significant if we recall Socrates' longing, at the beginning of *Timaeus*, to see his city in motion; Socrates—in the language of *eros*—identifies motion as the thing that is missing from the summary of *Republic*. If desire is for a static object that one might possess, then this desire will always be frustrated by an ephemeral, changing thing that resists objectification.

In *Plato's Erotic World*, Jill Gordon traces the function of eros through the dialogues, focusing especially on those dialogues not traditionally identified as erotic. In her reading of the origin tale of *Timaeus*, she writes, "in Plato's world eros has divine cosmological origins and is part of the original divine human soul. Eros is coextensive with the individuation of souls and thus with their alienation from divine being."[25] Separation from origins is a serious problem for Plato, as Gordon points out, for example, in his *Parmenides*: "Socrates feels trepidation precisely when Parmenides suggests that his theory of forms may carry the consequence of completely cutting off human access to the forms."[26] The binary system that identifies the sensible versus the intelligible creates a border between these worlds—a border that must be crossed, or the human soul remains alienated from its source. The practice of philosophy, which Gordon argues is an *erotic* practice, is the process of returning the soul to its origin.

Perhaps most familiar of the erotic dialogues, Plato's *Symposium* deals explicitly with the role and nature of eros. In Diotima's speech, she tells us that eros is a *daimon*, "between a mortal and an immortal."[27] Diotima goes on to identify the role of the *daimonic*: "interpreting and transporting

[23] Lynn Huffer, *Maternal Pasts, Feminist Futures: Nostalgia, Ethics, and the Questions of Difference* (Palo Alto: Stanford University Press, 1998), 83.

[24] Bianchi, *The Feminine Symptom: Aleatory Matter in the Aristotelian Cosmos.*

[25] Gordon, *Plato's Erotic World*, 2.

[26] Ibid., 121.

[27] Plato, *Symposium* 202e.

human things to the gods and divine things to men; entreaties and sacrifices from below, and ordinances and requitals from above: being midway between."[28] As Diotima's speech later outlines, the lover is led by eros from the realm of mere body to a communion with the Forms.[29] This communion is an experience of immortality—however paradoxically ephemeral for the embodied lover—as Diotima argues that "love is of immortality."[30] Diotima links reproduction with immortality, but sexual reproduction is distinguished from what she calls "pregnancy in soul"—all creatures desire immortality, but some, such as wise men, desire to give birth to beautiful ideas, while women and foolish men are only able to give birth to physical children.[31] While eros may manifest as lust, as in the intemperate character of Alcibiades, it may also be used to guide the philosopher (*lover* of wisdom) toward the divine, if he is able to properly manage eros using the rational soul.

Plato's characterization of eros in *Symposium* deviates significantly from the mytho-poetic tradition that preceded him, where eros is a powerful and chaotic force that cannot be controlled by human beings. In the *Iliad*, for example, Aphrodite compels Helen to fall in love with Paris—which begins the catastrophic Trojan War. In lyric poetry, eros is similarly a dangerous sensuous force, as in the poems of Sappho. She describes eros explicitly in fragment 130: "Eros the melter of limbs (now again) stirs me – sweetbitter unmanageable (*amechanon*) creature who steals in."[32] As in Diotima's speech, eros has a kind of double-nature—here, both sweet and bitter—but even more significant is Sappho's use of the term *amechanon*, translated as "unmanageable." The term literally means "without a scheme" but strongly connotes helplessness.[33] As Dodds has pointed out, ancient Greeks experienced *daemonic* influence as both supernatural and beyond human

[28] Plato, *Symposium* 202e.

[29] This movement from the sensible world of the body to the intelligible world of the Forms is most apparent at the end of Diotima's speech, where she describes the "ladder of love" (*Symposium* 211a–212c).

[30] Plato, *Symposium* 207a.

[31] Diotima's discussion of the two types of pregnancy begins at *Symposium* 206c.

[32] Anne Carson's translation from *If Not, Winter: Fragments of Sappho* (New York: Vintage Books, 2002), 265.

[33] For discussion of the meaning of *amechania* in Parmenides' poem, see Peter Kingsley, *Reality* (Inverness: Golden Sufi Press, 2003), 91 and 565.

control.[34] In discussing these daemonic events, Dodds remarks, "these things are not truly part of the self, since they are not within man's conscious control; they are endowed with a life and energy of their own, and so can force a man, as it were from the outside, into conduct foreign to him."[35] The tradition that preceded Plato is consistent in identifying eros as an ambiguous and uncontrollable force akin to madness, but Plato puts a different spin on eros in *Symposium*: he desires that eros be managed—precisely the opposite of Sappho's characterization as "unmanageable" – by the philosopher skilled in harmonizing opposite forces. Eros poses a problem for rational agency, if agency is only understood as active, independent, voluntary motion.

In *Symposium*, the speech of the physician Eryximachus introduces a method: the physician knows how to doctor opposite forces in the body to create harmony (health). Eryximachus claims that "medicine is simply the science of the effects of Love" and further tells us that "a good practitioner knows how to affect the body and how to transform its desires."[36] In the speech of Alcibiades that concludes *Symposium*, Socrates is a living example of what a well-harmonized philosopher would look like—Alcibiades tells us that Socrates is temperate, despite "the madness, the Bacchic frenzy of philosophy."[37] Not only is Socrates balanced in himself, he is also capable of bringing about this harmony in others—and his method is often described in erotic language. For example, in *Theaetetus*, Socrates describes himself as a midwife and goes on to comment on the ability of midwives to act as matchmakers, making a sly comment about how these midwives might be suspected of pimping.[38] As Gordon has persuasively argued, Socrates' skill in erotics is not merely of interest in the dialogues that

[34] See E.R. Dodds, *The Greeks and the Irrational* (Berkeley: University of California Press, 1951) for a detailed discussion of the *daemonic* in the psychological life of Ancient Greece.

[35] Dodds, *The Greeks and the Irrational*, 41. While the question of free will was not schematized as a philosophical problem in Ancient Greek thought, the problem of agency was a frequent theme in myths and tragedies. As Vernant has suggested, "the category of the will is portrayed in tragedy as an anxious question concerning the relationship of man to his actions: To what extent is man really the source of his actions?" Jean-Pierre Vernant and Pierre Vidal-Naquet, "Oedipus Without the Complex" in *Myth and Tragedy in Ancient Greece* trans. Janet Lloyd (New York: Zone Books, 1988), 89.

[36] Plato, *Symposium* 186c–d.

[37] Plato, *Symposium* 218b; Socrates as "sober and temperate" 216d.

[38] Plato, *Theaetetus* 149d, cited in Gordon, *Plato's Erotic World*, 132.

explicitly deal with eros (like *Symposium*), but is central to Plato's philosophical project. But is eros something that human beings—even those skilled in philosophy—are capable of controlling?

To return to the method introduced by Eryximachus, we are presented with an analogy between music and medicine: "music, like medicine, creates agreement by producing concord and love between these various opposites."[39] This comment follows a very significant passage in which Eryximachus profoundly misunderstands Heraclitus—he paraphrases Heraclitus' fragment 51, where the self-differing thing is described as a "backwards-stretched harmony like that of the bow or the lyre."[40] While Heraclitus emphasizes the paradox of tension between opposites, Eryximachus here claims that Heraclitus means to eliminate discord entirely and privilege only harmony: "it is patently absurd to claim that an attunement or harmony is in itself discordant. . .Heraclitus probably meant that an expert musician creates a harmony by resolving the prior discord."[41] In other words, Eryximachus entirely resolves the tension between opposites, and dissolves any trace of paradox—an almost comically inaccurate portrayal of Heraclitus unlikely to be accidental on Plato's part.[42] Just as Plato hopes to domesticate and tame *eros* for philosophical purposes, he strategically eliminates difference and paradox from his method—an operation already familiar, as the function of *khora* in *Timaeus* similarly quarantines difference in a kind of non-space that is neither sensible nor intelligible. The method of the demiurge in creating the cosmos of the *Timaeus* repeats these strategies, and furthermore, does so while consistently employing erotic language.

Plato's cosmological narrative emphasizes the work of the demiurge, who, like the physician of *Symposium*, combines and harmonizes elements in an orderly manner, eliminating the discordant. Before he begins his ordering of what will become the cosmos, the demiurge is confronted with a chaotic motion—Plato's word for this is *plemmelos*, which as Bianchi points out is a musical term "denoting playing a false note, or being out of

[39] Plato, *Symposium* 187c.

[40] Heraclitus, DK 51.

[41] Plato, *Symposium* 187a–b.

[42] Eryximachus' claim can be refuted simply by recalling Heraclitus' fragment DK 10: "*Syllapsis*: wholes and not wholes, convergent divergent, consonant dissonant, from all things one and from one thing all."

tune, and more generally, erring, faulty, harsh, or offending."[43] In describing the construction of the cosmos, the demiurge demonstrates the same preference for order over the discordant and disordered seen in Eryximachus' speech, Timaeus tell us: "for God [the demiurge] desired that, so far as possible, all things should be good and nothing evil...he brought it into order out of disorder, deeming that the former state is in all ways better than the latter."[44] Here, the discordant or disordered is not merely in opposition to order, but is cast as evil in contrast to the activity of the demiurge, repeatedly identified as good and beautiful.

Through intelligent mastery, the demiurge transforms this disorderly chaos, using the opposing powers of force and persuasion (*peitho*). In constructing the cosmic soul, the demiurge must mix together Being, Same, and Other, and this requires force: "and since they were three, he took hold of them and blended them into one entire look; and since the nature of the Other was loath to mix, he joined it to the Same with force."[45] In creating the cosmic body, however, persuasion (*peitho*) plays a significant role in contrast to force: "for mixed indeed was the birth of this cosmos here, and begotten from a standing-together of necessity (*ananke*) and intellect (*nous*); and as intellect was ruling over necessity by persuading (*peitho*) her to lead most of what comes to be towards what's best, in this way accordingly was this all constructed at the beginning: through necessity worsted by thoughtful persuasion."[46] Reading this passage, Brill writes, "perhaps we are to read persuasion as inserting a gentleness into the development of the cosmos."[47] This harmony of force and gentleness is prefigured in Socrates' strangely abridged summary of *Republic*, when he tells us that the "souls of the guardians had to be of a certain nature...so that they'd be able to become correctly gentle [to friends], and harsh

[43] Plato, *Timaeus* 30a: "for since he wanted all things to be good, and to the best of his power, nothing to be shoddy, the god thus took over all that was visible, and, since it did not keep its peace but moved unmusically and without order (*kinoumenon plemmelos kai ataktos*), he brought it into order from disorder, since he regarded the former to be in all ways better than the latter." Cited in Bianchi, "Receptacle/Chora," 135.

[44] Plato, *Timaeus* 29e.

[45] Ibid., 35a–b.

[46] Ibid., 48a.

[47] Brill, "Animality and Sexual Difference in the *Timaeus*" in *Plato's Animals: Gadflies, Horses, Swans, and Other Philosophical Beasts*, ed. Jeremy Bell and Michael Naas (Bloomington: Indiana University Press, 2015), 163.

[to enemies]."[48] In other words, their nature has to harmonize opposing forces in an orderly manner according to binary categories, just as the rigged lottery discussed in the *Republic* mates human beings like-to-like, and as Eryximachus tells us the doctor produces health.

Plato's invocation of *peitho* introduces several key associations, as Gordon points out: "there is a tradition preceding Plato, of course, in which the erotic is indispensible to the order and movement of the cosmos. Most notably, in Hesiod and Empedocles, respectively, we see such a role for eros in mytho-poetic cosmologies and proto-scientific cosmologies, the latter being similar to what Timaeus is presenting."[49] In Homer and Hesiod, Aphrodite is dangerous, deceptive, seductive, and capable of completely subduing mortals and immortals alike.[50] In Empedocles' poetry, Aphrodite is queen of a mortal world of mixture, a deceptive and seductive world; as Empedocles warns, "gaze on her with your understanding and do not sit with stunned eyes."[51] In Empedocles' cosmology, the force of Love (associated with Aphrodite) mixes the four roots (earth, air, water, fire) together and the force of Strife returns them to their unmixed state. Empedocles tells us that the "soothing assault of blameless Love" makes those things that had previously become immortal grow mortal once again—an effect of Aphrodite that would evoke terror, were it not for her magical seductive effect, like a soothing drug.[52] Kingsley's translation, "soothing assault," captures the paradoxical relation in the work of Aphrodite, as it is forceful, inexorable, and completely gentle.

As Kingsley describes, Aphrodite "forces whatever she likes, whatever she wants, to act against its own will and better judgment—without appearing to exert the slightest force."[53] This ability of Aphrodite is personified in the goddess Peitho (Persuasion). As Marciano has pointed out, Peitho is "a cult goddess who often belongs in the train of Aphrodite in archaic literature and iconography…the influence of Peitho is directly linked with magic

[48] Plato, *Timaeus* 18a.

[49] Gordon, *Plato's Erotic World*, 36.

[50] In *Iliad* 14.198–9, Hera addresses Aphrodite by saying, "give me now love and desire, with which you subdue all immortals and mortal men." Cited in Kingsley, *Reality*, 378.

[51] Empedocles DK 25, Brad Inwood's translation in *The Poem of Empedocles: A Text and Translation with an Introduction by Brad Inwood* (Toronto: University of Toronto Press, 2001), 225.

[52] Empedocles DK 61, Kingsley's translation in *Reality*.

[53] Kingsley, *Reality*, 377.

spells."[54] The character of erotic experience in Homer, Hesiod, lyric poets like Sappho, and the poetry of Empedocles is consistently described as an overwhelming seduction and a loss of control (recall the epithet "limb loosener" for *eros*, used by Sappho). If eros is a daemonic experience of this kind, as these ancient sources attest, it is no wonder that Plato would attempt to produce a model in which eros is rationally managed and controlled. Eros is a bodily experience, as Sappho's songs frequently demonstrate, but the body is a liability for a patriarchal metaphysics of mastery—the body is too unpredictable, too chaotic. Just as *khora* was made to contain the dangerous ambiguity between binaries, *peitho* appears as a borderland between voluntary action and compulsion through seduction. In turning to Octavia Butler's models of sexual reproduction and erotic relation, I will explore both her third kind—the ooloi—and this strange borderland between force and seduction: a common theme in both *Wild Seed* and her *Xenogenesis* series.

Shapeshifters and Alien Sex: Radical Alterity in Octavia Butler

In *Wild Seed*, Butler introduces two immortal beings: Doro, who is born a black male but is an incorporeal parasite who kills and takes on the bodies of his victims, and Anyanwu, who was born a black female but can shapeshift and take on multiple forms after first incorporating the living patterns of other creatures into her body. While both Doro and Anyanwu can manifest different forms—male/female, white/black, old/young, and so on—their gender identities are stable: even inside a male body, Anyanwu still experiences herself as a female, and Doro is always male despite his sometimes female form. These characters, presented in opposition, represent culturally inscribed masculine and feminine ways of being: Doro is a violent, dominating, incorporeal breeder of human beings who uses the bodies of his victims without identifying with them at all; Anyanwu is absolutely embodied and shifts her shape through a radical identification with the other—she *becomes* the other through incorporating it into her body.

Doro and Anyanwu model the qualities of Plato's demiurge (Father) and *khora* (Mother), respectively, though Anyanwu is a representation of *khora*

[54] Laura Gemelli Marciano, "Images and Experience in Parmenides' *Aletheia*," *Ancient Philosophy* 28, (2008): 14.

with agency and corporeality. The relation between Doro and Anyanwu is explicitly erotic, as they are not only sexual partners but are bound to one another because of their immortality. Doro is the personification of intelligent mastery and force, while Anyanwu can take on the shape of any living being—a kind of mimicry that is only possible through erotic receptivity to the other. While Doro is not dependent upon any particular body that he inhabits, Anyanwu exists in physical, erotic relation with other living things. Doro explains his nature:

> I kill, Anyanwu. That is how I keep my youth, my strength. I can do only one thing to show you what I am, and that is kill a man and wear his body like a cloth. . .This is not the body I was born into. It's not the tenth I've worn, nor the hundredth, nor the thousandth. Your gift seems to be a gentle one. Mine is not.[55]

Just as harshness and gentleness were opposites that the guardians' souls in Plato's *Republic* were made to harmonize, these two forces appear in the characters of Doro and Anyanwu. Doro seems incapable of empathy, while Anyanwu frequently intervenes to protect the various offspring that Doro breeds, over many generations. Anyanwu's vulnerability is deeply woven into the heterosexual matrix of reproduction: repeatedly, Doro manipulates Anyanwu because she loves her children: "it would not be hard to make her follow him. She had sons and she cared for them, thus she was vulnerable."[56] It is her relation to others that makes Anyanwu vulnerable to Doro's power; her love is a liability, from his perspective. For Doro, the other is always a conquest; for Anyanwu, love is radical intimacy with the other.

The erotic styles of Doro and Anyanwu represent very different models of *eros.* Doro is hierarchical, dominating, possessive, and thoroughly patriarchal, while Anyanwu desires communion with others and her existence is always bound up with those she loves. These contrasting models of eros are strikingly similar to the hierarchical model of eros in Plato (the pederastic relation between lover and beloved), contrasted with the non-hierarchical and deeply reciprocal model of eros in the songs of Sappho. The patriarchal model of eros requires hierarchy, as the lover is active while the beloved is passive (whether a woman or a boy); this model also involves domination,

[55] Octavia Butler, *Wild Seed* (New York: Warner Books, 1980), 13.
[56] Ibid., 20.

mastery over the other, and possession of the love object. As Ellen Greene has argued, the model of eros in Sappho offers "an erotic practice and discourse outside of patriarchal modes of thought."[57] The lovers in Sappho's erotic poems are not active versus passive, but exist in a reciprocal relationship to one another; instead of dominating or possessing the other, the lover loses herself in her beloved. This erotic "pattern of mutuality" reflects a non-binary understanding of *eros*, where both lovers are simultaneously active and passive, an ambiguous swaying like that of *khora* in Plato's narrative.[58] Anyanwu's ability to shapeshift involves different stages: first, through observation of an animal or person, she is able to mimic its appearance, but once she has ingested the flesh of an animal, she can truly *become* it. "I was not a true leopard, though, until I killed one and ate a little of it. At first, I was a woman pretending to be a leopard—clay molded into leopard shape. Now when I change, I am a leopard."[59]

Anyanwu's method still involves violence, but unlike Doro, her destruction of the animal's body does not eradicate it entirely, but allows her an understanding of the other so intense that she becomes it. Her intention in ingesting the other is not possessive or dominative, but motivated by curiosity and often, respect and admiration; when Anwanyu becomes a dolphin, she marvels at the agility and intelligence of dolphin bodies and is reluctant to return to her human form.[60] In dolphin form, her desire becomes dolphin-desire, as she is nearly seduced by a male dolphin before being interrupted by Isaac, a son of Doro, who was instructed to bring her back to their ship. Anyanwu does not forcefully project her own identity onto the others that she becomes, as Doro does, her body receptively "reads" the patterns of others in order to know them.[61] Unlike the

[57] Ellen Greene, "Apostrophe and Women's Erotics in the Poetry of Sappho," in *Reading Sappho: Contemporary Approaches*, ed. Ellen Greene (Berkeley: University of California Press, 1996), 234.

[58] Sappho's model of *eros* diverges significantly from the patriarchal model because she is describing love between women, where there is no difference in social status between them. In the patriarchal practice of pederasty, the older man (lover, *erastes*) had superior status and authority over the young man (beloved, *eromenos*). See Greene, "Apostrophe and Women's Erotics in the Poetry of Sappho" for detailed discussion of these differing models of eros.

[59] Butler, *Wild Seed*, 87.

[60] Ibid., 89–94.

[61] Anyanwu tells Issac, in explaining her ability, "my body reads it—reads everything." Ibid., 87.

incorporeal Doro, Anyanwu's identity is thoroughly embodied, and her agency is bodily intelligence without dominative mastery over others. As Stacy Alaimo suggests, "her way of knowing collapses the very division between subject and object, as one transforms into the other. Anyanwu's transformations dramatize an embodied epistemology that acts as an antidote to willful separations and masterful machinations."[62]

Octavia Butler's character of Doro is similar to the male demiurge in Plato's *Timaeus*, as both patriarch gods desire to create beings that resemble themselves. Timaeus tells us that the demiurge "desired that all should be, so far as possible, like unto himself."[63] In the case of Doro, who breeds human beings in his own image, "Doro is a possessor and producer of bodies...he is a genetic engineer bent on creating a family of bodies that will be most like himself."[64] The mastery involved in this eugenics is echoed in Plato's *Republic*, where the guardians would determine human breeding based on a system of like-to-like, completely undermining any agency that those human beings might have with regard to their own sexual reproduction. The violence and injustice of this approach are emphasized in *Wild Seed* by the fact that Doro is acquiring many of his "children" through the African slave trade. While Plato's guardians and his demiurge are not identified as slave-traders, the patriarchal method of mastery over bodies coupled with the use of force results in a decidedly pathological model of erotic relations: a family structure that is hierarchical, deeply heterosexual, and that ceaselessly undermines the erotic agency of subjects identified as "passive."

Hierarchical thinking is frequently critiqued in Octavia Butler's works. In her *Xenogenesis* series, the alien Oankali race retrieves the last living human beings from the dying and poisoned Earth, which has been destroyed by human war and violence. The protagonist of the first *Xenogenesis* book, a black woman named Lillith, is awoken to meet an Oankali face-to-face, as the Oankali have kept the human beings in stasis in order to learn about them. Jdahya, the ambassador Oankali, tells Lillith that one meaning of "Oankali" is "traders," and that they *require* continual genetic trading with

[62] Stacy Alaimo, "Skin Dreaming: The Bodily Transgressions of Fielding Burke, Octavia Butler, and Linda Hogan," in *Ecofeminist Literary Criticism: Theory, Interpretation, Pedagogy*, ed. Greta Gaard and Patrick D. Murphy (Chicago: University of Illinois Press, 1998), 129.

[63] Plato, *Timaeus* 29e.

[64] Gregory Jerome Hampton, *Changing Bodies in the Fiction of Octavia Butler: Slaves, Aliens, and Vampires* (Plymouth: Lexington Books, 2010), 29.

other species—if they do not "trade," they die.[65] The Oankali consist of male and female individuals as well as a third kind, the ooloi, experts at genetic arrangements. The violent demise of the human race, through the destruction of the earth, is diagnosed by the ooloi as a poisonous genetic combination: intelligence and hierarchical thinking. Jdahya explains to Lillith that, while the human species has grown to become intelligent, "you [humans] are hierarchical. That's the older and more entrenched characteristic."[66] Like Anyanwu, the Oankali lose themselves in the other; they have no static identity, but are continually assimilating new forms and changing shape. The ooloi, because they fall outside or between the binary of male and female, are particularly queer in their identity, as Patricia Melzer has argued, "the ooloi inhabit a special position that is decidedly queer – a phenomenon that is hard to comprehend in our dichotomous way of conceptualizing gender and sexuality."[67] When Lillith first meets an ooloi, she is disgusted and hostile, "looking at Kahguyaht [ooloi], she took pleasure in the knowledge that the Oankali themselves used the neuter pronoun in referring to the ooloi. Some things deserved to be called 'it'."[68]

The structuring of sexual reproduction in the *Xenogenesis* model involves five participants: a male and a female human, a male and a female Oankali, and one ooloi, who mixes the genetic material of all of them, to produce offspring called "constructs." Unlike the hierarchical, heterosexual nuclear family of Plato's *Timaeus*, this communal reproduction does not privilege any of the participants, nor does it require violent submission to a master. Human beings, habituated to their binary categories, have trouble with the subtlety and ambiguity of this arrangement. When Lillith meets another human man acquainted with the ooloi, he says "when they woke me up, I thought the ooloi acted like men and women while the males and females acted like eunuchs. I never really lost the habit of thinking of ooloi as male or female."[69] His understanding reflects an assumption about agency—that it must be *active* rather than

[65] He tells Lillith, "we do what you would call genetic engineering. We know you had begun to do it yourselves a little, but it's foreign to you. We do it naturally. We *must* do it. It renews us, enables us to survive as an evolving species." Butler, *Lillith's Brood*, 40.

[66] Ibid., 39.

[67] Patricia Melzer, *Alien Constructions: Science Fiction and Feminist Thought* (Austin: University of Texas, 2006): 236.

[68] Butler, *Lillith's Brood*, 49.

[69] Ibid., 89.

passive; in sexual reproduction, the males and females (whether human or Oankali) are passive participants while the ooloi are the orchestrators. Lillith characterizes this man's perspective as "a kind of deliberate, persistent ignorance."[70]

This stubborn misrecognition is repeated throughout the saga, as some of the human beings awakened by the Oankali refuse to integrate, protecting a purity of categories that Lillith herself initially expresses, when confronted with the Oankali plan of mating human and Oankali, "a rebirth for us [humans] can only happen if you let us alone! Let us begin again on our own."[71] The complexities of this situation are immense, when the Oankali are viewed as colonizers, but Butler stresses the inevitability of confrontation with the other, as the ambassador Oankali Jdahya tells Lillith, "I can't *un*find you...you're here."[72] He then offers Lillith a painless solution of suicide, if she desires it, and she finds that she does not prefer to die. Although Lillith later comes to love her ooloi mate Nikanj, Butler stresses the element of coercion in Lillith's situation. It is here that the borderland of seduction and force is most prominent in the *Xenogenesis* model of sexual reproduction: the bodies of human and Oankali mates begin to "know" one another through chemical signatures, and create a kind of dependency upon the ooloi of their mating group.[73] When a male or female human or Oankali has been touched by an ooloi's sensory arms, this chemical signature is initiated, and results in an erotic longing for communion with the ooloi.

Much like the action of *peitho* in Ancient Greek myth, this seduction has the nature of a drug or a magic spell: *is* the lover voluntarily participating, or does this chemical seduction mean passivity, or worse, coercion? The experience of eros in the tradition preceding Plato invokes precisely this problem, as agency is called into question by the overwhelming and irresistible nature of the desire. In contemporary language, this question can be posed as: do I choose who I desire, or is my body inexorably drawn by pheromones that I do not consciously will? In this ambiguous place, issues of biological destiny begin to erupt, particularly with regard to sexual

[70] Ibid.

[71] Ibid., 43.

[72] Ibid., 43.

[73] This is first explained to Lillith by the mature ooloi Kahguyaht: "humans and Oankali tend to bond to one ooloi....the bond is chemical." Ibid., 110.

orientation and choice of love objects. The loss of control that eros introduces is extremely threatening to an identity that grounds itself through mastery and domination; as in Plato's *Symposium*, this terror produces a powerful drive to control eros and possesses the other entirely, so as not to lose one's identity. The dissolution in the other that is described in Sappho's poems, or in Anyanwu's desire to live as a dolphin and forget her human body, is akin to death from the perspective of a dominative, patriarchal, stable identity. But from the standpoint of the Oankali, this dissolution is desired, and is the moving vehicle of their growth and transformation as a species—their identity is dynamic and living, ever in flux.

These questions about erotic agency are complicated by the dualistic tradition of conceptualizing the body as dumb, passive matter in opposition to the incorporeal soul or mind capable of intelligence. For Plato, mastering the power of eros is part of the philosophical project of disciplining the body using the rational mastery of the soul; the body cannot have agency because it is irrational and chaotic, like nature. In Octavia Butler's *Wild Seed* and in her *Xenogenesis* books, the body is not an unintelligent material, but a living, moving force capable of learning and understanding. As Alaimo has argued, Butler's depiction of the body, especially in the case of Anyanwu, "suggests a model of knowing that sees animal and human bodies as active, signifying forces, not abject, mute, passive, resources. Butler casts off the body as mere vestment or investment and transforms it into a liminal space that blurs the divisions between humans and animals, subjects and objects, nature and culture."[74] Anyanwu's body is able to take on the form of anything that enters into it, but her body is not a passive medium, like Plato's *khora*. She learns the patterns of life that she ingests and she uses her knowledge to heal, an ability that is responsible for her incredible longevity and is frequently used to lengthen the lives of human beings in her care. Anyanwu demonstrates a model of *khora* with agency, corporeality, and intelligence.

In her *Xenogenesis* series, Butler explores the agency of the body in relation to desire even more explicitly in developing the "construct" ooloi, who change shape according to the desire of the other. At first, human-Oankali mating only produced "construct" male and female beings, who

[74] Alaimo, "Skin Dreaming," 130.

were part human and part Oankali, but eventually, Lillith gives birth to the first construct ooloi, Jodahs.[75] Jodahs describes its power to transform to Yedik and Ayodele, human-Oankali construct children, "I can change myself. . .but it's an effort. And it doesn't last. It's easier to do as water does: allow myself to be contained, and take on the shape of my containers."[76] The resemblance to Plato's *khora* as receptacle is especially striking in this description. The children are disturbed by this and ask Jodahs when it is able to be itself, if it is always being contained and forced. Jodahs explains that it is not forced, and that its identity is not static, but changeable: "changing doesn't bother me anymore. . .at least, not this kind of deliberate, controlled changing."[77] The construct ooloi's body constantly tastes the world around it, through smells, touching skin, eating plants and animals, and perceiving body language—both apparent and chemical. It is infinitely adaptable, and transforms into the form most desired by the bodies around it, especially in relation to its erotic mates. For the construct ooloi, "constant change and adaptation to the object of desire becomes the self-defining act."[78] The Oankali need others to continue evolving through their gene trading, but the construct ooloi needs others in an even more explicit manner: without the desire of the other, the construct ooloi can lose all form and devolve into an unseeing, barely conscious, creature—this happens in *Imago*, when a construct ooloi is separated from its family, and it takes much nurture to bring it back to awareness.

Jodahs, a construct ooloi, presents us with Octavia Butler's most fully realized model of a third kind that exists through sensual, erotic relation with others. Its identity is entirely hybrid—part human, part Oankali, neither male nor female, even its appearance shifts based on its perception of others' desires. Jodahs is, like Anyanwu, thoroughly embodied, and experiences its bodily senses as erotic, seductive. Jodahs describes his metamorphosis into adulthood: "my first changes were sensory. Tastes, scents, all sensations suddenly became complex, confusing, yet unexpectedly

[75] Oankali children, and the human-Oankali construct children, are not born male or female, but "eka" (androgynous), until they reach metamorphosis and are drawn to one or the other sex. During the transformational period of metamorphosis, their bodies become male, female, or in the case of Jodahs, human-ooloi.

[76] Butler, *Lillith's Brood*, 612.

[77] Ibid., 612.

[78] Melzer, *Alien Constructions*, 240.

seductive."[79] Like all Oankali, it is driven to know others that it encounters—to deeply know them in their bodily, chemical, sensuous makeup. The agency of Jodahs, as third kind and construct ooloi, is never entirely active or passive, receptive or penetrating, but continually partakes of both. Jodahs' identity is dynamic and formed only in reciprocity with the others it encounters; Jodahs does not desire any stable identity or borders, but craves the continual motion and exploration of the world and others, using its skillful and intelligent bodily senses.

With Jodahs, Butler imagines a different kind of identity, a dynamic identity that is entangled with the others it encounters. The construct ooloi cannot be categorized according to binary models; they are creatures that continually change in concert with the other bodies they encounter. As Darwinian models of adaptation demonstrate, this is a much more accurate paradigm for understanding living things, as opposed to the essentialist categories of systems such as that of Plato. Butler's constructs demonstrate the manner in which bodies are themselves borderland spaces, simultaneously passive and active, constantly engaged in sensuous interactions that change them as they, in turn, change the bodies around them. If bodies, and identities, are imagined in this way, the picture that emerges is an image of motion, just as Socrates longed to see in the beginning of the *Timaeus* dialogue—bodies with permeable borders, constantly creating difference and multiplicity. Patriarchal models, like Plato's demiurge or Eryximachus' doctoring, require masterful ordering through domination, but these models are built on the fantasy of static identity, a frozen snapshot of structure rather than a living, moving world of embodied agents. Uncovering this fantasy, and the machinations that support it, reveals a messy and less predictable world than the patriarchal dream of ordered mastery—for a system of thought based in notions of certainty and control, this is a terrifying prospect, but for all those bodies who have been contained in their tight categories, squirming free of these oppressive, imaginary walls is a welcome invitation.

Bibliography

Alaimo, Stacy. 1998. "Skin Dreaming": The Bodily Transgressions of Fielding Burke, Octavia Butler, and Linda Hogan. In *Ecofeminist Literary Criticism:*

[79] Butler, *Lillith's Brood*, 523.

Theory, Interpretation, Pedagogy, ed. Greta Gaard and Patrick D. Murphy, 123–138. Chicago: University of Illinois Press.

Bianchi, Emanuela. 2006. Receptacle/Chora: Figuring the Errant Feminine in Plato's *Timaeus. Hypatia* 21 (4): 124–146.

———. 2014. *The Feminine Symptom: Aleatory Matter in the Aristotelian Cosmos.* New York: Fordham University Press.

Brill, Sarah. 2015. Animality and Sexual Difference in the *Timaeus.* In *Plato's Animals: Gadflies, Horses, Swans, and Other Philosophical Beasts*, ed. Jeremy Bell and Michael Naas, 161–178. Bloomington: Indiana University Press.

Butler, Octavia. 1980. *Wild Seed.* New York: Warner Books.

———. 1989. *Lillith's Brood.* New York: Grand Central Publishing.

Butler, Judith. 1993. *Bodies That Matter.* New York: Routledge.

Carson, Anne. 2002. *If Not, Winter: Fragments of Sappho.* New York: Vintage Books.

Derrida, Jacques. 1982. Differance. In *Margins of Philosophy.* Trans. Alan Bass, 3–27. Chicago: University of Chicago Press.

———. 1995. *On the Name.* Trans. David Wood, John P. Leavey, Jr., and Ian McLeod. Palo Alto: Stanford University Press.

Dodds, E.R. 1951. *The Greeks and the Irrational.* Berkeley: University of California Press.

Gordon, Jill. 2012. *Plato's Erotic World: From Cosmic Origins to Human Death.* Cambridge: Cambridge University Press.

Greene, Ellen. 1996. Apostrophe and Women's Erotics in the Poetry of Sappho. In *Reading Sappho: Contemporary Approaches*, ed. Ellen Greene, 233–247. Berkeley: University of California Press.

Hampton, Cynthia. 1994. Overcoming Dualism: The Importance of the Intermediate in Plato's *Philebus.* In *Feminist Interpretations of Plato*, ed. Nancy Tuana, 217–242. University Park: Pennsylvania State University Press.

Hampton, Gregory Jerome. 2010. *Changing Bodies in the Fiction of Octavia Butler: Slaves, Aliens, and Vampires.* Plymouth: Lexington Books.

Holmes, Brooke. 2010. *The Symptom and the Subject.* Princeton: Princeton University Press.

Huffer, Lynn. 1998. *Maternal Pasts, Feminist Futures: Nostalgia, Ethics, and the Question of Difference.* Palo Alto: Stanford University Press.

Inwood, Brad. 2001. *The Poem of Empedocles: A Text and Translation with an Introduction by Brad Inwood.* Toronto: University of Toronto Press.

Irigaray, Luce. 1985. *This Sex Which Is Not One.* Trans. Catherine Porter with Carolyn Burke. Ithaca: Cornell University Press.

Kahn, Charles H. 1979. *The Art and Thought of Heraclitus: An Edition of the Fragments with Translation and Commentary.* Cambridge: Cambridge University Press.

Kalkavadge, Peter. 2001. *Plato's Timaeus: Translation, Glossary, Appendices and Introductory Essay*. Newburyport: Focus Publishing.
Kingsley, Peter. 2003. *Reality*. Inverness: Golden Sufi Press.
Marciano, Laura Gemelli. 2008. Images and Experience: At the Roots of Parmenides' *Aletheia*. *Ancient Philosophy* 28: 21–48.
Melzer, Patricia. 2006. *Alien Constructions: Science Fiction and Feminist Thought*. Austin: University of Texas Press.
Plato. 1925. *Symposium*. Trans. W.R.M. Lamb. Boston: Harvard University Press.
———. 1929. *Timaeus*. Trans. R.G. Bury. Boston: Harvard University Press.
Vernant, Jean-Pierre, and Pierre Vidal-Naquet. 1988. Oedipus Without the Complex. In *Tragedy and Myth in Ancient Greece*. Trans. Janet Lloyd, 85–112. New York: Zone Books.

PART IV

Speculative Borderlands

Alice's Parallel Series: Carroll, Deleuze, and the 'Stuttering Sense' of the World

Andrea Oppo

Two Worlds, Two Meanings: An Introduction

What is the border between philosophy and literature? How might these disciplines be connected or differentiated? And in what form or *where* should such connection, or division, occur? If one looks at the history of philosophy in its very beginnings, the answer to those questions might seem slightly clearer than it does in present times. Greek philosophy stemmed precisely from denying any truth-value to myth, narratives, poetry, and, more generally, to the 'aesthetic domain' as it is expressed distinctively in what is best known today as the 'fine arts.'[1] From Parmenides onwards, and even more notably with Plato, the quest for Being should centre on the perfect (i.e. *identical* and *non-contradictory*) transparency of the *logos*. Significantly, in modern times—in order to achieve the highest level of

[1] The birth of an autonomous system of arts originates at the end of the seventeenth century and culminates in the eighteenth century with the concept of *beaux arts*, as opposed to the useful arts, as specified in particular by Charles Batteux in his book *Les beaux arts réduits à un même principe* (1746). Unlike other kinds of arts, the *beaux arts* have their own objective in pure pleasure: eloquence and architecture are, in fact, excluded by Batteux, whereas poetry remains the most important art as it embraces the possibility of grasping not only 'our world' but also 'other worlds': 'Si ce monde ne lui suffit pas, elle crée des mondes nouveaux, qu'elle embellit de demeures enchantées...' (Batteux, *Les beaux arts*, 3).

A. Oppo (✉)
Pontifical University of Sardinia, Cagliari, Italy

J. Elbert Decker, D. Winchock (eds.), *Borderlands and Liminal Subjects*, https://doi.org/10.1007/978-3-319-67813-9_11

transparency and incontrovertibility—the same *logos* has increasingly sought its best guarantee of truth in that which is objective, preferably *material* or related to matter, belonging to 'nature,' to the *external* (physical, verifiable) world, and consequently in that which can be labelled as a 'fact.' Throughout the centuries, in continuity with the development of modern sciences, Western philosophy has pursued and accumulated knowledge of the 'true world' precisely in the correspondence (*adaequatio*) between logical reasons and facts.[2] Strictly speaking, for the same exigency of incontrovertibility, a *fact* should not be assumed from beyond the empiric and tangible reality, and any *reason* that aims to be 'legitimate' should refer only to that reality: in such a reductionist version, this may well be a Quinean definition of modern naturalism—the philosophy of the *real world.*[3] It is no wonder, then, that at the beginning of this evolution the imitative representation of *another world* effected by artists and poets (whom Plato called, in fact, *hoi mimētikoí*, 'the imitators') was of no use for the classic Greek philosophy project—especially if one wants to read the latter as having marked out the initial outline for the path subsequently followed by Western scientific thought. Not by chance, Plato's condemnation of art was affirmed mainly on an ontological and epistemological basis. His famous arguments involve the criticism of art on the grounds of its unreality (i.e. however perfect it is, the artist's creation remains an illusion, a shadow without substance) and of the insufficient knowledge of its own reasons (i.e. everybody is capable of explaining his work, except for the artist

[2] However debated and articulated, not to mention ambiguous, this issue may be, the idea of a *correspondence* between a structure of beliefs and a structure of facts permeates the whole history of philosophy, from Plato (*Sophist* 262E-263D) and Aristotle (*Metaphysics Γ* 7: 1011b 26–27) to Frege, Russell, and Tarski, and is indeed to be considered 'the most venerable of all kinds of theories of truth' (Kirkham, *Theories of Truth*, 119). On this, cf. Kirkham, *Theories of Truth*, Lynch, *The Nature of Truth*, and Künne, *Conceptions of Truth.*

[3] For a definition of naturalism in Quine, see Quine, *Theories and Things*, 67–72. For a recent survey on this question in relation to the legitimacy of a subjective point of view on the world, see L. Rudder Baker, *Naturalism and the First-Person Perspective.* In its stronger construal, philosophical naturalism maintains that it is *only through science*, that is, an objective point of view on things, that we can achieve knowledge and understanding of reality. The existence of a tension in Quine himself between this kind of physicalism and the idea of 'inscrutability of reference' in his theory of meaning is well known, however.

himself).[4] Plato consigned any artistic invention or inspiration as such— for example, the literary world or any dream or fictional representation devoid of a philosophical *logos*—to the field of obscure and undetermined knowledge. From that moment onwards, philosophy and literature were 'officially' torn apart. With few exceptions, the classic path of Western philosophy has always swept poetry and literary narrative out of its path, that is, the path of objective and true reality, by relegating them to the realm of mere 'subjectivity.'

Nevertheless, in the history of philosophy the aesthetic experience has always been 'allowed' somewhere on the threshold of rationality, with its paradoxical perspective of being simultaneously both the object and the source of knowledge. And though this is a field where everything is relative, subjective, and nothing demonstrable (individual sensibility, changes in stylistic canons, fashions, etc.), aesthetic judgement—as Immanuel Kant acknowledges—tends intrinsically towards universality; it claims to be valid 'for everybody,' as if its inner motive, private and incommunicable, were governed by universal and binding laws.[5] There is a fundamental option—one might even say—that periodically returns in the history of philosophy: art is not truth versus art is the supreme truth. For many philosophers, this doubt acted as a sort of *siren song*: a fascinating but impossible idea. However, to some extent Immanuel Kant's considerations on aesthetic judgement opened up a decisive breach in this idea. Since the Romantic era, philosophical thought has tried to establish a bridge between rational knowledge and sensation, between the 'given' and the 'imaginary'

[4] Cf. these two arguments especially in Plato, *Republic*, X, 596c–597a and 601a. Much more directly, and with a particular focus on poetry, Plato examines the same problem in the *Ion*. In this dialogue, through Socrates' questioning of Ion the rhapsode, he explores the origin and impetus of poetry, the poet's relationship to the things he discusses, and that of the critic to the poet and his work. On the deceptive effect of arts, see also Plato, *Sophist* 235 E 5–236 A 2.

[5] The claim ('as if') for universal validity of the judgement of taste is a crucial juncture of the entire first part of Immanuel Kant's *Critique of Judgment* (cf. in particular I. Kant, *Critique of Judgment*, Book I, Second Moment, §§ 8–9). What is claimed by this purely subjective (aesthetic) judgement is an *exemplary* validity. Humankind itself demonstrates this exemplarity and thereby justifies the unity and universality of such judgement, so that taste may be designated a *sensus communis aestheticus*. Apart from this, however, for Kant such a judgement is not objective and does not improve our knowledge: it is merely a *free activity* of the faculties of cognition with the unique certitude of giving us pleasure and displeasure.

worlds, so that the *two*, as it were, became *one*.[6] Yet, it is not only within the context of Romanticism and of Idealism that the world of art rises to a higher epistemological dignity. At the end of the nineteenth century and for the whole of the twentieth, the linguistic turn in philosophy transposed the ontological problem concerning the aesthetic domain into the problem of the meaning of its own language(s).[7] The world of nature and the world of art began to be considered also as two different 'texts' whose significance must be deciphered. At the same time, the problem of the meaning of reference in the philosophy of language reduced the distance between the two worlds, since the philosophical question was no longer about the ontological unreality of a depicted-fictional structure but rather about its logical or phenomenological meaningfulness—hence, its truth-value was also reconsidered. In this regard, it is rather more than mere provocation when Quine famously asserts that the 'ontological' status of the gods in Homeric poetry and the particles of contemporary physics are epistemologically coequal.[8] Following the epochal division that marks philosophy in the twentieth century—the division between continental and analytic thought—one must note how a number of thinkers from both sides brought the narrative text, and by extension the contents of art, back within their horizon of interest. This manifestly happened with Nietzsche, with Heidegger, as well as with Adorno, Ricoeur, and Derrida, among others, on the continental side; but no less significantly with Quine, Davidson, Rorty, and also Cavell and Putnam, in what has been called a 'narrative turn' within analytic philosophy.[9]

Undoubtedly, there are relevant differences among contemporary philosophers: while rigid naturalism still considers the world to be impersonal,

[6] This is, roughly, the appearance of philosophical aesthetics as a modern discipline, which starts with Alexander G. Baumgarten (1750). For Baumgarten, aesthetics is the science of sensitive knowledge. For the first time—thereby marking the birth of modern aesthetics—an aesthetic view beyond logic is recognized that is neither moral, nor mystic nor practical, but fully cognitive and theoretical.

[7] See Jürgen Habermas, "Philosophy and Science as Literature?," in *Postmetaphysical Thinking: Philosophical Essays* (Cambridge, Mass.: The MIT Press, 1992), 207–208.

[8] Willard Van Orman Quine, *From a Logical Point of View* (Cambridge: Harvard University Press, 1953), 44.

[9] Bill Martin, "Analytic Philosophy's Narrative Turn: Quine, Rorty, Davidson," in *Literary Theory After Davidson*, ed. Reed Way Dasenbrock (University Park, Penn.: The Pennsylvania State University Press, 2010), 124–143.

so that there are no irreducibly first-person *facts*, at the opposite pole the hermeneutic position takes subjectivity as the most privileged point of view, so that the philosopher and narrator/artist may even merge into one single figure.[10] In between these poles, however, a more liberalized naturalistic philosophy can no longer deny the fact that the meaning of a narrative text and the meaning of texts whose references are only elements in nature can both be objective. Starting from Quine's principle of the 'indeterminacy of translation,' that is, the thesis that 'there is "no fact of the matter" as to which translation manual is the right one,' Hilary Putnam agrees that the assertibility of a particular sentence 'is pragmatic and depends on the entire context.'[11] Hence, Putnam writes, '*we should talk about interpretation and not about meaning*.'[12] This does not mean that any interpretation is absolutely relative but, in fact, that there are better and worse interpretations, namely, there is an objectivity and 'a fact of the matter in interpretation without making that fact of the matter unique or context-independent.'[13] For Putnam, an absolute Platonic and scientific conception of the world, as an 'uncaring machine,' 'may be all there is to the worlds of physics and chemistry and biology, but the worlds of physics and chemistry and biology are not the only worlds we inhabit [...].'[14] Some meanings more than others may be 'ontologically queer,' as for Plato they would certainly be. Yet, as Kant understood very clearly—Putnam writes—'they are nonetheless indispensable in epistemology.'[15]

Thus, to answer the initial question, the border between philosophy and literature is, then, the question of the meaning of reference. The two worlds, the natural world and the narrative world, at least on a linguistic level, have their own degree of reality depending on the context. Both can be *meaningful*. Above all, either as facts or as values, they influence our life in that they are an epistemologically and ontologically relevant part of

[10] According to Habermas, this is what nearly happens with philosophers like Blumenberg, Simmel, Derrida, and sometimes Nietzsche and Adorno. Nonetheless, for Habermas, a certain level of criticism and a validity claim on the objective and external world is what should define philosophy as opposed to literature. See Habermas, *Postmetaphysical Thinking*, 205–228.

[11] Hilary Putnam, *Realism With a Human Face*, edited by James Conant (Cambridge, Mass.: Harvard University Press, 1990), 209.

[12] Ibid., 209–210. Putnam's emphasis.

[13] Ibid., 211.

[14] Ibid., 137.

[15] Ibid., 138.

it. Yet, this reciprocal acknowledgement does not resolve another, more crucial, problem. While 'meaning as such' is the first border, what is the connection between further and *deeper* meanings? Between intensional and extensional references? Between intangible values and 'facts of the matter' or, in other words, between the meaning of the world from *within* and from *outside*? What *border* can connect these worlds?

In his ambitious book *The View from Nowhere*, Thomas Nagel states that the problem of problems in philosophy is 'how to combine the perspective of a particular person inside the world with an objective view of that same world.'[16] According to Nagel, it is from this tension, between an objective and a subjective (one could say a 'relational' and an 'adverbial') theory of meaning, that the most authentic philosophical questions arise. For the philosopher Michael Dummett, the failure to reconcile those two perspectives is also at the root of the main division in contemporary philosophy.[17] Nonetheless, trying to bridge that gap can lead, in many ways, to a mid-zone of language that forces philosophy up to a point of rupture—a point at which the concept is something that, literally, ***does not make sense.***

A Deeper Genesis of Sense: Deleuze Through the Looking-Glass

In a postface he wrote for the Italian translation of his book *The Logic of Sense*, five years after the original edition in French, Gilles Deleuze affirmed that he felt he had already moved beyond the spirit of that work: 'It was the first time I sought somehow a form that was not that of traditional philosophy [...]. I have nothing to change in it. Rather, I would question why I was in such need of Lewis Carroll and of his three great books, *Alice in Wonderland*, *Through the Looking-Glass* and *Sylvie and Bruno*.'[18] The 1969 *Logic of Sense* is in large part a reading of Lewis Carroll's work, including also chapters on Klossowski, Tournier, Zola, Fitzgerald, Lowry, and Artaud. But, as stated in this note to the Italian edition, it is above all through Carroll that Deleuze tries to demonstrate how thought 'organizes itself also

[16] Thomas Nagel, *The View from Nowhere* (New York: Oxford University Press, 1986), 3.

[17] Michael Dummett, "Frege and Husserl on Reference," in *The Seas of Language* (New York: Oxford University Press, 2003), 224–229.

[18] Gilles Deleuze, *La logica del senso* (1st ed. in Italian 1975), trans. M. de Stefanis (Milan: Feltrinelli, 2006), 293. My translation.

by means of similar axes and directions: for example the height and Platonism which would orient the traditional image of philosophy; the Presocratics and depth (the return to Presocratics as a return to the underground, to prehistoric caves); the Stoics and their new art of surfaces....'[19] In contrast to his former work, *Difference and Repetition*, which 'still aimed at a sort of classical greatness or even to an archaic depth [...] In *Logic of Sense*,' Deleuze writes, 'the newness for me consisted in that I wanted to learn something about surfaces.'[20]

The *surface* Deleuze is referring to is a 'new border,' an overcoming of the binary logic of height/depth, or of an external/internal state of affairs. *The Logic of Sense* for Deleuze is a discussion of the twentieth-century linguistic turn and is organized in thirty-four 'series' of issues, each in a certain sense 'parallel' to the others, in which Deleuze analyses the structure of sense in its dynamic genesis. In doing so, he anticipates the classic issues of logic, namely, the conditions of truth that make a proposition 'true' or 'false,' and points to the question of the foundation of this entire process. For Deleuze, there must be something unconditioned that presupposes any further designation, that is, an irreducible denotation. His quest for 'sense' is thus an attempt to search for a new dimension of propositions, which 'is exactly the boundary between propositions and things.'[21] The subjective/objective opposition finds a new frame to be read when the classic Fregean denotation is put to the test and is substituted by a third image whose sense is a thought on 'surface.' As in Alice's world, Deleuze considers everything as flattened or lacking thickness, just like the playing cards Alice meets in her adventures. There is neither any sort of bottom nor a bottom with no bottom. This is what Deleuze means by 'surface'—a *topologically* complex world, where any relation is inclusive, in that it draws together all the divergent series.

> Thus – as Deleuze writes in the book's preface – to each series there correspond figures which are not only historical but topological and logical as well. As on a pure surface, certain points of one figure in a series refer to the points

[19] Deleuze, *Logica del senso*, 293–294.

[20] Ibid., 294.

[21] Gilles Deleuze, *The Logic of Sense* (1st ed. in French 1969), trans. M. Lester (New York: Columbia University Press, 1990), 22.

> of another figure: an entire galaxy of problems with their corresponding dice-throws, stories, and places, a complex place; a 'convoluted story.'[22]

Once the illusion of heights and depths is won, the 'inside' and 'outside' belong to each other in a sort of disjunctive synthesis, as Deleuze would say. From that moment on, Deleuze passes through the 'looking-glass' and contemplates the land of that which starts to make no sense, that is, Carroll's nonsense world. In that world, events are both incorporeal and atemporal; bodies enlarge and shrink; actions are active or passive; and the verb tenses continually skip the 'present simple' to adopt an impersonal or infinitive timeless form where past and future coincide. The language's words themselves are not mere passive objects but have their own will and life: there are 'no longer states of affairs – mixtures deep inside bodies – but incorporeal events at the surface which are the results of these mixtures. The tree "greens"....'[23] When Alice tries to call to mind some poems she had learned, she comes up with new verses. Similarly, when she tries to grasp the meaning of a word, it reveals a brand-new meaning. These are the effects of the surface: '*The ideational or the incorporeal can no longer be anything other than an "effect."*'[24] 'The Stoics discovered surface effects. Simulacra cease to be subterranean rebels and make the most of their effects... The most concealed becomes the most manifest.'[25] Carroll's world is a world of card figures which have no thickness, and in which 'becoming unlimited comes to be the ideational and incorporeal event, with all its characteristic reversals between future and past, active and passive, cause and effect, more and less, too much and not enough, already and not yet.'[26] Without doubt, it seems we are dealing with a literary, impossible, nonsensical world.

Deleuze says that this nonsense is the root of every sense. It may not appear at a first level of analysis, when the designation of meanings is fixed more or less arbitrarily and, as it were, 'attached' to the most stable things we know—the natural world's objects. But the problem of sense begins to reveal itself in a second level of understanding, when one reflects on its deeper origin. In order to avoid an infinite chain of designations, Deleuze

[22] Deleuze, *Logic of Sense*, xiv.

[23] Ibid., 6.

[24] Ibid., 7. Deleuze's emphasis.

[25] Ibid., 6–7.

[26] Deleuze, *Logic of Sense*, 8.

assumes that sense has neither a physical nor a mental existence: rather, it has a dynamic structure which runs simultaneously from inside to outside, without presupposing an 'up' or a 'down.' In *Sylvie and Bruno*, in fact, Carroll describes Fortunatus' purse as being akin to a Möbius strip, which is made of handkerchiefs sewn in the wrong way, in such a manner that 'its outer surface is continuous with its inner surface,' so that 'it envelops the entire world, and makes that which is inside be on the outside and vice versa.'[27] In the same way—Deleuze observes—the pure event, as it emerges in the surface of things, is a sort of a mobile point, a zipper or a frontier between life and thought. As a frontier, it has a sort of 'static ontological and logical genesis'[28] and 'is not a separation, but rather the element of an articulation, so that sense is presented both as that which happens to bodies and that which insists in propositions.'[29] Sense is, therefore, a 'doubling up' and the '*neutrality of sense is inseparable from its status as a double*.'[30] In this regard, being an intangible point, it is beyond the range of our common sense, but is better explained by a series of paradoxes that, unlike Russell's paradoxes of signification, point to the impotence of the speaker or the neutrality of the various meanings of the proposition.[31] Thus Deleuze identifies sense as something having a status of 'pure event,' that is, a perennial gap within the meaning-production, something irreducible to any state of facts: be they material/objective, desire/belief, or universal/conceptual facts. For the French philosopher, Carroll shows better than anyone else the mechanism of production of sense by extracting the pure event from the denotational meaning, by organizing it in parallel series that never touch each other and that are finally linked only by a number of paradoxical elements.[32] In this whole process, there is no fixed designation for anything, but only a fragile and aleatory domain in which the parallel worlds are connected by means of a paradox—the paradox of the impossibility for the language to be meaningful.

[27] Ibid., 11.

[28] Cf. the sixteenth and seventeenth series.

[29] Deleuze, *Logic of Sense*, 125.

[30] Ibid. Deleuze's emphasis.

[31] Cf. in particular the fifth, eleventh, and twelfth series, in Deleuze, *Logic of Sense*, 28–35 and 66–81.

[32] Cf. 'Sixth Series on Serialization,' in Deleuze, *Logic of Sense*, 36–41.

While—as seen in the previous section—the first border between philosophy and literature was to be found in meaning, according to Deleuze, a further border between different *levels of meaning*, that is, an ultimate sense that encompasses all of them, lies in what he calls the 'pure event.' This element is 'the fourth dimension of the proposition' in that it 'merges neither with the proposition or with the terms of the proposition, nor with the object or with the state of affairs which the proposition denotes, neither with the "lived," or representation of the mental activity of the person who expresses herself in the proposition, nor with concepts or even signified essences.'[33] Deleuze defines this element or pure event simply as 'sense' and he maintains that it is by no means unknown in the history of philosophy of language, from the Stoics to Husserl:

> The Stoics discovered it along with the event: sense, *the expressed of the proposition*, is an incorporeal, complex, and irreducible entity, at the surface of things, a pure event which inheres or subsists in the proposition. The discovery was made a second time in the fourteenth century, in Ockham's school, by Gregory of Rimini and Nicholas d'Autrecourt. It was made a third time at the end of nineteenth century, by the great philosopher and logician Meinong. Undoubtedly there are reasons for these moments: we have seen that the Stoic discovery presupposed a reversal of Platonism; similarly Ockham's logic reacted against the problem of Universals, and Meinong against Hegelian logic and its lineage ... In each period the controversy is taken up anew (André de Neufchateau and Pierre d'Ailly against Rimini, Brentano and Russell against Meinong). In truth, the attempt to make this fourth dimension evident is a little like Carroll's Snark hunt. Perhaps the dimension is the hunt itself, and sense is the Snark. It is difficult to respond to those who wish to be satisfied with words, things, images, and ideas. For we may not even say that sense exists either in things or in the mind; it has neither physical nor mental existence. Shall we at least say that it is useful, and that it is necessary to admit it for its utility? ... Husserl calls '*expression*' this ultimate dimension, and he distinguishes it from denotation, manifestation, and

[33] Deleuze, *Logic of Sense*, 19. In this list, Deleuze sums up some classic conceptions of meaning, namely, 'denotation,' 'manifestation,' and 'signification.' The 'sense' is in fact extraneous to all of them, he says, just as it is irreducible to any 'individual state of affairs, particular images, personal beliefs, and universal or general concepts' (19). Indifferent to both particular and general, personal and impersonal, sense would be, therefore, 'of an entirely different nature' (19).

> demonstration. Sense is that which is expressed. Husserl, no less than Meinong, rediscovered the living sources of the Stoic inspiration.[34]

Sense is, thus, a further and unconditioned dimension, 'capable of assuring a real genesis of denotation and of other dimensions of the proposition.'[35] In this respect, it is a sort of '*perpetuum mobile*' and 'its function is to traverse the heterogeneous series, to coordinate them, to make them resonate and converge, but also to ramify them and to introduce into each one of them multiple disjunction.'[36] Yet, as Deleuze insists many times, the nature of this dimension is subject to an 'essential fragility,'[37] like that of the thinnest surface, that cannot but affect the same production of sense: indeed, the pure events—for example, Alice becoming larger than she was and shorter than she is[38]—are 'stuttering events' per se, in that, by 'eluding the present,' they make and do not make sense at the same time. As Deleuze argues, 'it pertains to the essence of becoming to move and to pull in both directions at once.'[39] Hence, the beginning of parallel series of meanings. To emphasize this, 'Lewis Carroll explored and establishes a serial method in literature. We find in his works several methods for developing series. We find first two series of events with slight internal differences being regulated by a strange object.'[40] This object is often a paradoxical operator which, like a blank word, keeps things in a sort of displacement, showing at one and the same time their possibility of being both meaningful and nonsensical.[41]

[34] Deleuze, *Logic of Sense*, 19–20.

[35] Ibid., 19.

[36] Ibid., 66.

[37] Cf. 'Fourteenth Series of Double Causality,' in Deleuze, *Logic of Sense*, 94–96.

[38] Deleuze, *Logic of Sense*, 1.

[39] Ibid.

[40] Ibid., 42.

[41] Deleuze gives an example, which he takes from *Sylvie and Bruno*, of such a 'strange object,' that is, 'an eight-handed watch with reversing pin which never follows time. On the contrary, time follows it. It makes events return in two ways, either in a becoming-mad which reverses the sequential order, or with slight variations according to the Stoic fatum. The young cyclist, who falls over a box in the first series of events, now proceeds uninjured. But when the hands of the watch return to their original position, the cyclist lies once again wounded on the wagon which takes him to the hospital. It is as if the watch knew how to conjure up the accident, that is, the temporal occurrence of the event, but not the Event itself, the result, the wound as an eternal truth' (Deleuze, *Logic of Sense*, 42).

'Language Stutters': The Fragility of Surface

In investigating its origin, Deleuze discovers that sense is an effect rather than a cause, and it has a determinate relation with nonsense. In this regard, he identifies two different types of nonsense. The first remains in the surface of sense and produces a world that still has a 'logic.' This logic is a word-device that paradoxically leaves the 'shelf' of meaning always empty by means of a 'mobile frontier' with *twofold* and *uneven* faces that connects every thought-aphorism. This is the case of the nonsensical phrases (like in the famous nonsense poem *Jabberwocky*: ''Twas brillig, and the slithy toves / Did gyre and gimble in the wabe'); of the so-called esoteric words (e.g. the 'Phlizz,' a fruit without taste, or the 'toves' [badgers-lizards-corkscrews] or the verb 'outgribe' [bellowing-whistling-sneezing]); and of portmanteau words, which create a condensation and a disjunction at one and the same time—the 'snark' is neither a shark nor a snake; 'frumious' is derived from furious + fuming; 'mimsy' from flimsy + miserable.[42]

The second type of nonsense, on the contrary, is the one that swallows sense to make it finally disappear into the night of exclusion: it is a terrifying nonsense that, for Deleuze, can be seen in the reading Antonin Artaud gave on Carroll's work and, in particular, on his poem *Jabberwocky*.[43] 'As we read the first stanza of "Jabberwocky," such as Artaud renders it,' Deleuze observes, 'we have the impression that the two opening verses still correspond to Carroll's criteria ... but beginning with the last word of the second line, from the third line onward, a sliding is produced, and even a creative, central collapse, causing us to be in another world and in an entirely different language.'[44] 'With horror,' Deleuze states, 'we recognize it easily: it is the language of schizophrenia.'[45] In this case, breaking the fragile world of surface can lead to radical loss or to madness. In this primary order of schizophrenia, Artaud puts the spotlight on a fundamental regression to the

[42] See Deleuze, *Logic of Sense*, 44–47.

[43] Cf. 'Thirteenth Series of the Schizophrenic and the Little Girl,' in Deleuze, *Logic of Sense*, 82–93.

[44] Deleuze, *Logic of Sense*, 83–84.

[45] Ibid., 84. 'Summing this up,' Deleuze concludes, 'we could say that Artaud considers Lewis Carroll a pervert, a little pervert, who holds onto the establishment of a surface language, and who has not felt the real problem of a language in depth – namely, the schizophrenic problem of suffering, of death, and of life' (84).

body, to a word that can be swallowed back by the mouth and converge in a unique series as in an unarticulated spasm.

Such a difference between the two ways of nonsense is also reflected by the 'logic' of Lewis Carroll's two main works. In Wonderland, Alice has to adapt to a world with no laws; in the Looking-glass world, she faces a place that is governed by unusual laws. In both worlds she is the only person who has self-control and who has some sort of competence. She is the one who tries to make sense out of those worlds. But her effort is a constant fight between the parallel series of meanings, so that the decision she/Carroll makes every time cannot but reflect the double and counter-effectual character of sense. Sense for Deleuze seems to be like a stutter: possibly a fundamental stutter of Being. This is revealed in Carroll's works through an unstable word or language in which the series converge to eventually find a sort of unbalancing operator. Interestingly enough, Carroll was himself a stutterer in real life. But what he depicts in his works is the stutter of language, of event, of a deeper sense of the world. Everything *seems* to make sense in that it makes unbalanced, double, counter-effectual sense. Whereas Heidegger's own 'linguistic turn' is clearly expressed in his 1950 seminal conference, 'Language,' with his mantra-phrase 'Language speaks' ('*Die Sprache spricht*') not man,[46] Deleuze (with Carroll) might well say: 'Language stutters.' For the language of sense, to correspond to all the heterogeneous and unreachable meanings, that is, the parallel series of meaning, is the same as to stutter. But while the stuttering of sense is equally meaningful, at least in its attempt and in its struggle to make sense, it is also dangerously close to another possibility that Deleuze would actually follow in subsequent years.

As already anticipated, the stutter is only one of the two possibilities of the 'nonsense underlying sense,' and as a matter of fact, is an option of secondary order. The other is a terrifying nonsense of primary order, which Deleuze would later develop with his theory of the 'body without organs' in his collaboration with Félix Guattari.[47] The shift to the second option is

[46] See Martin Heidegger, *On the Way to Language*, trans. P.D. Hertz (San Francisco, Ca.: Harper and Row, 1982).

[47] In *Anti-Oedipus* (1972) Deleuze and Guattari introduce the 'body-without-organs' concept to represent the experience of schizophrenics who feel organs as 'pure intensities' that can be linked together in an infinite number of directions. In this regard, what is called 'delirium' is no other than a wider and more complex matrix by which all the intensities are not reducible to personal and familiar coordinates, but are directed to the world-historical reality.

evident in Deleuze's retrospective review of *Logic of Sense*. In the note to the Italian edition of the book, the French philosopher reveals one of the main intents of his work ('I tried, however very timidly, to make psychoanalysis inoffensive by presenting it as an art of surface'[48]), and writes:

> So, what now? Luckily, I am no longer able to nearly speak in my own name anymore, as what happened to me after *The Logic of Sense* depends on my meeting with Félix Guattari, on my work with him, on what we do together. I guess we looked for other directions because we wanted so. The *Anti-Oedipus* has neither height nor depth, nor surface. There, everything happens, becomes, the intensities, the multiplicities, the events, on a sort of spherical body or a round-rolling picture: Body-without-organs ... The *Anti-Oedipus* is a good start, on condition that we break up with it.[49]

The place and importance of Lewis Carroll's writings in Deleuze's own philosophical path are summarized very clearly in a short text he dedicated to the British writer. 'In Lewis Carroll,' Deleuze writes, 'everything begins with a horrible combat, the combat of depths: things explode or make us explode, boxes are too small for their contents, foods are toxic and poisonous, entrails are stretched, monsters grab at us.'[50] Everything that is 'pre-sense' begins in depth and *that* depth is just like hell: 'things and words are scattered in every direction, or on the contrary are welded together into non-decomposable blocks. Everything in depth is horrible, everything is nonsense.'[51] Here, Deleuze analyses a linear path of 'ascension' in Carroll's output.

> *Alice in Wonderland* was originally to have been entitled *Alice's Adventures Underground*. But why didn't Carroll keep this title? Because Alice progressively conquers surfaces. She rises or returns to the surface. She creates surfaces. Movements of penetration and burying give way to light lateral movements of sliding; the animals of the depths become figures on cards without thickness. All the more reason for *Through the Looking-Glass* to invest the surface of a mirror, to institute a game of chess. Pure events escape from

[48] Deleuze, *La logica del senso*, 294.

[49] Deleuze, *La logica del senso*, 294–295.

[50] Gilles Deleuze, "Lewis Carroll," in *Essays Critical and Clinical* (1st ed. in French 1993), trans. W. Smith and M.A. Greco (Minneapolis, Mn.: The University of Minnesota Press, 1997), 21.

[51] Deleuze, *Essays Critical and Clinical*, 21.

> states of affairs. We no longer penetrate in depth, but through an act of sliding pass through the looking-glass, turning everything the other way round like a left-hander ... Mathematics is good because it brings new surfaces into existence, and brings peace to a world whose mixtures in depth would be terrible: Carroll the mathematician, or Carroll the photographer.[52]

Just like Alice, at the beginning Carroll 'still seeks the secret of events and of the becoming unlimited which they imply, in the depth of the earth, in dug out shafts and holes which plunge beneath, and in the mixture of bodies which interpenetrate and coexist.'[53] But as one advances in the story, everything progressively returns to the surface: 'It is not therefore a question of *the adventures* of Alice, but of Alice's *adventure*: her climb to the surface, her disavowal of false depth and her discovery that everything happens at the border.'[54] In parallel with the history of philosophy, from Plato to the Stoics,[55] Deleuze sees a climax in which, from the quest for hidden causes (Plato), one ends up considering the quest for effects as the sole result of 'becoming unlimited' (the Stoics).

> This is why Carroll abandons the original title of the book: *Alice's Adventures Underground*. This is the case – even more so – in *Through the Looking-Glass*. Here events, differing radically from things, are no longer sought in depths, but at the surface ... Alice is no longer able to make her way through to the depths. Instead, she releases her incorporeal double.[56]

Continuing in this direction, in the subsequent novel *Sylvie and Bruno* 'it is the little boy who has the inventive role, learning his lessons in all manners, inside-out, outside-in, above and below, but never "in depth." This important novel pushes to the extreme the evolution which had begun in *Alice*, and which continued in *Through the Looking-Glass*.'[57]

> Carroll's third great novel, *Sylvie and Bruno* – Deleuze writes in his article 'Lewis Carroll' – brings about yet a further advance. The previous depth itself

[52] Ibid.
[53] Deleuze, *Logic of Sense*, 9.
[54] Ibid.
[55] See Deleuze, *Logic of Sense*, 4–8.
[56] Ibid., 9–10.
[57] Ibid., 10.

> seems to be flattened out, and becomes a surface alongside the other surface. The two surfaces thus coexist, and two contiguous stories are written on them … Not one story within another, but one next to the other. *Sylvie and Bruno* is no doubt the first book that tells two stories at the same time, not one inside the other, but two contiguous stories, with passages that constantly shift from one to the other, sometimes owing to a fragment of a sentence that is common to both stories, sometimes by means of the couplets of an admirable song that distributes the events proper to each story.[58]

But, as the French philosopher argues, 'the world of depths still rumbles under the surface and threatens to break through.'[59] Finally, all this happens in a new, unexpected form. Depth (*Alice in Wonderland*) and surface (*Through the Looking-Glass*) become one in the final term of Carroll's trilogy. This is the genesis of the first and most fundamental 'parallel series' in which the most terrible combats of depths and the stutters of surface emerge in a disjunctive synthesis that is akin to the Möbius strip, in which 'the continuity between reverse and right side replaces all the levels of depth; and the surface effects in one and the same Event, which would hold for all events, bring to language-becoming and its paradoxes.'[60] 'With *Sylvie and Bruno*, Carroll makes a scroll book in the manner of Japanese scroll paintings.'[61]

Conclusion: A 'Tangled Story'

Deleuze's predisposition towards tripartitions brings us to the conclusion that the third and final parallel series is a disjunctive synthesis, where there are no longer terrible fights and oppositions, nor stutters and counter-effects that undermine sense itself. There is rather an ultimate nonsense, which gives 'an account of the entire universe, its terrors as well as its glories: the depth, the surface, and the volume or rolled surface.'[62] This nonsense, however, *stands in itself*: it is, as it were, continuous in its discontinuity. Evidently, following Deleuze with his *Logic of Sense* means also stopping, as he does, at the point at which it is still possible to 'speak in one's own name.'

[58] Deleuze, *Essays Critical and Clinical*, 22.

[59] Ibid., 21.

[60] Deleuze, *Logic of Sense*, 11.

[61] Deleuze, *Essays Critical and Clinical*, 22.

[62] Ibid.

The disjunctive synthesis is a sense that does not make sense in the way one was used to think in the *outside* and *denotative* world. In fact, from that perspective a disjunctive sense is a failure of sense. But at another, more foundational, level it is—at least for Deleuze—the sole feasible attempt to put things together. Beyond *Logic of Sense*, as Deleuze himself admitted, we face another story where the loss of all these possibilities is irreversible.

In a text published between 1880 and 1885, made of brief humorous stories and entitled *A Tangled Tale*, Lewis Carroll sets out a number of 'knots' that, as Deleuze observes, 'in each case, surround the singularities corresponding to a problem; characters incarnate these singularities and are displaced or rearranged from one problem to another, until they find each other again in the tenth knot, caught in the network of their kinship relationship.'[63] While *A Tangled Tale* was an attempt to anthropomorphize mathematics, its problematic result is the same as that faced at the end of Deleuze's *Logic of Sense*, in which all the singularities are equally 'displaced or rearranged from one problem to another.' *The Logic of Sense*'s 'finale' is, in fact, a tangled story, in which, as Deleuze says, 'the mode of the event is the problematic.'[64]

This might be also a good metaphor for the relationship between philosophy and literature (as well as between a scientific-external view of the world and a psychoanalytic-internal one) from which this chapter started. Trying to make sense of those series—or in other words, trying to find the border between them—may lead to a disjunctive synthesis, in which only the *logos* as a surface keeps the questions: the questions as 'effects.' Whereas the answers—just as in Carroll's tales—may stand on the other side in a mirror image as 'causes,' and would therefore be useless answers in that they would not *answer* questions that come 'after.' A simple and linear *correspondence*, even that between questions and answers, never really works at this level of the discourse, where the limit of difference is *transgressed* and the fields (the series) one has to deal with are irreducibly heterogeneous. As Derek Attridge argues in commenting on Derrida's position on literature, the question 'what is literature?' 'is, after all, a philosophical, not a literary question; it asks for a statement of the essence of literature.'[65] 'The question of its origin,' says Derrida, with reference to literature, 'was immediately the

[63] Deleuze, *Logic of Sense*, 55.

[64] Ibid., 54.

[65] Jacques Derrida, *Acts of Literature*, ed. D. Attridge (New York: Routledge, 1992), 1.

question of its end. Its history *is constructed* like the ruin of a monument which basically never existed.'[66] Thus, 'what is literature?' is an answer, not a question. On the other hand, from an authentically 'literary' point of view, as Deleuze points out, 'literature rather moves in the direction of the ill-formed or the incomplete ... Writing is a question of becoming, always incomplete, always in the midst of being formed, and goes beyond the matter of any livable or lived experience.'[67] In this regard, literature is 'delirium,' in a Deleuzian sense, 'and as such its destiny is played out between the two poles of delirium,' namely, delirium as 'a disease, the disease par excellence' and as the highest 'measure of health,' 'a possibility of life.'[68] For to write in a literary way is also to become something other than *a writer*; to think 'literarily' is another thing from the thinking of a philosopher. 'To those who ask what literature is,' Deleuze concludes, 'Virginia Woolf responds: "To whom are you speaking of writing?" The writer does not speak about it, but is concerned with something else.'[69]

Bibliography

Baker, Lynne Rudder, ed. 2013. *Naturalism and the First-Person Perspective.* New York: Oxford University Press.

Batteux, Charles. 1746. *Les beaux arts réduits à un même principe.* Paris: Ed. Durand.

Deleuze, Gilles. 1990. *The Logic of Sense* (1st ed. in French 1969). Trans. M. Lester. New York: Columbia University Press.

———. 1997. *Essays Critical and Clinical* (1st ed. in French 1993). Trans. W. Smith and M.A. Greco. Minneapolis: The University of Minnesota Press.

———. 2006. *La logica del senso* (1st ed. in Italian 1975). Trans. M. de Stefanis. Milan: Feltrinelli.

Derrida, Jacques. 1992. In *Acts of literature*, ed. D. Attridge. New York: Routledge.

Dummett, Michael. 2003. Frege and Husserl on Reference. In *The Seas of Language*, 224–229. New York: Oxford University Press.

Habermas, Jürgen. 1992. *Postmetaphysical Thinking: Philosophical Essays.* Cambridge, MA: The MIT Press.

66 Ibid., 42.

67 See Deleuze, "Literature and Life," in *Essays Critical and Clinical*, 1.

68 Deleuze, *Essays Critical and Clinical*, 4.

69 Ibid., 6.

Heidegger, Martin. 1982. *On the Way to Language*. Trans. P.D. Hertz. San Francisco: Harper and Row.
Kirkham, Richard L. 1995. *Theories of Truth. A Critical Introduction*. Cambridge, MA: The MIT Press.
Künne, Wolfgang. 2003. *Conceptions of Truth*. New York: Oxford University Press.
Lynch, Michael P., ed. 2001. *The Nature of Truth. Classic and Contemporary Perspectives*. Cambridge, MA: The MIT Press.
Martin, Bill. 2010. Analytic Philosophy's Narrative Turn: Quine, Rorty, Davidson. In *Literary Theory After Davidson*, ed. Reed Way Dasenbrock, 124–143. University Park: The Pennsylvania State University Press.
Nagel, Thomas. 1986. *The View from Nowhere*. New York: Oxford University Press.
Putnam, Hilary. 1990. In *Realism with a Human Face*, ed. James Conant. Cambridge. MA: Harvard University Press.
Quine, Willard Van Orman. 1953. *From a Logical Point of View*. Cambridge: Harvard University Press.
———. 1981. *Theories and Things*. Cambridge, MA: Harvard University Press.

Cultural Liminality: Gender, Identity, and Margin in the Uncanny Stories of Elizabeth Bowen

Paromita Mukherjee

Elizabeth Bowen has always been ambivalent about her cultural identity. While she has an Anglo-Irish heritage, she spent most of her adult life in England. Her roots in the Protestant ascendancy separated her from Catholic Ireland. Like her female characters, Bowen is a marginalized figure in her own culture. Her cultural liminality is reflected in her representation of the liminal or transitional figures in her uncanny stories. Bowen deconstructs what we call 'normal' or 'real' by writing about the ghostly, haunting, and the irrational in a realistic mode, the manifestations of which are shown through hallucinations, anxieties, memories, and histories of the fictional characters. How women are overwhelmed, crippled, and marginalized by terror, lies, trauma, violence, and alienation are significant in these stories. Several of Bowen's female characters in her novels and short stories are either at the transitional phases of maturation or clinging to the thin line that separates life and death. The 'self', in these texts, gains access to the 'other' from the consciousness at the threshold of intermediary moments, only in the environment of the *phantasm*. As a result, the reader encounters certain identities that illuminate interesting issues about gender,

P. Mukherjee (✉)
Amity University, Kolkata, India

J. Elbert Decker, D. Winchock (eds.), *Borderlands and Liminal Subjects*, https://doi.org/10.1007/978-3-319-67813-9_12

which otherwise never come to the surface. These identities are marked by difference and marginalization, which destabilize the cultural assumptions of 'selfhood' and make us rethink the meaning of feminine subjectivity.

The theme of this chapter is the transitional and liminal figure, which under the duress of excessive emotion and anxiety clings to the border or margin of the real and unreal world. I am going to focus on some of Bowen's short stories to show how they highlight the ideas of the liminal and the margin. How space, location, and structure act as vessels of memory and history, and how that helps in the reconstruction of gender and identity, is also a significant part of my analysis. Further, drawing upon the Freudian idea of the 'uncanny', I will explore how in Bowen's stories, the cultural assumptions of selfhood and identity are redefined at the liminal conditions created by the phantasm.

The Short Story, the Ghost Story, and the 'Uncanny'

The short stories by several authors often get neglected because of the critical attention given to their novels. The ghost story within the genre of short story hardly gets any scholarly consideration. Diana Wallace argues that the ghost story, like gothic novel, has allowed women writers special kinds of freedom to offer critiques of male power and sexuality, but the ghost story has hardly received any critical attention and is doubly marginalized for being short story and also ghost story.[1] In the light of this remark, it is also necessary to note Bowen's own ideas about short stories. In a Preface to one of her collection of stories, Bowen writes:

> The short story is at an advantage over the novel, and can claim its nearer kinship to poetry, because it must be more concentrated, can be more visionary, and is not weighed down (as the novel is bound to be) by facts, explanation, or analysis .... [It] revolves round one crisis only, [which] allows for what is crazy about humanity: obstinacies, inordinate heroisms, 'immortal longings'.[2]

[1] Diana Wallace, "Uncanny Stories: The Ghost Story as Female Gothic", *Gothic Studies* 6/1 (Manchester University Press: Manchester, UK, 2004): 57–58.

[2] Elizabeth Bowen, *Afterthought: Pieces About Writing* (London: Longmans Green, 1962): 79–80.

In another Preface, she wrote that the short story is "semi-poetic" and requires "a central emotion".[3] Bowen has written about a hundred short stories apart from ten novels and several non-fictions, spanning over fifty years, before, during, and after the Second World War. However, her novels have received much critical attention, whereas only few of her war-time stories have been considered by critics.

Bowen's short stories are the kernels of inventive ideas and intense emotions. The moments of crises arising in her stories take more developed shapes and get a steadier, calmer, and stricter treatment in her novels. The focus of this chapter is on particularly some early and pre-war stories of Bowen, such as "The Shadowy Third", "Foothold", and "The Apple Tree".[4] In these stories, Bowen merges the boundaries between realism and supernaturalism. These stories do not necessarily portray a visible spectral figure or a ghost. More often, what gets dramatized is the idea of the haunting and feelings of uncertainty, indeterminacy, instability, uneasiness, fear of the seemingly unknown, and dread of something spectral and enigmatic. This destabilization occurs through hallucinations, anxieties, traumas, fantasies, memories, and histories of places and people that create an aura of the *phantasm* and uncanniness. This chapter will explore the transitional moments of crisis arising in the above-mentioned uncanny stories before they pass over to the comparatively rational arena of Bowen's novels. Not only these stories highlight some of the important elements of all of Bowen's works, but they also open up certain questions relating to her own marginalized, transitional, and undecidable position in her culture.

Bowen pushes the boundaries of the traditional ghost stories, as she works on the ambiguous edge between the explained and unexplained supernatural. She considered it to be 'unethical' to allow the supernatural into a novel.[5] However she used it often in her short stories. In her ghost stories, the readers are not taken to a parallel world of fantasy where a different rationale is at work; nor are we provided an explanation of the supernatural occurrences within the reality of human ambience. Instead, amid the uncanny and undecidable moments created in the stories, we are

[3] Bowen, *Collected Impressions* (London: Longmans Green, 1950): 41, 43.

[4] Bowen, "The Shadowy Third", *Encounters* (1923), "Foothold", *Ann Lee's* (1927), "The Apple Tree", *The Cat Jumps and Other Stories* (1934) in Angus Wilson edited *The Collected Stories of Elizabeth Bowen* (Hopewell, NJ: Ecco Press, 1981).

[5] Bowen, Preface to *A Day in the Dark and Other Stories* (London: Jonathan Cape, 1964): 9.

left wondering 'what really happened?'. In this context, one may refer to Clare Hanson's proposition that short stories may be structured like dreams where the relation between events and images are often random and arbitrary, which are an expression of the repressed or unconscious desire through the combination of elements of strangeness and familiarity.[6] Thinking along that line, one can argue that the uncanny stories of Bowen are like dreams: an amalgamation of events and images most of which remain unexplained. The female characters in most of these stories are in a perpetual dream-like and transient state, drifting at the borderline of sleeping and waking, and roving at the threshold of being dead and living.

Sigmund Freud, in his essay "The Uncanny", uses the German word *unheimlich*, which literally means 'unhomely' and is translated into English as 'uncanny'.[7] The uncanny is not just a feeling of the mysterious or weird, but also something strangely familiar and yet unhomely. It is a return of the repressed and basic fear of death or the dead who returns. It is something random, incredible, disturbing, unexpected, and shocking. As Nicholas Royle mentions, the uncanny effect may be produced by darkness, solitary houses and forests, silence, margins and borders, half-lives, alienation, repetitions, doubling, and multiplying.[8] Bowen shows the uncanny effects through a character's subjective feeling of trauma and reiterations of the past, in the familiar settings of cities, houses, forests, gardens, and so on. Her stories are filled with incidents of haunting, disturbing, and occasionally uncanny events, inexplicable gaps in narrative logic or rationale, and the frequent disruption of identity and the supposition of any stability to identity. This is most often witnessed when the 'self' in its certainty is shown to be disturbed, whether internally or from outside, by some 'other', the acknowledgment of which causes the boundaries of identity to become blurred.

According to J. Hillis Miller, either in real life or in fiction, the self may or may not exist as an independent, substantial, extralinguistic entity. On one hand, whatever can only be named in figure may exist as only a figure, that is, "a phantasmal effect of the displacements and exchanges of language.

[6] Clare Hanson, Introduction, *Re-reading the Short Story* (London: Macmillan, 1989): 26–27.

[7] Sigmund Freud, "The Uncanny", *Writings on Art and Literature* (Stanford: Stanford University Press, 1997): 193.

[8] Nicholas Royle, *The Uncanny* (New York: Routledge, 2003): 109, 190.

On the other hand ... [self] may exist, but in a realm inaccessible to direct seeing and naming".[9] The idea of the self is thus open to questioning. That is to say, what we may assume as identity may merely be an agreement between the speaking creatures, who have agreed to acknowledged boundaries of being in common. However, this still does not guarantee the stability of identity. The 'self' can assume wandering and different guises.

The 'other' may appear as the reflection or variation of the 'self' arising from its consciousness and manifesting itself in the figure of a ghost. The figure of phantom or ghost, in ghost stories, may give a form to the undecidability. A ghost, in its appearance, is not undecidable. However, it highlights the idea of semantic and ontological undecidability by being one figure that, in being neither present nor absent, is neither alive nor dead. It gives decidable categories that are limited in their ability to fix meaning. The ghost or phantom or the haunting figure is disturbing because, while it takes a human form, it clearly is not alive. It is thus almost human but not quite. And yet it is disturbing because it is a figure of someone who is dead and so should not be able to appear. Thus it is unsettling because it causes us to reflect on the fact that we too are mortal. We will die, and thus this ghostly figure 'figures' us outside ourselves, as in fact, the 'other'. The fluid nature of the 'self' thus can make way for the figure of the 'other', a phenomenon that happens often in Bowen's stories.

The Liminal and the Margin

In Bowen's early stories, we often encounter certain female characters that are clinging to the thin line that separates life from death. These liminal figures, at the threshold of life and death, are mostly alienated from the rest of the world because of their fears and anxieties that are rooted in the indifferent behavior of their male partners. "The Shadowy Third" shows two such examples of the marginalized women. In this story, a sense of the unseen lingers around the house of Martin and Pussy, a married couple expecting a child. Pussy feels the presence of Martin's dead wife in this house. She never sees the ghost, but feels as if a shadow of the previous wife lingers at every corner and near every object reminding Pussy that once she existed. It almost becomes an obsession for Pussy as she starts thinking

[9] J. Hillis Miller, *Ariadne's Thread: Story Lines* (New Haven: Yale University Press, 1992): 32.

herself to be the usurper of her husband's affections and also is afraid that she might end up like the dead wife, forgotten by the husband. While Pussy craves for her husband's permanent affection, the readers are given a glimpse that the coldness and death associated with her husband will alienate her anyway. The history of the house is a powerful presence in this story. As Allan E. Austin comments, the houses in Bowen's stories are "haunted by presences that prey upon susceptible imaginations and so feed fears. This openness to haunting is one way the author exposes the resourcelessness of seemingly sophisticated moderns".[10] Not only do these reactions open up several channels to allow the characters to experience the house's history, they also create new identities by redefining the selfhood for each character.

Bowen describes Pussy as a frail young woman with "features and light hair and eyes", who waits for her husband "very near the edge of the platform" that corresponds to her own weak condition at the edge of life.[11] Her borderline and liminal condition is reflected by her desire to stay at the garden. Garden seems to be symbolic of a space at the threshold: it is neither an integral part of the solid structure that a house is, nor a space that is completely separated from the house. Pussy seems to be fonder of the garden than of the house as she wants to stay out of the house more:

> 'Let's stay out,' she begged. 'It isn't time for supper. It isn't beginning to get dark yet. Do stay out – dear Martin!'
>
> 'Why,' he said, looking round at her, 'one would think you were afraid of the house.'
>
> 'Hoo!' she laughed, 'afraid of *our* house!'
>
> But he was still dissatisfied. Something was making her restless; she was out in the garden too much. And when she was not in the garden she was always walking about the house. One or two days, when he had stayed at home to work, he had heard her on the stairs and up and down the passages; up and down, up and down. He knew that women in her state of health were abnormal, had strange fancies.[12]

A pregnant woman is described by her male partner in terms of 'abnormal', 'strange', and fanciful. Martin refers to their house in a detached tone as 'the

[10] Allan E. Austin, *Elizabeth Bowen* (Boston: Twayne Publishers, 1989): 72.

[11] *The Collected Stories of Elizabeth Bowen* (Hopewell, NJ: Ecco Press, 1981): 76.

[12] Ibid., 77.

house' while Pussy tries to affirm some sort of possession by referring it as 'our house'. It appears as if Pussy is trying hard to convince herself that she is able to convert someone else's thing as her own. She is almost competing with the Martin's dead wife in terms of creativity and renovation as she takes pride in thinking of certain changes that she is about to bring to the garden and the house.

Martin's dead wife is never named in the story. Pussy refers to her as 'Anybody' while Martin thinks of her as '*She*'.[13] It is revealed that the dead wife was pregnant too, but the child had not lived. Pussy wonders what the name of that child could have been, as she discovers certain nursery pictures from the attic. There is a mention of a chest with locked drawers that alarms Martin, as if some hidden secret from the past will soon be exposed. Martin remembers his dead wife sitting by the fire and making baby clothes, while he remained engrossed in reading books. He did not like her glasses and never returned home by the earlier train to spend more time with her, even during her pregnancy. Pussy tries to understand the pain and loneliness that the dead wife must have experienced, as Martin was neglectful of her. Martin, on the other hand, remembers how he had alienated his dead wife. It seems that to make amends, he is ready to give more attention to his present wife. His current attention toward Pussy and previous neglect of the dead wife make Pussy feel guilty of a pleasure that the dead wife had missed. Hence she tries to imagine what she would feel like if Martin did not care for her also like his dead wife. The history of the dead wife in the house casts a shadow on the present wife, who can only understand the 'other' by imposing a self-inflicted pain of imagination on her 'self'. Pussy's insecurities and fears pave the way for the shadowy third to exist, as she feels herself to be the usurper who has taken away 'somebody else's happiness'.[14] To realize that guilt, it becomes necessary for the 'other' to exist as the 'self'.

Maud Ellmann describes "The Shadowy Third" as a "story of a serial killer" where the "very blankness of this pale commuter is his murder weapon: the women who have loved him – one pale, one dumb, two dead – seem to have blanked out of existence, nullified".[15] Bowen begins this story with the description of paleness, death, and resentment that seems

[13] Ibid., 77–79.

[14] Ibid., 82.

[15] Maud Ellmann, *Elizabeth Bowen: The Shadow Across the Page* (Edinburgh: Edinburgh University Press,2003): 84.

like a premonition of further morbidity. The house here links the events of the lives of the dead and living wives. It appears as if the fate of the present wife has been determined by the fate of the dead wife. While Pussy's self-exploration and quest for identity begin through morbid thoughts and resentful questions, the dead wife seems to be silently questioning through the objects of the house as Martin feels "as though those windows were watching him; their gaze was hostile, full of comment and criticism".[16] Pussy even implants the question of 'murder' implying that perhaps Martin had murdered his first wife through neglect:

> 'Do things like that happen? Could a person go on loving and loving and never be wanted?'
>
> 'How should I know?'
>
> 'I think,' she said, 'that not to want a person must be a sort, a sort of murder. I think a person who was done out of their life like that would be brought back by the injustice much more than anybody who was shot or stabbed'.[17]

Through the silence of the dead wife and the wonderings of the present wife, Bowen shows that these marginalized women are trying to find their identities. However, their explorations never become a reality as they are sacrificed for the domestic purpose of maintaining houses and family. While the 'self' as embodied in the character of Pussy is haunted by the history of the 'other' dead wife, and will perhaps share the same tragic fate, the story also shows that history can enable the 'other' to appear and offer silent resistance.

Gender, Identity, and History

Space, location, and structure function as the vessels or bearers of memory and history in Bowen's stories. The houses and the gardens in her stories act as agents of psychological oppression. In "The Shadowy Third" we have already seen how the history of the house with the memories of the dead wife has affected the lives of Martin and Pussy. The supernatural has been presented here as a feeling or anticipation. In "Foothold", we will encounter a crisis created by the possibility of a ghost of Clara, a former inhabitant of

[16] *Collected Stories*, 80.

[17] Ibid., 82.

the house in which a modern and educated couple, Janet and Gerard, move in. Janet insists on seeing the ghost of Clara, while her husband Gerard thinks that it is Janet's psychological problem arising from loneliness. Their writer friend Thomas visits them and they hope that Thomas will be able to bring closure to the problem of the ghost. The history of the house and its inhabitant in this story create the phantasmic 'other' and open up the channel of communication with the 'self'. The crisis, in this story, directs one to rethink about the issues of gender and identity.

Janet is a lonely housewife with a husband busy at work and children away in schools. To fill up her idle time, she devotes her energy to the redecoration of the house and beautification of the garden. Janet's loneliness is described in terms of space and size of the house:

> I do feel the house has grown since we've been in it. The rooms seem to take so much longer to get across. I'd no idea we were buying such a large one. I wanted it because it was white, and late Georgian houses are unexigeant, but I promised myself – and everyone else – it was small.[18]

When Thomas wonders if Janet is bothered by the presence of the ghost of Clara, Janet clearly says that Clara helps to fill up the emptiness of the house and then reflects upon the emptiness of her life:

> ... my life – this life – seems to have stretched somehow; there's more room in it. Yet it isn't that I've more time – that would be perfectly simple, I'd do more things ... I've never been able to see how one's day could fail to be full up, it fills itself. There's been the house, the garden, friends, books, music, letters, the car, golf, when one felt like it, going up to town rather a lot. Well, I still have all these and there isn't a moment between them. Yet there's more and more room every day. I suppose it must be underneath.[19]

This makes Janet uncomfortable, and like Thomas, even the readers may wonder that perhaps Clara is a figment of Janet's imagination that helps Janet with her loneliness.

Janet is the only one in the house who ever meets the ghost of Clara. Gerard decides to look for it but inevitably fails. As a result, he becomes

[18] *Collected Stories*, 299.

[19] Ibid., 302.

skeptical of its existence. Thomas jokes about it, hinting that Janet has probably created a fictional ghost:

> 'If I had a ghost,' said Thomas . . . 'she should be called "Celestina". I like that better than Clara.'
>
> 'If I have another daughter,' said Janet agreeably, 'she shall be called Celestina.'[20]

The above conversation clearly points that Janet ignores Thomas's implication about creating a ghost and counteracts with the suggestion that one creates a daughter, not a ghost. While Thomas may insist upon the ghost being Janet's imagination, Janet provides a historical fact that someone named Clara existed in the house, years before they moved in:

> Her name occurs in some title-deeds. She was a Clara Skepworth. She married a Mr. Horace Algernon May and her father seems to have bought her the house as a wedding present. She had four children – they all survived her but none of them seems to have left descendants – and died a natural death, middle-aged, about 1850. There seems no reason to think she was not happy; she was not interesting. Contented women aren't.[21]

It is to be noted here that Bowen carefully rejects all the usual associations that one makes regarding the appearance of ghosts—unfulfilled desire in lifetime, yearning for revenge, unusual death and as a result a wandering soul, and so on. Instead she highlights a comment made by Janet that contented women are not interesting. For a woman to be interesting, she needs to be discontent, perhaps like Janet herself.

Thomas also experiences the presence of the ghost of Clara, but he is at first mistaken because he thought it to be Janet. His modern, uninhibited, academic mind refuses to acknowledge its presence. It is easier to discard something unusual than actually confronting it, especially when it shakes the rational mind. Also there is no evidence in the story that the ghost really existed. It is possible that Janet was pretending to be the ghost because Thomas never sees the two of them together. What becomes interesting here is the crisis in Janet's life that encourages Clara to show up and as a result disturb the perfect suburban household. Thomas academically

[20] Ibid., 301.

[21] Ibid., 304–5.

thought Janet to be "the most attractive woman of his acquaintance: her bodily attraction was modified and her charm increased by the domination of her clear fastidious aloof mind over her body".[22] Thus it becomes disturbing for him to admit that Janet's relationship with Clara is neither of friendship, nor of love, but a result of her being unfulfilled in life: "'A peevish dead woman where we've failed,' he thought, 'it's absurd.' Gerard and he – he thought how much less humiliating for them both it would have been if she'd taken a lover".[23] It is easier for Thomas to dismiss Clara's ghost as an idea in Janet's mind than to seriously probe into the reason of why would Janet need a ghost for companionship by rejecting her husband and friend, or rather why would Janet choose female companionship over male.

As Phyllis Lassner observes, the "triangular arrangement" among the couple and Clara threatens the "men's domestic model of stability", and the men are humiliated because "Janet's communion with Clara reflects an intimacy that transcends male desire and subverts male hegemony".[24] Janet's idea of one living "two lives, two states of life" disrupts the domestic harmony.[25] Her life with Clara seems to have been waiting the whole time. The house and domesticity that had engulfed Clara, and is engulfing Janet, show the limitation of happiness in the traditional order of family: "Oh, Clara, ... I can't bear it. How could you bear it? The sickening loneliness ...".[26] Clara, as Gerard worries, "has got a foothold".[27] For him, as a husband, it is difficult to fathom that his wife is no longer interested in him and has formed a relationship with a ghost. The existence of this ghost, for him, is perhaps a power game that Janet is playing. It is somewhat strange that Janet, who had been complaining about the house growing larger, is the one who doesn't want to leave the house for a trip abroad that both Gerard and Thomas suggest. The identity of Clara, in this story, represents a feminine possibility of knowing something instinctively and emotionally, and is then juxtaposed with the masculine understanding

[22] Ibid., 302.

[23] Ibid., 305, 308.

[24] Phyllis Lassner, *Elizabeth Bowen: A Study of the Short Fiction* (New York: Twayne Publishers, 1991):13.

[25] *Collected Stories*, 301.

[26] Ibid., 313.

[27] Ibid., 309.

that is done logically and intellectually. It helps Janet explore a feminine identity outside the framework of a mother or a wife.

Culture, Selfhood, and Difference

Every culture has its complex assumptions concerning selfhood and identity. The culture tries to maintain these assumptions by incorporating enough characteristics to maintain an illusion of wholeness. However, every cultural group has its misfit that cannot be incorporated and explained by the preconceived notions of identity and 'selfhood'. These misfits are the victims of the environment who suffer from alienation, isolation, and lack of self-esteem. Bowen's female characters live in extreme conscious states of hallucination, hysteria, fear, and loss. In some of her stories, a woman's sensibility is taken to an excess. Hanson argues that this excess help in exploring "the complex and contradictory elements which go to form 'feminine' identities" in women-centered texts.[28] The kind of story-telling that Bowen takes up in her fiction is distinctive, where she shows several innovative possibilities for thinking about the female identity. In the stories discussed above, one can see how the burden of domesticity, household responsibilities, and motherhood can stifle certain female characters such as Pussy and the dead wife in "The Shadowy Third" and Janet and Clara in "Foothold". Myra Wing is another such alienated and marginalized character who appears in the story called "The Apple Tree", and the corresponding dead female character in that story is Doria.

The interpersonal relations that connect the 'self' and the 'other' in the stories of Bowen help to illustrate the relations between memory, history, and hallucination, and also highlight the notion of 'difference'. Memory and hallucinations lead to the possibility of seeing the 'self' as the 'other' in "The Apple Tree". The guiding forces behind the event of seeing the 'other' in this story are the feelings of being an outsider and lurking in the borderline or threshold, and a desire to be accepted by the society. Wing is driven by guilt and remorse that she had abandoned her childhood friend Doria and thus had been a catalyst in Doria's suicide. She describes herself as haunted by the incident of Doria's hanging herself from an apple tree. Guilt

[28] Clare Hanson, *Hysterical Fictions: The 'Woman's Novel' in the Twentieth Century* (New York: St. Martin's Press, LLC, 2000): 2.

makes her sleepwalk and recreate the incident in the library when some of her husband's friends come to visit the house.

Myra considers herself to be the source of the apple tree as she hysterically tells, one of the guests, Mrs. Bettersley: "Its roots are in me".[29] One cannot be sure if there is a real apple tree in the library or not. Even if there is one, it is not visible to any of the other people who were present at the scene. However, all of them have a feeling of the tree's presence in the room, and the feelings are described in an ambiguous way. Lancelot, another guest, sees Simon, Myra's husband, coming toward him "bumping, as though in a quite unfamiliar room, against the furniture, one arm stuck out ahead, as though pushing something aside, or trying to part a curtain".[30] A feeling of strangeness is produced as Simon tries to push through something invisible. However, a rational explanation is provided immediately as the light runs into the library and Lancelot sees big chairs and bookcases around Myra. Possibly, Simon was just trying to push through the large pieces of furniture and was waving his hand aimlessly for moving faster, but one can never be certain about it. The dreamlike incident in the library could have been dismissed as a matter of mere sleepwalking, but Lancelot hears three thudding sounds that seem to him like the sounds of apples falling. The narrator even points out that the idea of apples falling in a room makes Lancelot wonder if he is hallucinating or becoming mad. The uncanniness is further developed when Mrs. Bettersley fails to approach Myra in the room: "One can't get past ... it's like an apple tree".[31] What Lancelot and Mrs. Bettersley see, hear, or feel cannot be explained by means of rational thinking.

The unexplainable force, which has made its presence felt in the library in "The Apple Tree", is the 'other' that one cannot fathom with bodily or sensory perceptions. The force could be a figment of Lancelot's imagination originating from his previous discussion with Mrs. Bettersley about something strange regarding Myra. The force could also be Mrs. Bettersley's knowledge of the past incident at Myra's childhood school as reported in the newspapers. However, there are certain gaps in the story that invite the reader to wonder why Lancelot would associate the thudding sound in the library with an apple falling. He had no prior information about the apple

[29] *Collected Stories*, 470.

[30] Ibid., 464–65.

[31] Ibid., 466.

tree where the suicide was committed. It is also not explained how Myra could be cured by Mrs. Bettersley. Although there are no manifestations of some ghostly 'other', such instances cause the reader to encounter an aporetic moment within the structure and logic of the narrative. In being moments of aporia, the gaps confront the reader with an experience at the level of form that is analogous with the inexplicable for the characters in the story. Thus the story is structured around moments that are more than merely strange; they are literally undecidable. The idea, that an unexplainable can cease to unsettle people once it can be explained through articulation, is emphasized by Mrs. Bettersley's assurance: "Make it come into words. When it's once out it won't hurt any more".[32] This seems almost therapeutic. The event of understanding something that is otherwise unfathomable, as Bowen may like us to think, leads to the final effect of disappearance of the happy couple into "a sublime nonentity".[33] The visibility of the 'other' requires an acknowledgment of the inexplicable in a way, which rationalizes away the very thing that disturbs Myra's confession of guilt.

Mrs. Bettersley's success in exorcizing Myra can be read as the ultimate imposition of power and authority, and meaning as well, by the hegemonic culture over the 'otherness'. We see this kind of imposition in "Foothold" as well, where the Georgian house compels Janet to embrace an identity other than that of a mother and a housewife. The overwhelming and claustrophobic domestic life that Janet had been living obstructs any expression of 'self', and thus the appearance of Clara as the 'other' becomes necessary, where the house becomes the medium. The large library in the house of "The Apple Tree" also produces a similar overwhelming effect on Myra. She is afraid to shed her childhood and embrace an adult life. Her dependency on Simon is expressed in "I thought he'd save me ... I felt so safe with him".[34] Myra has a yearning for domestic life, which is challenged by the instability that her past causes. In this story, Bowen captures the liminal moments of Myra's initiation into conjugal life. Unlike Janet in "Foothold", who has already lived the life of a mother and a housewife, the exorcized

[32] Ibid., 467.
[33] Ibid., 470.
[34] Ibid., 467.

Myra embarks into the life of domesticity by rejecting the 'other'. She loses the 'self' in "a sublime nonentity".[35] In both of these stories, the 'other' appears at moments of crisis, but the hegemonic forces try to prevent it from fulfilling any promises of stronger or more unconventional identities.

The issues of 'otherness' and 'difference' are embedded within the identities in several ways in the story. The account of Myra's childhood shows the strong connection between the two young girls who are ostracized by the rest of the girls in their school:

> Doria and I were always in trouble. I suppose that was why we knew each other. There were about eighteen other girls, but none of them liked us. We used to feel we had some disease – so much so, that we were sometimes ashamed to meet each other: sometimes we did not like to be together. I don't think we knew we were unhappy; we never spoke of that; we should have felt ashamed. We used to pretend we were all right; we got in a way to be quite proud of ourselves, of being different. I think though we made each other worse. In those days, I was very ugly. Doria was as bad ... We did not even care for each other; we were just like two patients in hospital, shut away from the others together because of having some frightful disease. But I suppose we depended on one another.[36]

Myra's desire to be accepted by the rest of her social circle, where 'difference' is considered to be a "disease", led her to deny her own 'difference', resulting in the nervous breakdown. This is certainly another narrative means of presenting the 'otherness' and 'difference' through the apprehension in the 'self' that Bowen hints upon. However, the disturbance created by the apprehension of 'self' and the fluidity of being in the story is pacified by a rational and authoritative figure like Mrs. Bettersley, who puts an end to any possible alterative that hinders the norms of an established and pre-existing social order.

"The Apple Tree" raises several questions about friendship, inclusion, rejection, identity, and communication. Myra's need for inclusion in the dominant group of the girls in her school had compelled her to reject her friendship with Doria. In the beginning of the story, Simon's friends reject Myra because she is young and inexperienced. They are surprised at Simon's choice of a wife because Myra is different. She is a "mannerless, sexless

[35] Ibid., 470.
[36] Ibid., 468.

child", who is inept at dinner-table conversations and "this wraith" is "not considerable as a mother of sons".[37] Lassner aptly describes that, by "refusing to relinquish her childhood trauma for married love, she weakens her husband and withholds the generative power of fertility".[38] In the end of the story, Myra had to be exorcized before she could be included as one of them. The identity of the group in which Simon belonged required sameness from Myra before she could be accepted. The haunting in this story provides a platform that highlights the idea of 'difference', but the 'difference' is soon subsumed into the category of sameness by the act of exorcism. The haunting allows Myra to be different and in the liminal stage, whereas the exorcism forces her to cross the threshold and get absorbed into the community surrounding her.

The Liminality and the Possibility

The various tropes used by Bowen to explore aspects of otherness and difference in her texts are elements of reveries, hallucinations, shadows, fantasies, fears, fascinations, images of ghosts, and absurd or irrational actions. These contribute to the production of uncanny and phantasmic effects. Along with that, they also serve the purpose of giving rhetorical force to the narrative concerns with matters of individual apprehensions of difference. This further disturbs the readers' notions of culture, and other broader notions of identity. The strange and disturbing events occurring in the texts that have been considered so far are not always supported with rational explanations. Although certain events can be explained by stretching the rational, most supernatural, unnatural, or illogical activities are left undecided for the reader. Answers are left in a liminal and uncertain condition, at the thin border between the two binaries. Bowen's female characters in these uncanny stories are left in this liminal position, where these transitional identities may not always complete the conversion or cross the borders, but definitely show the possibilities. Pussy in "The Shadowy Third" either will die at childbirth or will probably survive if Martin remains attentive consistently and if she is able to ignore the presence of the shadow of the dead wife. Janet in "Foothold" either will be marked as a delusional

[37] Ibid., 463.

[38] Phyllis Lassner, *Elizabeth Bowen: A Study of the Short Fiction* (New York: Twayne Publishers, 1991): 52.

woman or will probably reject the ghost of Clara and seek out the company of her husband and friend. Myra Wing in "The Apple Tree" is a child-woman haunted by her dead friend Doria, and she is given the possibility of a happy married life at the cost of surrendering her 'difference'. The phantasm in these stories highlights the anomalies of these female identities that are roving at the threshold of two different states of being, and their repressed fears and anxieties are channelized through the haunting. These identities are in the process of 'becoming' something but not there yet. The phantasm in these texts facilitates their cultural visibility.

In Bowen's works, the cultural history is constructed through an individual's sense of 'self' and its reactions with social and political forces. Her loyalty was torn between England and Ireland due to her dual condition of being an Irish woman and yet spying on Ireland for the English as she was working for the British Ministry of Information during the Second World War. Despite her Irish origins and her tendency to describe herself as an Irish novelist, Bowen felt identified with England in its battle with Germany. Yet, Ireland always seemed to offer her some sort of stability and reliability.[39] This dilemma gave rise to an intense form of self-questioning and fracturing of the self. Bowen's own hesitant attitude toward her nation and culture is reflected in the uncertainties that her stories produce, which investigate several possibilities and refuse to provide definite endings. The unusual aspects of Bowen's works are, as Ellmann rightly describes, the "frictional disjunctions between modes of writing" that makes the "lunatic giant" inside each individual to produce "knockings and batterings" within the structure of social realism.[40] Events in Bowen's works are shown through psychological experience of the characters reacting to their surroundings. Uprooted from Bowen's Court in Ireland, Bowen was living in London during the war when her London house was bombed. The fragile position of the marginalized female characters, crippled by terror, trauma, and violence, corresponds to Bowen's own liminal position. Bowen experiments with narrative possibilities that produce the undecidable factors in her works, which further reflect the uncertain traits of her own cultural identity. They show the variation of the "selfhood". Her main female characters are marked by 'difference' and are misfits to the

[39] Victoria Glendinning, *Elizabeth Bowen: Portrait of a Writer* (London: Weidenfeld & Nicolson, 1977): 145.

[40] Ellman, 4.

norms and order of the society they live in. The ghosts appear in her stories to highlight the qualities of 'otherness' and 'difference' in the female characters re-evaluating the feminine subjectivity.

Bibliography

Austin, Allan E. 1989. *Elizabeth Bowen*. Revised ed. Boston: Twayne Publishers.

Bowen, Elizabeth. 1950. *Collected Impressions*. London: Longmans Green.

———. 1962. *Afterthought: Pieces About Writing*. London: Longmans Green.

———. 1964. Preface. In *A Day in the Dark and Other Stories*. London: Jonathan Cape.

———. 1981. In *The Collected Stories of Elizabeth Bowen*, ed. Angus Wilson. Hopewell: Ecco Press.

———. 1986. In *The Mulberry Tree*, ed. Hermionee Lee. New York: Harcourt Brace Jovanovich.

Ellmann, Maud. 2003. *Elizabeth Bowen: The Shadow Across the Page*. Edinburgh: Edinburgh University Press.

Freud, Sigmund. 1997. The Uncanny (1919). In *Writings on Art and Literature*, 193–233. Stanford: Stanford University Press.

Glendinning, Victoria. 1977. *Elizabeth Bowen: Portrait of a Writer*. London: Weidenfeld and Nicolson.

Hanson, Clare. 1985. *Short Stories and Short Fictions, 1880–1980*. Basingstoke: Macmillan.

———. 1989. "Introduction" and "A Poetics of Short Fiction". In *Re-reading the Short Story*, ed. Clare Hanson. London: Macmillan.

———. 2000. *Hysterical Fictions: The 'Woman's Novel' in the Twentieth Century*. New York: St. Martin's Press.

Lassner, Phyllis. 1991. *Elizabeth Bowen: A Study of the Short Fiction*. New York: Twayne Publishers.

Lee, Hermione. 1981. *Elizabeth Bowen: An Estimation*. London: Vision Press Ltd.

Miller, J. Hillis. 1992. *Ariadne's Thread: Story Lines*. New Haven: Yale University Press.

Royle, Nicholas. 2003. *The Uncanny*. New York: Routledge.

Wallace, Diana. 2004. Uncanny Stories: The Ghost Story as Female Gothic. In *Gothic Studies*, vol. 6/1. Manchester: Manchester University Press.

Crossing the Utopian/Apocalyptic Border: The Anxiety of Forgetting in Paul Auster's *In the Country of Last Things*

Dylan Winchock

Space exists in relation to the narratives which map out its limits, accreting meaning through the stories we recite to ourselves and one another, and through a tension between these contesting narratives. Paul Auster's speculative novel, *In the Country of Last Things*, reveals the modernist Utopian project as a flattening of narrative interaction through an apocalyptic erasure of the past in order to maintain a singular, self-contained, and uncontested spatial and temporal narrative. This highly policed border between apocalypse and Utopia is a fantasy, however, where Borderland testimonies 'rooted' in fragmentation and mobility become tactics of political resistance against disappearance and amnesia.

Among the seemingly endless possibilities of speculative fiction, the critique of Utopia has been a long-running tradition. Utopia, itself a speculative space, has been desired by many as a political reality; this reality, however, is based on an unattainable perfection. A Utopia must be self-contained in that the very existence of an outside beyond its border threatens the validity of its 'seamless' interior. This specialized and radical form of interiority risks a disruption of its limits if even a single discrepancy emerges in its overarching narrative. Utopian space is thus always one

D. Winchock (✉)
California State University, San Marcos, CA, USA

J. Elbert Decker, D. Winchock (eds.), *Borderlands and Liminal Subjects*, https://doi.org/10.1007/978-3-319-67813-9_13

tenuous step away from collapse—it is wrapped in a narrative that teeters on the edge between fulfillment and apocalyptic disaster.

The threat of apocalypse necessarily looms at Utopia's horizon: it promises an obliteration of the complications and nuances that are revealed by the palimpsestic polyvocality (the Babel and the babble) of multiple narratives. Apocalypse, according to Fredric Jameson in *Archaeologies of the Future*, refers to an act of absolute destruction that is easier to imagine than an end to capitalism.[1] It serves, then, as a narrative that obscures the unthinkable failure of the economic base; however, this does not mean that apocalyptic narratives cannot also be examined at a superstructural level. Apocalypse may mask the failure of the base, but it can simultaneously exist to mask the unthinkable failure of any number of reified ideologies and institutions that exist to reinforce that base. It serves as an erasure of contradiction, a re-blanking of the slate, and an assertion of a single new narrative. In Christianity, for example, apocalypse replaces the sins of a sophisticated world with a singular narrative of salvation through a return to Eden. This disturbingly Utopian erasure of the historical past and the material present for a simplified and static future is the key element of most apocalyptic messages and the key criticism embedded in most post-apocalyptic novels.

Post-apocalyptic literature[2] reflects the failure of Utopian narratives to truly erase contradiction. Such novels tend to focus on the residue of the past in the aftermath of destruction. Maya Merlob claims that they rarely earn the "post-" prefix, as they engage in an "ongoing apocalypse" that "encourages us to believe there is and was no past."[3] This ongoing nature of apocalypse defers the desirable—yet unthinkable—end of things, locking time in a "cyclic order."[4] Though a self-contained temporal loop might seem a perfect closed system for Utopia, the residual past is never fully

[1] Fredric Jameson, *Archaeologies of the Future: The Desire Called Utopia and Other Science Fictions* (New York: Verso, 2005), 199.

[2] Some may critique my seemingly casual usage of generic terminology. Technically, there are some notable differences among Utopian, anti-Utopian, inverted Utopian, dystopian, and post-apocalyptic novels (for a complete description of these types, please see Fredric Jameson's *Archaeologies of the Future*—in particular, the chapter entitled "Journey Into Fear"). However, my conflation of terms is intentional in that I believe the separation of these genres has somewhat obscured their shared roots in the binary tension between Utopia and apocalypse.

[3] Maya Merlob, "Textuality, Self, and World: The Postmodern Narrative in Paul Auster's *In the Country of Last Things*." *Critique: Studies in Contemporary Fiction* 49, no. 1 (2007): 27.

[4] Ibid.

erased. Post-apocalyptic novels describe instead of an erasure a place of ruin—a space of *incomplete*, or failed, apocalypse where the tatters and shreds of former worlds hang onto a fragile monovocal narrative. It is a new beginning, to be sure, but it comes with many strings attached. Even as the multiplicity of voices are erased, residual narratives rush forward to stake a claim, pushing against the border between utopia and apocalypse. The old complications, now erased, are thus frequently replaced with equally complicated new mixtures, blends, and narrative hybrids.

Because Utopian and apocalyptic narratives both believe themselves to be self-contained and absolute, the tension between the two reveals a Borderland whose limits resonate throughout this binary structure. Utopias are preoccupied with patrolling their borders and carefully monitoring the limits of their own definition against the threat of the outside world, even as the Apocalyptic aspect of Utopia wipes away evidence of that outside. However, some of those who have been forced into the margins of society have found a sense of home in the ambiguity of a Borderland identity and have become adept in inventing creative ways to penetrate supposedly impenetrable borders. Gloria Anzaldúa, in *Borderlands/La Frontera*, suggests that this struggle against othering and exclusive binaries is a struggle that "has always been inner, and is played out in the outer terrains."[5] The production of Borderland space is thus a physical conflict, but always as a manifestation of the ideological: it is rich site of hegemonic struggle. The refused, hidden away in the margins of dominant space, are forced to survive through conscious disruptions of a binary power system. "To survive the Borderlands/you must live *sin fronteras*,"[6] argues Anzaldúa: the reified permanence of borders is called into question as their permeability is made visible; and in doing so, the twinned aspect of the Utopia/Apocalypse binary is also revealed.

While Anzaldúa was most certainly focused on Chicana and lesbian identities, she does not anchor her concept of Borderland tactics of survival solely within these two binary disruptions; the idea of Borderlands can be applied to post-apocalyptic literature as well. From the Utopian side of the binary we see the silenced and forgotten—their narratives locked outside of the monolithic and dominant mythology—emerge as manifestations of the contradiction within the very framework of the Utopian/apocalyptic

[5] Gloria Anzaldúa, *Borderlands/La Frontera* (San Francisco: Aunt Lute Books, 1999), 109.
[6] Ibid., 217.

border. These ideologies, identities, and narratives find ways to negotiate with a necessarily totalitarian geography. Hidden Borderlands, once revealed, are particularly destabilizing: the mere hint of a narrative that cuts across both sides of the binary and, therefore, beyond the Utopian, can disrupt—if not effectively topple—the fragile space that the mythology circumscribes. On the reverse side of the binary, we see the apocalyptic process of erasure leaving behind a tattered narrative space; and as the multitudes of alternative voices spill in to fill the void, an overwhelming Borderland is produced. It is no neat third space where everyone is acknowledged and heard within the context of their own voices. People are instead thrown into a consciousness of shifting and blending voices that must be embraced in order to survive. It is in the moments when the characters succeed in forming this fluid identity that the space surrounding is transformed into one of potentially mutual understanding, possibility, and change.

Auster's novel, *In the Country of Last Things*, calls into question the simple categories of Utopian and post-apocalyptic literature by critiquing the hidden destructive element embedded within the Utopian fantasy. While his novel does contain elements of Utopian thought and structure, it leaves characters and readers alike dissatisfied with the result. The totalitarian oversight needed to maintain the sham of a Utopia in the nameless city mocks the Utopian project; and the government's ineffectuality, along with the city's shattered infrastructure and the population's complete lack of Utopian optimism, suggests that Utopia is nothing more than fantasy. As a result, the nameless city uneasily dreams of Utopia even as it drifts ever closer to apocalypse. The apocalyptic aspect of the novel reveals a city slowly decaying and crumbling, society drifting apart, and a people left not in a blank slate, but sifting through the rubble of what came before. It is a city of lost citizens attempting to locate themselves in the context of a Borderland between Utopia and Apocalypse, preoccupied with the search for a means to connect their narrative memories to spatial and temporal landscapes.

The process of apocalyptic erasure in the nameless city of *Last Things* manifests most clearly in its primary ideological maze: the Sea Wall. The government's Sea Wall Project becomes a physical macrocosm of the Utopian enclave behavior that can be seen throughout the city. Anna Blume writes in her undeliverable letter (Auster's novel) that her earlier ability to freely enter the city does not equate to an analogous ability to leave.[7] The

[7] Paul Auster, *In the Country of Last Things* (New York: Penguin, 1987), 85.

government has begun the construction of a great wall that will surround the city, keeping the sea itself at bay. The sea, conventionally a symbol of the unknown and the unconscious, becomes an enemy of the state and stasis. Government officials inform Anna that the wall exists for her protection and "to guard against the possibility of war."[8] She is told that "the threat of foreign invaders was mounting,"[9] but the only 'invader' we see is Anna herself, who enters the city from the outside, insisting on a permeable border, and questioning the dominant reified order. The government officials nevertheless plod on in their Kafkaesque fashion, explaining to Anna that there are no longer any ships ferrying people out beyond the wall: "if nothing comes in, nothing can go out."[10] They force onto Anna the rhetoric of a Utopian binary that, in the erasure of the outside, also imprisons those on the inside.

The Sea Wall is a manifestation of an anxious narrative about the Other that is but a reflection of the city's own self-destructive trajectory toward the intersection of Utopia and apocalypse. The government expects to work on the Wall for at least the next fifty years,[11] even though governments in the novel seem to collapse every few months. The Sea Wall, then, represents the never-ending process of a Utopian drive toward the impossible goal of total self-enclosure and the inability to see beyond the ideological goals of maintaining the illusion of an impermeable border. Similarly, the government focuses on the thousands of jobs that construction will produce, but ignores the destructive nature of the project. The Wall is not built from raw materials, but of the remnants of crumbling and collapsed buildings throughout the city.[12] While the border is meant to erase the outside world, it is in fact bringing apocalypse inside by slowly laying waste to the city's interior.

Furthermore, instead of creating a channel of communication between 'us' and 'them,' or opening a dialogue that acknowledges narratives beyond the Utopian myth, the city takes refuge in reinforcing a closed system. With the Sea Wall denying Anna passage back to the home she left behind, she moves down the borderline, seeking weaknesses to be exploited. She hears

[8] Ibid., 86.

[9] Ibid.

[10] Ibid.

[11] Auster, *Country*, 86.

[12] Ibid.

talk of travel permits that might allow her to leave through walls in other directions, but quickly learns that the permits exist mostly in name. If such permits indeed exist, Anna's bureaucratic shuffling between government agencies informs her that they cost more than she could possibly afford.[13] In fact, there are very few in the city who possess enough money to survive, let alone purchase luxuries. The permits, then, create an illusion of freedom that in reality exists only for those who have no need to leave a hierarchical system guaranteeing their continued privilege and dominance. Giving up on the official route, Anna considers rumors of underground organizations that know of tunnels to the outside world. Counter-rumors suggest, however, that this may be nothing but stories repeated by the government in order to round up and "disappear" dissidents at the other end.[14] Those who are caught trying to escape are reportedly sent to labor camps in 'the south,' where they are never heard from again. These narratives of fear are themselves ideological walls around the city: those who are taken away may indeed be in labor camps, but the rumors ignore the unlikelihood of ever again hearing from escapees within the limits of the city walls.

Since the Sea Wall has replaced production with salvage, there exists a fear among those trapped within that objects from the past—like the narratives from beyond the Wall—will vanish forever. Anna's journal informs us that "nothing lasts [...] Once a thing is gone, that is the end of it."[15] The apparent permanence of disappearance deeply concerns Anna, and there is a persistent anxiety that any given object may be the last of its kind. Once gone, what will it take to evoke the memory of this 'last thing?' Indeed, she states: "A thing vanishes, and if you wait too long before thinking about it, no amount of struggle can ever wrench it back. Memory is not an act of will, after all."[16] For Anna, then, we have no control over memory; rather, it is implicitly linked to the physical world around us. Without these monuments to the past, time cannot be fixed in place.

The disappearance of objects and the failure of memory lead to an anxiety that language, too, will fade. As we lose the ability to recall lost objects, we also lose the ability to communicate the ideas behind them. Anna worries that "little by little, the words become only sounds, a random collection of

[13] Ibid., 90.

[14] Auster, *Country*, 90.

[15] Ibid., 2.

[16] Ibid., 87.

glottals and fricatives, a storm of whirling phonemes, and finally the whole thing just collapses into gibberish."[17] Like the city that hollows out its center in search of perfection, the act of erasing the past hollows out a system of language. When the center no longer holds, language shreds and tatters like the disparate narratives erased by the Utopian project. The nameless city, then, calls into question the ability to successfully communicate as a society: without a transcendental signifier through which to anchor language, how does a society of people continue to hear one another?

A fragmented narrative, like the dismembered identities of those swept into the Borderlands, can be used to fluidly reconfigure itself across multiple contexts; those who do not take on a Borderland identity, unfortunately, tend to fall victim to the fear of the failure of language. Boris Stepanovich, Anna's friend and mentor, tells Anna of the "language of ghosts" that many in the nameless city speak.[18] It is a language that recalls a now vanished capitalism—a narrative of wealth and abundance that fixes the speaker in a language game that cannot adapt to the failure of Utopia. The speakers of this language become paralyzed by their attempt to maintain a totalizing Utopian narrative through a fetishization of capital. The paralysis of those who cannot adapt to changing conditions parallels Anzaldúa's *coatlicue state*, or a sense of helplessness and loss[19] in the face of a crumbling worldview: "Digging in your heels you refused the reality – always your first line of defense to emotional pain." Those who speak the language of ghosts fall into the dangerous trap of remaining in the coatlicue state, as "transforming habitual feelings is the hardest thing you've ever attempted."[20] Consumed by their stories of consumption, the speakers of the language of ghosts wither away and die on the equally withered avenues of the Utopian dream.

It is in this way that the speculative critique of Utopia speaks to an underlying human dilemma: the inability to fix oneself in space, memory, or language (common anxieties of the postmodern condition) reveals an underlying anxiety about self-disappearance. What happens when our physical presence has been forgotten? Who will remember us? Can words

[17] Auster, *Country*, 89.

[18] Ibid., 115.

[19] Gloria Anzaldúa, *Light in the Dark/Luz en lo Oscuro* (Durham: Duke University Press, 2015), 123.

[20] Ibid., 131.

adequately contain us across time? In a minor episode, the chauffeur in *Last Things* is buried by a number of people who lived with him. The city forbids burial in favor of recycling the dead: gravesites are monumentalized objects that recall the past and are therefore not permissible. The willingness of Anna to help in this illegal endeavor, however, indicates a desperate desire for a permanent connection to history.

This anxiety over disappearance is rooted in the fear of forgetting.[21] Paul Ricoeur, in *Memory, History, Forgetting*, suggests that memory is tied to an ambition to be faithful to the past, which leads to an endless struggle against forgetting.[22] The "unsettling character" of forgetting is not that we forget, but that we can never know until the moment of recall whether this loss of memory is temporary or final.[23] Further unsettling is its reminder to us of the inevitability of death, as we will forget everything in time.[24] Laurence J. Kirmayer argues that these feelings of "terror and loss" come from the "gap" between the stories we tell about our past and our "frailty and impersistence of memory."[25] Ricoeur, however, reminds us that this sense of frailty, if present, is partially unfounded in that we receive great pleasure when suddenly recalling a memory long lost. He argues that in actuality "we forget less than we think or we fear."[26] While Anna initially tells the readers that we cannot willfully recall the past, Ricoeur more hopefully claims that it is quite difficult to willfully *erase* the past; much of what we forget and remember occurs regardless of our efforts. Even intentionally erased memory (the repressed) is under erasure only, and therefore leaves external "traces" on the physical world around us.[27] These traces connect our memories—and the abstraction of time—to the concrete spatial world in which we live.

[21] This fear of forgetting is manifested in the Borderland between the Utopian fantasy of permanence and its repressed apocalyptic fantasy of annihilation.

[22] Paul Ricoeur, *Memory, History, Forgetting*, trans. Kathleen Blamey and David Pellauer (Chicago: University of Chicago Press, 2004), 21.

[23] Ibid., 27.

[24] Ibid., 417.

[25] Laurence J. Kirmayer, "Landscapes of Memory: Trauma, Narrative, and Dissociation" in *Tense Past: Cultural Essays in Trauma and Memory*, eds. Paul Antze and Michael Lambek (New York: Routledge, 1996), 174.

[26] Ricoeur, *Memory*, 440–41.

[27] Ibid., 425.

In order to survive erasure, then, one must learn to "inhabit" the world by locating oneself in space, thus creating a bond between space, time, and self. Words alone, according to Ricoeur, are easily lost with the passing of memory, but place can serve as a reminder against forgetting.[28] He argues that the memories of inhabited places allow for "corporeal space [to be] immediately linked with the surrounding space of the environment, some fragment of inhabitable land."[29] In a sense, the physical world becomes a place marker for the maps that we construct and the narratives that shape our identities. One could say that identity itself exists at the intersection of our narratives of space (the maps we make) and our narratives of time (the memories we recall): the two, through us, become interwoven and inseparable. Ricoeur, then, suggests that the inability to locate oneself in place also disconnects oneself from time, from memory. This inability to inhabit the world situates us in a "realm of emptiness."[30]

Ricoeur concedes that a permanent personal link between place and time is unrealistic: "In truth, it is always possible, often urgent, to displace oneself, with the risk of becoming that passerby, that wanderer, that flâneur, that vagabond, stray dog that our fragmented contemporary culture both sets in motion and paralyzes."[31] Ricoeur's statement echoes the ideas of Anzaldúa's Borderland consciousness. Narrative and existential paralysis in the form of the coatlicue state, sets in motion a process[32] of "dismemberment and fragmentation" in order to begin a "reconstruction and reframing" that "allows for putting the pieces together in a new way."[33] This is not a break from the past, but rather a fluid and continual process. In the context of the Utopian/apocalyptic binary, the border between the two is fractured and the narratives that we tell about time, place, and identity are destabilized and scattered. We are forced then to see new patterns, new configurations, and new understandings of these stories and images. The old are not swept aside and erased; they are instead reconfigured. But what is produced is an emergent permeable narrative that, while containing

[28] Ibid., 41–42.

[29] Ibid., 148.

[30] Ibid., 149.

[31] Ricoeur, *Memory*, 149.

[32] Anzaldúa, in *Light in the Dark/Luz en lo Oscuro*, personifies this movement out of paralysis through the Aztec god who dismembers his sister, Coyolxauhqui, in order to protect his mother, Coatlicue.

[33] Anzaldúa, *Luz*, 19.

aspects of residual and dominant narratives,[34] also produces something wholly new. It is this Borderland tactic of survival that the residents of the nameless city must embrace—a positioning that in many ways parallels the tactics necessary to navigate postmodernism, postcolonialism, transnational globalism, or a contemporary world that has become incredulous toward the underlying Utopian trajectory of modernism. The fragmented world in which we (and the residents of the nameless city) live demands tactics of mobility that threatens coatlicue state paralysis if we are unable to balance between and among different spaces, narratives, and identities. Though society may paradoxically label us as 'stray dogs' for the displacement that it has forced upon us, it is through a willingness to 'stray' that new possibilities can be written within the cracks of a fragmented world.

Testimony is thus substantially different from a history or archive. A testimony of mobility—such as the witness borne in Anna's journal—is a subjective tactic of survival in the midst of events bigger than any individual's personal story. This form of testimony is a willing record of one's relationship to these events, but also an ability to maintain balance amidst narratives transforming under temporal, spatial, and social pressures. Hayden White explains that history is unlike testimony in that it "reveals to us a world that is putatively 'finished', done with, over, and yet not dissolved, not falling apart."[35] The historical narrative, distanced from the subjectivity of testimony, produces a closed and teleological system—a totalizing and self-contained epoch of time fitting for a Utopian project. Archives, similarly, are a contained and complete collection of a particular subset of knowledge. Like history, it departs from the subjective and is self-contained. While no one is arguing that events occur regardless of human participation, testimony makes visible the people who experience, organize, and narrate these events.

Testimony, such as that found in private letters, suggests the impossibility of total containment and the artificiality of the beginnings and endings imposed upon linear time by history and archives. Samuel Hynes, in his anthropological work on personal narratives of war, explains that "meaning

[34] Raymond Williams' explanation of residual, dominant, and emergent ideologies in the hegemonic process can be found in chapter 8 of his book, *Marxism and Literature*.

[35] Hayden White, *The Content of the Form: Narrative Discourse and Historical Representation* (Baltimore: Johns Hopkins UP, 1987): 21.

is not fixed but emergent."[36] Indeed, testimony is as close as we can come to the event itself; time moves on, and in its passing we can never return to the moment. The referent of testimony, Ricoeur agrees, is not the irrecoverable event, but the speaker who testifies.[37] Testimony is fact, in that "we have nothing better [...] to assure ourselves that something did happen in the past"[38]; but it is a multivalent fact that emerges in the spaces left empty by the inadequacies of other narratives. One hundred people witness a single event, and the one hundred testimonies, individualized to varying degrees, retain their own validity in reference to the memory of the speaker. Testimony is a permeable narrative, a language act that remains incomplete, much like the memory from which it is constructed. In this way, an event becomes wrapped in endless palimpsests of testimony based on which memories are revised, emergent, residual, and forgotten.

Anna, through several failed attempts to navigate disappearance, learns the importance of a Borderland testimony. Sam, her ally, lover, and eventual husband, provides an early lesson for Anna on the fragility of a closed archival narrative. His obsession with interviewing every individual that he can speak to and transcribing their stories into his manuscript is an attempt to lose himself in the Utopian narrative of the city to fix the city permanently in time. The archive becomes a memorial to those things that have been lost along the way, the things that disappear in the aftermath of silence. Without memory and without a past, there is no context through which to register change; and in a city that is literally crumbling around him—and a Utopian narrative that is doing the same—being aware of change seems the only way to maintain balance. Sam's archive becomes a map of the labyrinth: a reference point from which he can plan his next step through uncertain terrain. Unfortunately, the archival project is itself terribly flawed. Matti Hyvärinen notes the difference between the participatory and performative nature of Anna's testimony[39] and "the idea of a 'total representation' of the city, in the form of Sam's huge manuscript, [which] was burned to ashes

[36] Samuel Hynes, "Personal Narratives and Commemoration," in *War and Remembrance in the Twentieth Century*, eds. Jay Winter and Emmanuel Sivan (Cambridge: Cambridge University Press, 1999): 206.

[37] Ricoeur, *Memory*, 180.

[38] Ricoeur, *Memory*, 147.

[39] Matti Hyvärinen, "Acting, Thinking, and Telling: Anna Blume's Dilemma in Paul Auster's *In the Country of Last Things*," *Journal of Literature and the History of Ideas* 4 no. 2 (2006): 62.

years before."[40] Sam's desire to contain every story, palimpsest, and narrative is an endless project as damaging to its keeper as any modernist Utopian trajectory. Rather than reconfiguring the fragments of space and time, and, therefore, finding the balance of a Borderland identity, Sam becomes paralyzed by the impossibility of his project. The task does not connect him with the city that surrounds him, but rather isolates him from the outside world as effectively as the Sea Wall; indeed, the burning of the library from the inside—the place in which he and his work resides—seals the archive's fate to the same as the Utopian city. Losing oneself in a coatlicue state is the danger of the archive: it is a distant and dispassionate act of storytelling, a recording of the past without an authorial presence. Memory is memorialized and etched in stone anonymously. The past is closed up tightly in the confines of the archive and the personal present is left with no means of access.

This is not to say that bearing witness is without danger. Anna's time working as an interviewer of prospective temporary residents at Woburn House first echoes Sam's project: she approaches her job in a purely archival fashion, spending her time "putting their names on a list, organizing schedules of who would be moving in and when."[41] The act of scheduling here resembles a dispassionate chronicling of stories, where she places no more importance on one than another. In other words, she becomes a bureaucratic reader interested only in typologically compartmentalizing the lives of those around her. She produces a wall between herself and the world similar to the ones found around Sam and the nameless city.

The fragility of this border, however, is revealed as she learns to genuinely hear the stories of others. The distance between herself and the storyteller is eliminated—the border between the speaker and the audience becomes permeable through first-hand testimony. Anna is confronted with something more than a simple series of stories devoid of authors or any direct relevance to the world around her. Hearing the stories of these lost people as testimonies, she consciously enters a Borderland, and in doing so, she loses her defensive distance: "I spoke to twenty or twenty-five people a day. I saw them repeatedly, one after the other, in the front hallway of the house [...] One by one, they stumbled in to see me, an endless, unremitting flow of people."[42] Anna, though dispirited by the task before her, intimately

[40] Ibid., 74.

[41] Auster, *Country*, 142–43.

[42] Auster, *Country*, 143.

experiences the urgency of people seeking a way out of the dominant narrative of erasure and containment. They have wandered the labyrinth of Utopia and suffered the violence of apocalypse for too long, and Woburn House represents an alternative of inclusivity, even if it proves ephemeral. Anna sees a fragmented people come together through the common dream of having their disparate and fragmented stories collectively heard.

The desire for an alternative space within the city is intrinsically linked to a desire to remember that which has been forgotten. One cannot produce a Woburn House without also producing a rich palimpsestic depth in narrative that reveals possibilities exceeding the limits of the monological Utopian narrative of the State. Anna's job was to ask the 'necessary questions' for data collecting, but she finds that intoning name, sex, and age was insufficient: "They all wanted to tell me their stories, and I had no choice but to listen. It was a very different story every time, and yet each story was finally the same. The strings of bad luck, the miscalculations, the growing weight of circumstances."[43] It is here that Anna is exposed to the way in which the subjectivity of bearing witness can produce a larger communal narrative. Each individual has his or her own story to tell, based on his or her own direct personal experiences and relationships with the terrain. The place in which they are bound, however, produces commonalities across stories and a sense of continuity between them. The acts of telling and listening, as well as residing communally, produce an intimacy with space and time that had been lost under the violence of the Utopian fantasy. The common threads across the stories help to remind the people of the city that their memories of the past have a legitimacy even while under erasure.

Testimony is in this way a living performance of memory that reconstructs personal and communal identities through a Borderland inclusivity. Anzaldúa argues that stories are never "inert and 'dead' objects," but rather "acts encapsulated in time."[44] They produce an intimate relationship between the speaker, the word, and the audience, like a bridge that spans the distance between two sides of a border.[45] As subjective and personal as that narrative might be, it is—like memory—not completely in one's control. Some aspects may be consciously constructed, but it is also a reaction beyond our control to events at hand: "through narrative you formulate

[43] Ibid.

[44] Anzaldúa, *Borderlands*, 89.

[45] Anzaldúa , *Luz*, 5.

your identities by unconsciously locating yourself in social narratives not of your own making."[46] Indeed, Anzaldúa believes that to bear witness is to evoke the repressed and forgotten, "to step back and attempt to see the pattern in these events (personal and societal) [...] to expose this shadow side that the mainstream media and government denies."[47] This in-between state is what Anzaldúa calls *nepantlas*, or the Borderland spaces formed by the tension between cultural and personal narratives, where the forgotten and erased can be recalled and reconfigured in order to produce an ephemeral wholeness.[48] In the context of the nameless city, the 'shadow' is the hidden apocalyptic aspect of Utopia. Anna's testimony allows the two sides of the binary to bleed into one another, recalling the repressed memories of the marginalized people, and reconfiguring their disparate narratives into a temporary communal voice that critiques the violence of an apocalyptic project.

The elimination of distance through the opening of this border produces an empathy contrary to the order of modern Utopia. Empathy requires the individual to step between narratives, balancing across varied terrains, simultaneously experiencing both similarity and difference. It is a realization that memory is not entirely one's own. Because we never have complete control over memory or forgetting, we build testimonial narratives that are shared and retold, broken and reassembled by others, and recombined with elements of narratives not our own. From this perspective, an acceptance of the imperfection of memory can be achieved; the linearity of time can be reconsidered if empathy, community, and process is privileged over telos.

Within a Utopian project, there is little room for alternative narrative, time, or space. To establish a narrative that in any way contradicts the ideological belief in impermeability threatens the stability of the project as a whole. The production of alternative space is thus necessarily Borderland act of improvisation. Indeed, Anna learns to resist erasure in the nameless city through Boris' acts of improvisational testimony. Anna becomes Boris' protégée by following him on his outings to sell random goods to various city dwellers. She learns that narratives are not just words, but extensions of the material body and its relationship to the physical space that surrounds

[46] Ibid., 6.
[47] Ibid., 10.
[48] Ibid., 2.

it. She realizes that things indeed disappear and the memory does fade, but "what strikes [her] as odd is not that everything is falling apart, but that so much continues to be there. It takes a long time for a world to vanish."[49] She learns to disregard the static language of ghosts and to situate herself in nepantla, or a testimony of the past that is mobile, shifting, and fragmented. She models her tactics of survival on Boris:

> Boris had an aversion to being pinned down, and he used language as an instrument of locomotion – constantly on the move, darting and feinting, circling, disappearing, suddenly appearing again in a different spot. At one time or another, he told me so many stories about himself, presented so many conflicting accounts of his life, that I gave up trying to believe anything.[50]

The words themselves, then, take on the traits of a Borderland identity. They are in constant motion as mobile sites of resistance against the crushing grand narrative of the city. They disappear when necessary and reappear in new locations, new angles, and new positions. They consciously coincide and contradict, producing a story that does not demand unification and a singular truth, but rather revels in the sharing of fragmentation and difference.

Boris' physical movement through the city matches the movement of his narratives: "He would take me through back alleys and deserted paths, stepping neatly over the gutted pavement, navigating the numerous hazards and pitfalls, swerving now to his left, now to his right, not once breaking the rhythm of his step."[51] An adept at navigating the labyrinth around him, Boris does not falter as he balances between the very real Utopian 'fantasy' that dominates the city and the alternative narratives that he and other border-crossers provide as counterpoints in a growing dialogue. Boris may seem hopelessly lost from the perspective of a grand narrative due to the uncertainty of his truth, the fragmentation of his identity, and the shifting nature of his movement; however, both his physicality and narrativity reconstellate these elements into a temporary whole. He is complete in a postmodern sense, living by shifting rules that baffle a teleologically bound project like Utopia. James Peacock describes this dynamic form of identity as "an ethical imagination alive to the reality of suffering in social

[49] Auster, *Country*, 28.
[50] Auster, *Country*, 146.
[51] Ibid., 148

relationships, but at the same time negotiating it anew, embellishing it, and making it livable."[52] Boris is subverting the labyrinth, taking what is useful and discarding the rest, changing the rules of the game and finding new pathways to an exit long believed lost. His words and his steps, acting as one, "make inert things come to life"[53] and open up the closed totalitarian state around him to new possibilities.

Rather than fixing herself in a singular narrative, Anna begins to understand that the stories we tell are transformed by the spatial and temporal contexts in which they currently exist. She learns that space and time are transformed in turn by these very same stories. Anna, then, tells stories that permit dialogue and possibility, marking the world that surrounds her through her body, her memory, and her language. She can "zero in on these little islands of intactness [...] to create new archipelagoes [sic] of matter."[54] Rather than lose herself in erasure and the end of things, she approaches every "last thing"[55] as though it were "the first time."[56]

The labyrinthine pitfalls of the Utopian narrative, however, do not disappear simply because an alternative narrative is explored. Finding balance in nepantla is a struggle that tempts Anna to fall back into the paralyzing coatlicue state of a Utopian faith in endings:

> Now the entire notebook has almost been filled, and I have barely even skimmed the surface [...] I've been trying to fit everything in, trying to get to the end before it's too late, but I see now how badly I've deceived myself. Words do not allow such things. The closer you come to the end, the more there is to say. The end is only imaginary, a destination you invent to keep yourself going, but a point comes when you realize you will never get there. You might have to stop, but that is only because you have run out of time. You stop, but that does not mean you have come to the end.[57]

The Utopian narrative of time may not be as cyclical as Merlob suggested earlier. Rather, it is a linear sense of time that mimics cyclicality by spiraling

[52] James Peacock, *Understanding Paul Auster* (Columbia: University of South Carolina Press, 2010): 91.

[53] Auster, *Country,* 150.

[54] Ibid., 36

[55] Ibid., 1.

[56] Ibid., 7.

[57] Ibid., 183.

asymptotically closer toward a center that can never be directly addressed: it leads its inscribed subjects down a singular path and toward the center of the labyrinth, where they are supposedly rewarded with the timelessness of perfection. The unspoken transcendental signifier, however, is the violence of apocalypse, just as the transcendental signifier of apocalyptic narratives is the containment of Utopia. If the Utopian narrative masks a hidden apocalypse, then all paths leading to the center are dead ends. The inadequacy of transcendent endings is what Anna learns through her writing. Ilana Shiloh agrees, stating that Anna finds through her writing that the "end remains forever deferred."[58] Anna comes to realize that though she indeed must stop writing her letters to the outside world, her cessation of writing is not the same as an ending. Time does not halt at the center of Utopian ideology; apocalyptic dead ends are also made of permeable walls. No testimonial act will ever adequately address all aspects of the world in which we live. Katherine Washburn suggests that one can never successfully "escap [e] into the ease of the oracular or the comfort of the grand historical explanation."[59] Rather, Borderland tactics of survival allow one to construct a narrative that skims the multitudinous surfaces, suggests possibilities, and carves out temporal—yet temporary—stories. These stories, like memories, will have holes, but those holes must be accepted as part of the structure, leaving room for endless revisions and entry points for differing narratives. To take on a temporal Borderland identity is to find comfort in the incomplete, to seek dialogue over monologue, and to revel in the understanding that limits will necessarily be exceeded.

Auster's novel appropriately blurs the boundaries between Utopia and apocalypse. Just as every Utopian narrative is incomplete, so too is every apocalyptic narrative mid-apocalypse. Just as absolute containment is akin to the impossibility of permanent memory, so too does absolute erasure fail once memory is acknowledged as a shared process. Anna's letter—and Auster's novel—is an instructional one, and we are its recipient. The author and protagonist demonstrate the importance of testimony through a Borderland identity. While such a tactic is a means of survival through fragmentation and a straddling of identities, it is not an erasure of the self. Rather, it

[58] Ilana Shiloh, *Paul Auster and Postmodern Quest: On the Road to Nowhere* (New York: Peter Lang, 2002): 154.

[59] Katherine Washburn, "A Book at the End of the World: Paul Auster's *In the Country of Last Things*," *Review of Contemporary Fiction* 14 no.1 (1994): 62.

is a rooting of the self in the permeability of narrative, memory, and body. Roots, too, must shift; but this does not make them any less potent. It is a deeper form of intimacy, where the walls between people are broken down, where narratives intermingle, where the infinite possibilities of space and time are endlessly celebrated.

Bibliography

Anzaldúa, Gloria. 1999. *Borderlands/La Frontera*. San Francisco: Aunt Lute Books.

———. 2015. *Light in the Dark/Luz en lo Oscuro*. Durham: Duke University Press.

Auster, Paul. 1987. *In the Country of Last Things*. New York: Penguin.

Hynes, Samuel. 1999. Personal Narratives and Commemoration. In *War and Remembrance in the Twentieth Century*, ed. Jay Winter and Emmanuel Sivan, 205–220. Cambridge: Cambridge University Press.

Hyvärinen, Matti. 2006. Acting, Thinking, and Telling: Anna Blume's Dilemma in Paul Auster's *In the Country of Last Things*. *Journal of Literature and the History of Ideas* 4 (2): 59–78.

Jameson, Fredric. 2005. *Archaeologies of the Future: The Desire Called Utopia and Other Science Fictions*. New York: Verso.

Kirmayer, Laurence J. 1996. Landscapes of Memory: Trauma, Narrative, and Dissociation. In *Tense Past: Cultural Essays in Trauma and Memory*, ed. Paul Antze and Michael Lambek, 173–198. New York: Routledge.

Merlob, Maya. 2007. Textuality, Self, and World: The Postmodern Narrative in Paul Auster's *In the Country of Last Things*. *Critique: Studies in Contemporary Fiction* 49 (1): 25–45.

Peacock, James. 2010. *Understanding Paul Auster*. Columbia: University of South Carolina Press.

Ricoeur, Paul. 2004. *Memory, History, Forgetting*. Trans. Kathleen Blamey and David Pellauer. Chicago: University of Chicago Press.

Shiloh, Ilana. 2002. *Paul Auster and Postmodern Quest: On the Road to Nowhere*. New York: Peter Lang.

Washburn, Katherine. 1994. A Book at the End of the World: Paul Auster's *In the Country of Last Things*. *Review of Contemporary Fiction* 14 (1): 62–65.

White, Hayden. 1987. *The Content of the Form: Narrative Discourse and Historical Representation*. Baltimore: Johns Hopkins University Press.

Williams, Raymond. 1977. *Marxism and Literature*. Oxford: Oxford University Press.

Index

Note: Page number followed by 'n' refers to notes.

J. Elbert Decker, D. Winchock (eds.), *Borderlands and Liminal Subjects*, https://doi.org/10.1007/978-3-319-67813-9

I

J

N

O

FSC
www.fsc.org
MIX
Papier | Fördert
gute Waldnutzung
FSC® C083411

Kolibri 360 GmbH
Ferdinand-Jühlke-Straße 7
99095 Erfurt, Deutschland
produktsicherheit@kolibri360.de